THE REMBRANDT HEIST

THE REMBRANDT HEIST

THE STORY OF A CRIMINAL GENIUS, A STOLEN MASTERPIECE, AND AN ENIGMATIC FRIENDSHIP

ANTHONY AMORE

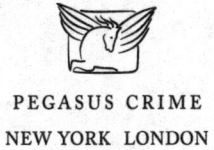

PEGASUS CRIME
NEW YORK LONDON

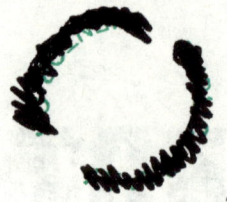

THE REMBRANDT HEIST

Pegasus Crime is an imprint of
Pegasus Books, Ltd.
148 West 37th Street, 13th Floor
New York, NY 10018

Copyright © 2025 by Anthony Amore

First Pegasus Books cloth edition November 2025

Interior design by Maria Fernandez

All rights reserved. No part of this book may be reproduced in whole or in part without written permission from the publisher, except by reviewers who may quote brief excerpts in connection with a review in a newspaper, magazine, or electronic publication; nor may any part of this book be reproduced, stored in a retrieval system, or transmitted in any form or by any means electronic, mechanical, photocopying, recording, or other, or used to train generative artificial intelligence (AI) technologies, without written permission from the publisher.

Library of Congress Cataloging-in-Publication Data is available.

ISBN: 978-1-63936-995-9

10 9 8 7 6 5 4 3 2 1

Printed in the United States of America
Distributed by Simon & Schuster
www.pegasusbooks.com

For Gabriela and Alessandra
My own priceless treasures

It's a wicked world, and when a clever man turns his brain to crime, it is the worst of all.
—Sherlock Holmes

CONTENTS

Preface	xi
Chapter 1. The Office	1
Chapter 2. 1975: A Very Busy Year	17
Chapter 3. Opening Acts	33
Chapter 4. Vengeance	50
Chapter 5. The Fugitive	66
Chapter 6. The Boost Effect	80
Chapter 7. On the Rocks	96
Chapter 8. A Seed Is Planted	108
Chapter 9. Smash and Grab	123
Chapter 10. Crises	141
Chapter 11. The Young Woman	159
Chapter 12. On the Run Again	166
Chapter 13. High Fidelity	180
Chapter 14. Preservation	194
Chapter 15. Trials and Tribulations	207
Epilogue	217
Timeline	227
Acknowledgments	231
Notes	235

PREFACE

For more than a decade, I avoided meeting with Myles J. Connor. Connor is a legendary figure in the long and astonishing history of Boston crime. He was infamous for a shootout with the police on the rooftop of a building in the Back Bay. He sensationally broke out of a jail cell in Maine using a fake gun he fashioned from a bar of soap and some shoeblack. He was the subject of a half-dozen separate manhunts. And he twice stood trial for a notorious double murder he didn't commit. It was, however, his fondness for stealing art and antiques that made him a near-mythical figure, and none of his many heists were bigger than his theft in 1975 of a Rembrandt then thought to be a painting of the artist's sister.

Since 2005, I had been investigating the most famous unsolved heist in history: the 1990 theft of thirteen works of art from the Isabella Stewart Gardner Museum in Boston, Massachusetts. The crime was committed overnight by two men disguised as police officers who used subterfuge to gain entrance to the museum. Once inside, they subdued the two young guards on duty, handcuffed them, wrapped their faces in duct tape, and secured them in the basement while they spent the better part of an hour and a half upstairs taking paintings by Édouard

Manet, Edgar Degas (including a few of his charcoal sketches), Govert Flinck, three works by Rembrandt van Rijn, and, most notably, a Johannes Vermeer. They also took a Napoleonic flagstaff finial and an ancient Chinese beaker, or *gu*. Despite the world's largest private reward ($10 million since 2017), my own work, and the combined efforts of dedicated agents from the Federal Bureau of Investigation (FBI) and prosecutors from the Department of Justice, nothing has been recovered as of this writing.

When the Gardner theft first hit the news, one suspect came to the minds of criminals and cops alike: Myles J. Connor Jr. The trouble with that suspicion was that Connor was safely locked up in a federal penitentiary in Bloomington, Illinois, on charges related to narcotics and possession of stolen art. Nevertheless, there's word, possibly apocryphal, that investigators working the Gardner case placed an urgent call to the Bureau of Prisons for a bed check, just to be sure that Connor had not again escaped incarceration and made his way to Boston that night; it was confirmed that he was indeed in his Bloomington cell while thieves pillaged the Gardner Museum. Though investigators had no strong early leads, the one thing they knew for sure was that the perpetrator was not Massachusetts's—and arguably the world's—most notorious art thief. At least not directly, that is.

Fully aware of this, I was unwilling to reach out to him. Over the years, I interviewed dozens of people who had stolen art. I was, and remain, determined to learn everything possible about the psychology of people who commit this sort of crime. Connor is one of a handful of people who have stolen masterworks more than once. As such, one would see him as a natural subject for a meeting to discuss why he is different in this regard. But I kept my distance for several reasons.

First, while incarcerated and thereafter, Connor made no secret of his theory as to who pulled off the Gardner heist. He told reporters that a local small-time criminal, the late David Houghton, had visited him shortly after the theft and told him that he and an associate of Connor's, Robert Donati, had stolen the paintings to broker his release from prison. The persistent problem for us who have investigated the case is that, like Houghton, Donati is dead, having been brutally murdered in Revere, Massachusetts, eighteen months after the heist. Moreover, Houghton's physique (he was, by all accounts, morbidly obese) surely would have been noted by the two Gardner Museum guards who were the victims of the thieves. Instead, they described two men of average and unremarkable stature; David Houghton could not have been one of the thieves. Nevertheless, Connor had every reason to provide his best guess. As a federal prisoner, information about the paintings was his best shot at bargaining with federal prosecutors for freedom. It was a ploy he knew better than anyone. Several people I trust had spoken with Connor about the heist, not least of all Tom Mashberg, a Boston-based reporter who made major headlines in the latter half of the 1990s reporting on the missing Gardner paintings. He and I forged a friendship and authored a book together. Tom confirmed to me his belief that, based on the many hours he spent interviewing him, the Houghton angle was what Connor truly believed. I believe Tom, and I do not believe Connor is lying about Houghton and Donati.

Moreover, my initial partner in the case was the legendary Scotland Yard detective sergeant Jurek "Rocky" Rokoszynski. Rocky was fresh from having pulled off one of the great recoveries in the annals of art theft by getting back two stolen multimillion dollar paintings by J.M.W. Turner that belonged to Tate Gallery in London. He had met Myles and felt that he had nothing new to offer beyond what he had told the media.

Lastly, upon his release, Connor had reunited with famed criminal defense attorney Martin K. Leppo. Leppo had taken to seeking media deals based on Connor's life so that they could both capitalize on the fame he had garnered from his long and legendary career in crime. There was talk—though never confirmed—of Leppo being behind a website that had popped up as an independent solicitor of information about the heist. This made me hesitant to seek a meeting with him, as an overture from the museum's own investigator might be deemed newsworthy. At that point in time, I didn't believe it would serve the interests of the overall investigation into the whereabouts of the paintings to have this become a viral news story. Media distractions and their aftershocks soak up an enormous amount of time that could be better spent on actual investigative work. So, I decided not to pursue a meeting with Connor, at least not for the time being.

On an early Saturday evening in September 2015, I was considering the imminent end of my tenth year without recovering the paintings. The frustration and disappointment weighed like thirteen albatrosses slung over my neck—they still do. Though many advances in the case had been made in the prior decade, the disappointment augmented my already melancholic disposition. I was sitting at an outdoor table at Starbucks accompanied only by my laptop and a manila folder overstuffed with case information. Nothing I was reading was new. I was re-re-rereading the files looking for something—anything—I had previously missed. It's a tedious but essential part of working on an old unsolved case. A Massachusetts State Police detective I greatly respect, Gerry Mattaliano, told me more than once "the answer is in the files," so I revisit them often. I opened my investigative journal and the first name I saw was MYLES. I wrote his name at the center of a blank page and circled it. From that hub, I drew spokes to the names of all the major figures who had consistently reemerged time and again as potential players in the heist. There was no mistaking it: the master thief knew them all and knew them well. I leaned back in my chair, took one last peek at the setting sun, and came to a decision.

"It's time to finally meet Myles," I said aloud to myself.

In the time since Rocky had met him, I had uncovered too many previously unknown connections between Connor and so-called people of interest. I could no longer justify avoiding the art thief who may have inspired the culprits. It was no secret that Myles claimed that he and Bobby Donati had cased the Gardner Museum years before the heist. He described Donati pointing out the Napoleonic finial as a personal prize he'd take if they robbed the place. Myles coveted the uniquely well-preserved Shang Dynasty *gu*, which was located in the Dutch Room, just an arm's length from Rembrandt's far more valuable, and also stolen, masterpiece, *The Storm on the Sea of Galilee*. Both pieces, in fact, fit his taste in art: Dutch and Asian works. His story, again, made sense.

I knew I couldn't reach out to him directly, because I was still concerned that Marty Leppo might try to turn my overture into a headline. There were many who believed that even if they couldn't snag the huge reward the museum was offering ($5 million at that time), attaching themselves to the Gardner theft could lead to a payday via media attention. That's why so many people jump at the chance to appear in television shows and documentaries, or create podcasts and social media videos, about this and all manner of true crime. So, I turned to Tom Mashberg. I knew Tom had a good relationship with Connor and his best friend, Al Dotoli, and I had learned that I could trust Tom. I immediately messaged him.

"I think it's time for me to meet Myles," I wrote, cutting straight to the chase. I knew he wouldn't take this lightly. Few, if any, understood the gravity of such a meeting. I also could trust him not to try to turn it into a story. He replied within seconds.

"Good, I think you should."

"Can you make it happen?" I asked.

"I'll try," he said.

Soon, Tom reached out to Al Dotoli. He had grown up with Connor, played bass behind him in his rock and roll days, and managed his music career. The two were inseparable. Al had even appeared alongside Myles in Rebecca Dreyfus's documentary *Stolen*. Dotoli also tried his best to keep his friend in line—to the extent possible.

Soon, I learned Myles would be quite happy to meet with me if, in return, I would be willing to appear in a documentary that was being filmed about his life. I'd need the approval of the Gardner Museum's public relations person, but, like me, she was willing to sniff out any opportunity to advance the case and quickly approved my appearance in the film.

Before long, it was showtime. We'd film my interview at the Sheraton Hotel in Braintree, a prime location to meet all sort of players in the investigation, so I had been there often. I barely noticed the typically tedious, gridlocked traffic from the North Shore where I lived; my mind was completely preoccupied with the meeting. Upon finding the conference room where the filming was to take place, a middle-aged man introduced himself as Bruce Macomber, the film's director, who explained, "We're focusing this film on Myles as a rock and roller. We want to tell the story of how his successful music career was derailed by his criminal behavior. We're almost done but wanted to get some statements in it from people like you and Tom who are familiar with his crimes." I knew this but was glad to get the reassurance. If the film had been about the Gardner Museum, I'd have not participated. He led me toward a long table. "Would you like to see what we've shot so far?"

"Sure, but where's Myles?" I asked, as he led me over to a laptop that was playing raw footage of the film.

"He went to the men's room," interjected a very tall, very slim older man whom I recognized from photos as Al Dotoli. "He got lost coming back to the room the last time he excused himself. He's probably lost again," Dotoli said, amused.

Al introduced himself, holding out a hand and offering a warm smile. Though he was then nearing seventy, he had a young air about him and a permanent gleam to his eye. He wore a plaid collared shirt and blue jeans and spoke in a friendly manner. I knew from Mashberg that Myles is deeply fond of Al, and it didn't take long to see why. Dotoli is generous, gregarious, and funny, and I took to him immediately. There is no pretense about the man.

Macomber set the scene for the footage they showed me on a small screen, with Al injecting some jocular context. The film focused on the 1970s, when Myles was the prototypical local rock star on the verge of making it big. Unfortunately for his bandmates and Al, their front man just couldn't put away his penchant for thievery. It was sort of like *Eddie and the Cruisers*, if Eddie had been obsessed with the challenge of stealing the world's great masterpieces.

Finally, Myles entered the improvised film set. Al let out a lighthearted, "Well there you are!" as his friend moseyed in, hands in his pockets and an easy smile on his face. He sported a tatty cream-colored blazer over a black T-shirt featuring the acid-green name of what I think was an energy drink. We caught each other's eye instantly, and he approached as if we were long-lost friends who were meeting to make the peace.

"Anthony," he said with twinkle in his eye, "good to meet you."

"Likewise, Myles. Thanks for having me," I replied, reaching out my hand.

We exchanged small talk about the documentary, and the director soon interrupted. It was time for my onscreen appearance. With cameras rolling, the interview began. What did I think of Myles's career given that he was seemingly destined for success in the world of rock music before crime derailed it? I replied, "If Myles had put as much effort into his music as he did art theft, he'd be in the Rock and Roll Hall of Fame today." It wasn't a platitude meant to ensure I didn't end up on the cutting room floor. It was and remains the absolute truth. The man is the Elvis Presley of art heists.

After my cameo, Myles and I watched some of the raw footage. Because little live concert video of Myles's early career exists today, the filmmaker decided to shoot re-creations, hiring an actor who bore Connor some resemblance to portray him as a young man giving it his all in concert. Actual images of Myles performing call to mind a cross between Jerry Lee Lewis and Marlon Brando. There was a reenacted scene in which "Myles" was carried onto the stage in a casket from which he jumped to perform Bobby Lewis's "Tossin' and Turnin'," and another re-creating the time when he and Al snuck two strippers into a concert they performed at Walpole State Prison—perhaps the most dangerous prison in the country during the seventies. To the great delight of the inmates, the ladies, disguised as crew members, undressed as he played. It all required the suspension of disbelief, and had I not studied his life so closely I might have thought it sensationalized. But I knew better. He was larger than life in ways both benign and malignant.

Finally, as the crew started wrapping up its movie equipment, Myles and I sat down to talk, while Tom and Al listened in. Though Mashberg is a journalist, writing then for *The New York Times*, I had complete confidence that he would keep the meeting secret. Along with Al, he sat by silently while Myles and I began our conversation.

Connor seemed to take a liking to me right away and, as the feeling was mutual, I decided to lay it out on the table. "I've waited a long time to talk to you, and in that time, I've talked to a lot of people who know you. I'm sure you've heard."

He smiled and nodded, and the cat-and-mouse aspect of the prior decade made me grin, too. I continued, "Here's what I know: you live by a certain code, and you take that code very seriously. And I've yet to meet a single person who has said your adherence to that code is anything less than genuine. For that reason, I respect you." He smiled. He was pleased that I knew this. "And," I added, "I also I think you'll deal honorably with me." Honor was an important concept to Myles. I knew that he has long been enamored of Japanese culture, especially the way of the samurai, and honor is valued nowhere more than it is amongst them. Though Myles lived his life by a different set of rules than the rest of us, he was known to abide by those rules—the good and the bad—with great discipline.

"Thank you," he said, quietly, almost modestly, pleased with how our meeting was beginning.

Encouraged, I went on. I asked him about the mindset of people who steal masterpieces. I wanted his view on the motive, the modus operandi, and where they would most likely be hidden. He was open and honest with me, sharing all his perspectives. We talked for about an hour without interruption and discussed things that I will never repeat. We also meandered onto topics like our kids, guitars, and our favorite artists. On all these, we were of like mind. We spoke in hushed tones to be sure that the crew couldn't hear us as they went in and out of the room lugging equipment. To my left, Tom and Al had begun their own conversation. I leaned into Myles from across the narrow table.

"Myles, I really need your help. What is it going to take to get these paintings back? I'm willing to do anything." It wasn't an offer; rather, it was a declaration that I wasn't just going through the motions. I wanted to know what a thief hoped to hear that could make things right from those seeking stolen art.

He sat back in his chair and looked up at the ceiling, stroking his chin with his left hand. His hair, still clinging to a hint of its once-red color, was mussed, and he needed a shave. As he considered my question, the twinkle in his eye disappeared momentarily, replaced with utter sincerity. "I think whoever has them wants to know that they aren't going to get in trouble for dealing with you," he said.

I agreed. I have always believed this, but hearing it from the man who has held countless stolen works of art temporarily captive was an important confirmation. Perhaps my greatest mission has been to convince whoever has one, or some, or all, of our artworks that the museum is dealing in good faith.

"I've worked really hard to get the message out there that the reward is real, and that the immunity overtures from the feds are real," I said. "That's why I do all these TV shows and interviews. I'm putting myself out there, on the record for the world to see, that we aren't looking to screw anyone."

Myles was genuinely interested in what I was saying. He too was leaning forward now, mirroring my posture: relaxed, but listening intently.

"You know better than anyone how all of this stuff works," I said, looking him in the eye.

He nodded with a humble yet flattered smile.

"You know that we're just a museum, we're not in the business of double-crossing criminals," I reasoned. I leaned back in my chair, having explained our position. "We just want our paintings back on our walls, where they belong."

"That's right," he replied. "They belong back in the Gardner Museum."

At that point, I was as confident as I could be that Myles and I were speaking the same language. And I was pleased. Everything I knew about the man, all my years of researching him, told me that though there was no crime too big for Myles Connor—he truly did understand the cosmic importance of Mrs. Gardner's collection being made whole again. That was important to me. I liked knowing that the two of us—though at polar opposite ends of the art world—shared a common belief in justice. Though his wasn't always exacted through official means, or in the manner that society demands, both of us understood that some things just ought to be, and the restitution of the artistic gifts that Isabella Stewart Gardner left "for the enjoyment and education of the public forever" was one such thing. Mrs. Gardner and her museum were innocent victims, and neither of us could abide that.

Still leaning forward, Myles folded his hands in front of him. He repeated the story that he's been telling for years, and I looked forward to hearing it from him in person, face-to-face. His memory had been somewhat impaired by a medical episode in prison years before. He had even reportedly tried hypnosis in a desperate search of his memory for any forgotten details of what David Houghton had said to him when he visited Connor in prison in 1990 to tell him about the Gardner robbery.

I asked a few more questions and gave him a copy of my first book, *Stealing Rembrandts: The Untold Stories of Notorious Art Heists*, which he asked me to autograph. I signed it: "To Myles, with grudging admiration. Anthony."

He and Al read the inscription and laughed. Then he took a pen and signed something for me. The inscription read: "To Anthony, with full blown admiration. Pals Always, Myles."

The time passed quickly because I was honestly enjoying the company, but it was time to wrap it up. I told Myles it was good to finally meet him. "Myles, I want you to know that my reasons for avoiding a meeting all these years was not a sign of disrespect. Frankly, I was worried that a meeting between the two of us would be a headline in the papers, like it was in the late nineties when your name surfaced about our thing."

He nodded. "I figured as much," he said, adding, "Thank you for appearing in the documentary."

"Well, I meant what I said, Myles. After all, you're the best art thief who has ever lived," I said, looking him in the eye.

I was surprised to see he appeared moved by my comment. While Myles certainly knew that he was as good as anyone and had led an incredibly colorful life, it struck me that perhaps he hadn't fully grasped his place in the annals of criminal history.

I continued. "I've studied the subject for a decade and looked at thousands of heists. Only one other person comes close, a guy in France who was basically a compulsive thief and constantly swiped pieces. But he's not in your league. He's prolific but his taste is boring." I was speaking of Stéphane Breitwieser,* a French waiter who stole more than two hundred pieces of art from a variety of museums and galleries in the late 1990s. He hit a large number of institutions, allegedly taking pieces that he liked for a personal collection. His story is especially notable for the fact that when the police closed in on him, his mother appears to have destroyed several stolen pieces in an attempt to conceal evidence that might incriminate her son.

Myles seemed flattered by my confirmation that he was at the top of his (albeit dishonest) field. Perhaps that is why he was interested in continuing the conversation. "Do you guys want to go have some lunch?" he asked. I accepted, fully aware that an invite to lunch from

---

* For more on Breitwieser, see Michael Finkel's excellent book *The Art Thief: A True Story of Love, Crime, and a Dangerous Obsession* (Knopf, 2023).

Myles did not mean he intended to pay. The meal was fun and free of the intensity of our earlier conversation. Tom and I prodded Al to tell us about his career in show business. He had a hundred great stories about superstars ranging from Aerosmith to Frank Sinatra.

The meal ended and, as expected, the bill was deposited in front of me. But I felt like George Steinbrenner must have after he bought the Yankees—it was expensive, but it was worth it. Al dropped us off back at the hotel, and as we parted, Myles and I shook hands.

"Let's stay in touch. There's a lot I can learn from you," I said.

Myles smiled, as if to say he knew exactly what I meant. "Definitely," he said, with his unmistakable lilting Boston accent. He didn't let go of my hand, and with a charming smile and his head tilted slightly to the left, he asked if I knew anyone at the Metropolitan Museum of Art in New York City.

"I'd like to see their Japanese sword collection," he told me.

My response was an unusual but necessary interrogatory. "Well, have you ever robbed them?" He fell back on his memory issues, which are sometimes real and sometimes a crutch. While he pondered this, I said, "I think it would be difficult for me to get you an appointment at a place you robbed, Myles."

He laughed, then tried a different request. "Okay, then do you know anyone who can put me in touch with Morihiro Ogawa?" He's nothing if not persistent, especially when it comes to anything related to Japanese swords.

"I just might, let me make a few calls," I told him. Truth be told, if I hadn't been meeting with Myles, I would've guessed Morihiro Ogawa was a pitcher for the Los Angeles Dodgers. But in advance of our get-together, I did a little bit of reading on samurai swords and learned that Ogawa was the world's top expert in the field. Myles told me he had a few swords—all legitimately obtained, he promised—that he'd dreamt of having the expert evaluate. But Ogawa resides in Japan and makes only infrequent visits to the United States with very specific itinerary. How I would convince this esteemed expert to meet with a legendary thief was something I didn't consider. But I wasn't afraid to try.

Back at home, I did more research on Ogawa and found through some of my museum sources that, serendipitously, he was coming to the Northeast the following month to take meetings at a few top institutions, including the Museum of Fine Arts, Boston. I contacted a colleague, my counterpart at the MFA, Nicki Luongo. "I'm hoping to have a friend show a few swords to Morihiro Ogawa, can you help?" Nicki was very receptive, but I knew it would be wrong to not be more forthcoming. "I must tell you that the friend I am hoping to accommodate is Myles Connor," I wrote in an email. "And in case you don't know, he has robbed your place." I held my breath and clicked SEND. I was shocked when, a few days later, a reply came, informing me that if I accompanied Connor for the visit, the institution would allow a meeting outside of public view. Nicki said that if I felt it would help my efforts to recover the Gardner's stolen art, she was willing to help. I'll never forget the gesture.

Myles was elated by the news, and I could tell he was impressed that I made it happen. On the appointed day, he and Al met me outside of the Gardner. Al parked his SUV, and Myles emerged from the front empty-handed.

"Where are the swords?" I asked.

"Oh, they are in the back," he replied, ambling toward the rear of the vehicle as Al popped open the rear hatch.

To my surprise—and, frankly, alarm—was a large, hard-sided, gray rifle case. Several decades earlier, such a sequence of events involving this man would have been cause for the person in my shoes to immediately dial 911. Instead, I laughed, slightly incredulously. "You have the swords in a rifle case?"

Myles had to laugh, too. Before he removed the case from the vehicle, I stopped him. "If we run into the police and they see you carrying a rifle case, we're getting arrested. Let me carry it." The fact of the matter was that even if the Boston Police saw me carrying the case in Myles's presence, all of us would be in cuffs, with lots of backup headed to our location. Luckily, no law enforcement personnel were in sight, but the whole thing was surreal: a museum security professional and a seasoned art thief, walking in lockstep down the Boston streets on a beautiful early evening, a rifle case swinging between them.

Myles was surprisingly mum on the walk to the museum, but he was grinning from ear to ear. He had a slight spring in his step, his excitement palpable. This was something he had wanted for a while. I must admit that I was too focused on his demeanor to consider what I would do once I arrived at the museum. It wasn't until I reached the employee entrance that I realized I was going to have to attempt entry with a rifle case. Not wanting to cause a stir for the watch desk guard, I told Al and Myles to go inside and check in with the guard while I texted the security director from outside with the case.

No sooner had they left when it hit me: *I just told Myles Connor to announce himself to a museum security guard.* I called out for them to wait a second, but it was too late.

Nicki arrived very quickly. Fortunately, she was unperturbed by the rifle case. Even luckier, the watch desk guard had never heard of Myles, so there was no panic. As we walked quickly to an elevator, I made quick introductions. She asked me to open it, and she saw the swords. At the time, Nicki was also a reserve police officer in her town. She is a pro and isn't the type to get shaken easily.

"This is Myles Connor," I said to her.

Myles thanked her, and she said with a smile, "You're not going to cause us any trouble, right Myles?"

Myles replied, "No, no, no" with an *aw shucks* sort of smile. We all laughed and took it in good humor.

We were led up to an administrative office and laid the case on a table where Myles opened it and revealed five swords, each in their impressive scabbard, or *saya*. He had three katanas and two *tantos*, swords with smaller blades. It wasn't hard to notice the pride he had in these items, most of which he had inherited from his grandfather, who was himself a major collector. After a short wait, Ogawa entered the room. In his early sixties, he was handsome, well-dressed, in a deep blue suit with cufflinks and a striking light blue tie. He moved with grace and distinction.

Beaming, Myles bowed and spoke a greeting to Ogawa in Japanese, and the expert returned the gesture, clearly appreciative of Myles's courtesy. Myles took a *tanto* from the case, and as he unwrapped a silk fabric to reveal it, Ogawa spoke. "I know this sword," he said, even before it was out of the *saya*.

"You're familiar with this style?" Myles asked, pleased that the great scholar recognized his most prized piece.

"No, I know *this particular sword*," Ogawa said respectfully. "It is one of a family of three. I have seen the other two."

Myles handed it to him with the reverence one sees displayed by altar servers as they offer the chalice to the priest. And Ogawa received it as a parishioner would accept the Eucharist. The whole meeting proceeded that way. Myles clearly was the real deal. His swords were not some cheap knockoffs, or even run-of-the-mill pieces from years past. His collection was world-class. Ogawa examined each in the same exact manner: methodically, using a magnifying glass to inspect the blade, the *hamon* (tempered line), the *hada* (grain), the *shinogi* (blade ridge), and every inch of the *tsuka* (handle).

All his life, Connor had been the center of attention. As a rock and roller playing in clubs around New England, his audiences adored him. As a criminal, he had the eyes of law enforcement officers from every agency centered on him. When incarcerated, he was the inmate that the administration looked to in desperation to broker peace with the prisoners. And as a thief, he was revered by his associates and underlings. His charisma was such that the guys who had done so many scores with him over the decades remained loyal to him forever, always proud that they could say that they had once run with the great Myles Connor. But now he was the humble student, obediently following the movements and methods of Ogawa, the master.

We departed the MFA after closing, passing through a room full of priceless art. We were about halfway to the building's exit when suddenly and unexpectedly the lights to the gallery went out. It was pitch black.

No, I thought, half-panicked. *Please tell me he isn't pulling something here.* I reached for him in the darkness and grabbed his left tricep. Though now seventy years old, his arm was muscular and as hard as the marble floor we were standing on.

"Myles! Don't even think about it." I said firmly. He started laughing, as did our host Nicki, who told me that they were just closing for the night.

"I wouldn't do that to you, pal," Myles said. I believed him. At least, I think so.

In the years since, Myles, Al, and I have formed an unlikely friendship, but one that has benefited all of us. For my part, I have gained a valuable source of information and advice about the field in which I work. Over the innumerable hours the three of us spent together, they came to tell me the true story behind Myles Connor's most famous and audacious heist in fine detail. And, for the first time, Al Dotoli has revealed to me all the intricacies of his successful plan to undo the crime his best friend committed. This is their tale.

CHAPTER I
THE OFFICE

As soon as the news broke in the late afternoon on April 14, 1975, Al Dotoli knew exactly who had stolen the Rembrandt. It had to be his best friend, Myles J. Connor, or MJ, as he sometimes called him. It usually was. No matter, though. Al was a businessman, not a criminal, and the heist had nothing to do with him. Being friends since adolescence with the country's most capable thief meant tolerating his habitual heists. It also meant occasionally having to help get him out of trouble. That was fine. That's what friends do—as long as it didn't involve Al having to do anything illegal. At least, not knowingly.

Dotoli was focused on a blossoming and respectable career in the music industry, a path that would lead him to work supporting some of the biggest names in the business. Besides, he had two daughters for whom he needed to provide, and he had recently begun dating a beautiful woman he wanted to impress. The last thing he needed was trouble with law enforcement, or anyone else for that matter.

Myles's criminality was always a tacit part of their long friendship, a camaraderie that had formed over electric guitars in their teens. They would be nearly inseparable over the course of seven decades—except when one of them was robbing banks, ripping off bikers and drug dealers, or, most notably, stealing precious art from museums. It was an immutable part of Myles's life, and Al accepted it, often with an inward laugh, but also with exasperation at what he saw as the shortsightedness of immediate gains that usually brought a long-term loss.

So, when the local news reported that a major heist had been committed in broad daylight at the Museum of Fine Arts, Boston, Al wasn't shocked like the rest of the world. He just grinned and shook his head. "A Rembrandt?" he said aloud to himself as he watched the broadcast. Then, with a shrug, "Sounds just like him."

Was it big news? Yes. Did Al care? Not especially. It was more a source of bewildered amusement to him. His friend had already committed more spectacular crimes than a dozen crooks would pull off in a lifetime. Unfortunately, Al had by now come to realize that his dream of making Myles Connor into a nationally known rock star was perhaps more important to him than it was to Myles and, as a result, the prospects were dwindling. This was just another of Myles's criminal exploits. Al had no idea it was going to happen, of course. Myles kept him far from the part of his life where he would get into trouble, except on those occasions when he needed Al's help to get out of it. Crime "was never part of my thing," said Dotoli. "He never brought me into any of that. I didn't want any part of it. I didn't have to. And if I had to [commit a crime], I don't think that I would."[1]

What separated Al from the rest of Myles's friends, aside perhaps from his moral compass, was his business acumen. A musician whose first band, The Internationals, formed before he was even in high school, he eventually formed another act, the Druids, while doubling as a bassist in Myles's band. Throughout his high school years, he saved every dollar he made and invested it in top-notch equipment: Fender guitar amplifiers, a Vox bass amp, high-end speakers, treble horns, and even a sound mixer. They proved percipient investments. In 1967 the

Kingsmen, themselves a garage band until recording the famous if not incomprehensible "Louie, Louie," were performing in Massachusetts and needed a first-class sound system. The venue owner rang Al, who agreed to rent out his equipment. He made $500 that night, far more than he ever earned performing a single show, and a career was born. He and a partner formed All Sound Audio, established an office in Quincy, and were soon renting out a growing inventory of equipment to bands who were from, or visiting, the Boston area. He even hired out guitars and amps to a local hard rock band that would eventually call themselves Aerosmith.

Business was booming. In 1969 the Woodstock Music and Art Fair led to an explosion in new bands, and Dotoli's was the only business of its kind in the area. What's more, major national acts like Sly and the Family Stone and Ten Years After turned to him for their sound production. Dotoli knew Chip Monck, the legendary emcee at Woodstock and fellow Massachusetts native, and was set to supply amplifiers at Woodstock until he saw the nightmarish gridlock of traffic leading to the now-famous Max Yasgur's dairy farm and opted out. Monck later brought Dotoli on board to handle the sound for all Grateful Dead shows in New England (at the time, production for concert tours was handled regionally). So impressed was he with Dotoli's system that he asked him to do the same for the Rolling Stones. But it came with a special request.

"Al, nobody has a system that can do what we want it to do," Monck told him. "Give me sixteen Dotoli Doubles."[2]

Dotoli Doubles were large sound systems devised by Al featuring two fifteen-inch JBL speakers in each. The cabinets for the speakers had to be specially made to his liking and were constructed in his office space. Monck rented eight for each side of the stage, an unheard-of setup in its day. Dotoli's speakers can be seen onstage with his company's name emblazoned in silver on each cabinet in the 1970 rock and roll documentary *Gimme Shelter*, depicting the Rolling Stones' famous yet tragic show at Altamont. Monck had arranged for the Hells Angels to provide security for the show, and they ultimately killed a fan and injured several others.

By 1972, Al was renting equipment to legendary musician James Cotton as well as his fellow blues performers the James Montgomery Band. He was equipping bands and venues throughout the region with his sound systems while his business partner was touring the world with the rock group Poco, a band formed by members of the recently defunct Buffalo Springfield. It was heady stuff for two young guys from Quincy who started out with onstage dreams of their own but quickly and successfully took to the business side of the industry.

Over time, Al fell in love with production management, eventually buying out his partner and shutting down the sound system rental business. So, in 1975, as his best friend Myles was off stealing masterpieces, Al was on a completely different course, providing tour production for national acts like Dionne Warwick and Sha Na Na, in addition to Cotton, Montgomery, and local favorites the Fat City Band. He was also handling smaller-scale concerts held at local arenas and radio stations. Business was good, the money was pouring in, and Al's career couldn't have been more detached from crime.[3]

After hearing the news of the MFA heist, Al turned his attention back to his paperwork, tending to bookkeeping duties in a series of detailed ledgers he obsessively maintained. This was before the days of personal computing, when fastidious recordkeeping by hand was essential. Tour dates, invoices, accounts receivable—they were all his to manage as he dug into the pile of work on his desk. Thankfully, executive functioning was one of Al's great assets, and he had a practice of keeping everything neatly organized. He took his work very seriously, and over the years this level of focus and dedication would bring him to the very heights of show business. In fact, in just one month, he would be overseeing production for Frank Sinatra's second-ever show at the Providence City Civic Center, a show so noteworthy that Jacqueline Kennedy Onassis planned to attend.

Later in the day, when he had finally finished his administrative tasks, Al called Myles. "Did you?" was all he had to ask. The question was met with laughter—Myles's inimitable high-pitched cackle. That response had them both laughing. It was all Al needed to hear. No one, not even his friend's long-since estranged wife, could communicate with Myles in fewer words than Al. It was the sort of cryptic exchange that develops over many years between the closest of friends. The language of blood brothers. There was nothing more to discuss, and they quickly moved the conversation to more innocent matters. Given his friend's history, the odds were always high that their conversations might be joined surreptitiously by a silent third party from any of a host of local, state, or federal agencies—even if it would take a team of code breakers from the National Security Agency to decipher their dialogue. They were religiously circumspect on the phone. In the strange world that was Al's, for what was then more than fifteen years since they had become fast friends, incidents like the theft just didn't seem like that big of a deal anymore. They had plenty to discuss about Myles's own music career and his upcoming gigs, all which would be produced and managed by Al, of course.

Nothing more about the theft was mentioned between the two. At least, not for some time. To Dotoli, his wayward pal had pulled off just another heist. It was what he did. Besides, Dotoli wasn't into fine art or antiques, just his family and his business. He tucked away a rationalization his friend told him long before, after one of his many prior thefts: "Any antique that is worth something has been stolen at one point from somebody in its history."[4] While this wasn't exactly true, it was enough of a justification for Dotoli. No need to sully it up like the specialists who studied crimes involving art. He didn't know any of them anyway. And both Myles and Al believed that they were the sorts who would look down their noses at the two of them, especially by Boston Brahmins.

Meanwhile, Boston was abuzz with talk about what happened at the Museum of Fine Arts. The city was still in its heyday of lawbreaking—something akin to a modern East Coast version of Wild West outlaw gangs committing every manner of crime one can imagine. And one would have to have quite a twisted imagination to dream up everything that was happening at the time. There were mass murders, Mafia wars, gangland hits, bombings, crooked feds, and even heists that *weren't* the work of Myles Connor. It was a crime reporter's dream and a district attorney's nightmare. These were the days before everyone flipped on everyone else (though, ironically, one of the city's most notorious gangsters, James "Whitey" Bulger, was informing to a corrupt FBI agent named John Connolly). Just ten years earlier, the city was terrorized by a serial killer and rapist known as the Boston Strangler. And days before, the media reported that inmates in the isolation cellblock at the Walpole State Prison had embarked on hunger strike over the harsh treatment and conditions there.

For years, Walpole was a source of headlines in the region's newspapers. The prison revolts that peppered the United States throughout the 1970s were nowhere worse than were seen there, just twenty-five miles outside of Boston. And the goings-on there were closely watched by the city's most hardened criminals for the simple fact that most of them had served time within its walls. They were keenly aware of the severe conditions there—a climate so dangerous that Howard Zinn described it as "a concentration camp in Massachusetts."[5] Even Albert DeSalvo, the Boston Strangler himself, couldn't survive the prison—he was murdered there in 1973. So, the hunger strike resonated with the former convicts, many of whom knew Myles Connor from his long stretch there beginning in 1967, when he was sentenced to twelve to twenty years for wounding a state police officer in a shootout. The trooper shot first, Myles argued, and he returned fire in self-defense. Incredibly, when his attorney pleaded for leniency on his behalf of his client, he claimed that Myles suffered from "an inferiority complex."[6]

Once he arrived at Walpole, Myles soon assumed a leadership role amongst his fellow inmates. A man of considerable charm and intellect, at only twenty-four years old he displayed the charisma, toughness, and obvious intelligence necessary to win the confidence of even the older inmates in one of the nation's toughest prisons. The fact that his crimes had captured headlines for their daring and drama—the shootout had occurred when he was fleeing police officers along the rooftops of Boston's Back Bay—gave him an undeniable cachet within the prison population. But that episode was just one of what would be many scenes in his life that were fit for the big screen.

On St. Patrick's Day 1972, Walpole prisoners rioted after a knifing took place in the maximum-security wing of the prison while many inmates were attending the showing of a film. As they filed out, they found fires in two wings of the prison. Fights erupted, items were flung, locks were broken, and guards found themselves cornered and retreating with inmates on the upper tiers locked in their cells and in danger from the smoke from the fires. With guards having abandoned their posts, inmates used weightlifting equipment as impromptu sledgehammers to free others from their cells. The violence only subsided when the warden decided to approach the inmate who was previously elected president of the Walpole Prison Jaycees: Myles Connor. The warden and Connor came to an agreement that the latter presented to the inmates, and a five-man arbitrating team was convened.[7] Connor was able to win several concessions on behalf of his fellow inmates, including conjugal visits, televisions, furloughs for certain prisoners, and even lectures from Harvard professors.[8] Peace was restored, and Connor was the key to it.

"I deemed it an honor to be so trusted by my fellow inmates," he said at the time. "In my opinion, the [warden] made a mistake, a judgmental error. He lived up to it. Every person here would not be here if he hadn't made a mistake." He added, "It's the best man who lives up to it and tries to better himself."[9] Thanks to the accolades he received from prison officials for his role in brokering a peaceful resolution to the dangerous turmoil at Walpole, and a letter of support from a Massachusetts State Police detective named John Regan—a good friend of Connor's father—he was released on parole in October 1972. "After I did all that, when the parole board hearing came up, they felt that they owed it to me to release me. And so they did."[10]

Despite Connor's success, unrest at Walpole was far from over. There was another uprising a year later in March 1973 when the guards' union went on strike, leading to the facility being run by the inmates under the careful eye of citizen observers. And by 1975, when the Rembrandt was stolen from the MFA, there was a full takeover of the prison that was covered extensively by the city's crime reporters.

The day before the heist, one of Myles's closest friends from Norfolk State Prison, Jimmy Martorano, was the subject of a front-page story in *The Boston Globe*. Martorano, and an associate named Edward Halloran, fled an approaching police officer, crashed into a wall, and were found to be in possession of guns, violations that meant a year in prison thanks to a new law enacted just thirteen days prior.[11] The pair were well-known in criminal circles, and their arrest was an immediate and stark warning to the criminal element about the legislation. But by the next day, all focus would be directed toward the Museum of Fine Arts.

The heist was the talk of the town, and it wasn't just the police who were wondering whodunit; everyone from pipefitters to professors tossed around their theories. The media, though, offered no clues, for few were left behind. The reports simply said that two men had purchased tickets to the MFA, went directly to the gallery where Rembrandt's *Portrait of Elsbeth van Rijn* was on display, and removed it from the wall. Guards who attempted to intervene as the thieves snatched the work were manhandled, and one of the robbers brandished a gun. As they made their quick getaway, the crooks fired warning shots that scared off anyone who tried to intervene. One guard who gave chase and tried in vain to stop them as they left the building was pistol-whipped and taken to the hospital to be treated for lacerations.[12] The description of the culprits, broadcast to police officers via an all-points bulletin, was somewhat lacking in detail. It reported "two unknown white males, one with long blond hair and glasses and a leather cap, both armed with 9mm automatics."[13] Not much to go on, especially in an era when long hair was in vogue for men. Discard the hat and glasses and the perpetrator would be virtually invisible. There was no great description of his partner, either. They did have eyewitness reports of the alleged getaway vehicle: a black and gold Buick or possibly an Oldsmobile bearing Massachusetts license plate 961-544.[14] Police officers expected that the car would likely have been ditched as soon as the thieves were certain they hadn't been tailed, and they were correct. By four o'clock the next morning, the car was located less than a mile away abandoned at Roxbury Crossing. It had been stolen from Norwood, Massachusetts, with different license plates on the front and rear replacing the authentic New Hampshire plates registered to the car.[15]

The director of the Museum of Fine Arts, Merrill C. Rueppel, offered his opinion to the media as to the pedigree of the unknown thieves. "I don't think a professional art thief would use violence to steal a painting," he said, adding that selling it would be difficult. "It would be almost impossible to find any kind of reputable dealer for it."[16] Rueppel's latter opinion was correct. He accurately reasoned that the painting was likely far too recognizable to sell, at least legitimately. But he was wrong on the other points, ignoring recent and nearby widely reported armed art thefts in Worcester (1972) and Cambridge (1973) where highly valuable artifacts were stolen and the thieves had used firearms and violence against museum guards.

While the lack of solid descriptions or evidence might have meant that Al's friend was—at least for now—in the clear, guesses were bandied about Boston like Super Bowl predictions. Everyone in the city and its environs believed they were in the know or claimed to know someone who was. Adding fuel to the speculation were reports that the painting was very highly valued. As if stealing a painting by the world's most famous artist from the New England's most famous museum wasn't eye-catching enough, half a million dollars in 1975 (roughly the equivalent of $3 million today) got everyone's attention.

Crime stories have long been Boston's passion. So, while news was still breaking, Al's circle of friends started gently prodding him for information. Did Myles do this? But in the days following the theft, Dotoli kept his mouth shut regarding what he knew about the Rembrandt heist. The truth was that he knew nearly nothing about the heist beyond Myles's tacit laugh that Al understood to be an admission. Sure, he knew what that meant, and he harbored no doubts. But he had no details, either. He also had no idea why it was taken. While most would assume that, like any other heist of high-value items, it was for money, most also didn't know Myles like he did. Rare was the art heist that Connor committed with largesse as his motive. Perhaps more important, the motive genuinely didn't matter to Al. All that mattered was no one was killed, Connor hadn't been caught, and no one was knocking on his door. Al had never even set foot into the MFA in his life. He couldn't have identified the Rembrandt, or any piece from the museum's massive collection, if it was hanging on the wall in front of him. He didn't have the palest idea of where it was. What's more, he neither wanted nor needed to know the answers to any of these questions.

The locals at the bars Al frequented weren't too surprised that he didn't speak a word about the MFA job. Naturally, they assumed he knew more than he actually did. After all, everyone was aware that he and Myles were like brothers. So, when he'd walk into the local pub, the regulars would shoot him a wink or a nudge him with a playful elbow. Everyone was aware that Al's friend was, by reputation, the obvious top suspect. Al just responded with a shrug, his virtually omnipresent smile, and his endearing high-pitched giggle, and that was the end of it. But that was about to change.

On April 28, 1975, two weeks after the heist, an ad appeared in *The Boston Globe* that was so noteworthy it elicited its own separate news story. The ad's heading, in large block letters, was the attention-grabbing word REWARD with the words FOR MISSING REMBRANDT in all caps beneath. It wasn't something one typically saw in a newspaper anywhere in the world. It continued, "A Reward is offered by the owners for the information resulting in the safe recovery of Rembrandt's *Portrait of Elsbeth van Rijn*, recently taken from the Boston Museum of Fine

Arts. All replies are confidential." At the bottom, contact information for the "owner's representative" was provided in the form of a phone number and a Boston PO box mailing address.

The term *owner's representative* was especially pertinent, for the Rembrandt was not owned by the Museum of Fine Arts. Rather, *Portrait of Elsbeth van Rijn* was a long-term loan. The painting's owners were descendants of Robert Treat Paine, a signer of the Declaration of Independence. But the wording was just vague enough to avoid that technicality.

The advertisement was sure to attract attention, as was, of course, its aim. The day after it ran, *The Boston Globe* reported that the painting was insured by its owners for $750,000, with museum officials describing it as "priceless." Thus, the stakes were raised even higher, especially among those in the criminal underworld. A spokesperson for First Security Services Corporation, the agency that placed the ad, provided only a prepared statement, saying, "We have been retained by agents of the owners of Rembrandt's painting of Elsbeth van Rijn, recently removed from the Museum of Fine Arts in Boston. It is our intention to negotiate with anyone who might be helpful in the safe recovery of this art work [sic]. All negotiations will be handled in a totally confidential manner, and at this time we are not prepared to comment further."[17]

The wording was clearly very deliberate. Rather than referring to the painting having been *stolen* from the MFA, the authors chose the word *removed*. That subtle distinction exchanged a criminal accusation for a word that implied something more akin to an error in judgment. As an official first communique with the thieves, it tacitly established a less adversarial relationship. It also avoided a specific dollar figure for the reward, which is often a difficult number to set and at times even more difficult to negotiate. What is an appropriate amount of money for something so valuable? Will the holders of the painting see the amount as a starting point for negotiations? If they are willing to ransom it back, will they expect the $750,000 figure that the *Globe* reported, surely much to the chagrin of the insurer? And was that even an accurate estimate?

It was clear from the ad that the owner's agent—most likely, the insurer—was extremely serious about getting the painting back. The very presence of an advertisement also signaled that the insurance company's investigators were desperate for information. The ending of the *Globe*'s story was telling: "Boston police and FBI agents are working the case, but reported no new developments."[18] At that point, this should hardly have been a surprise. There was little forensic evidence to work with aside from an abandoned rubber glove and a few spent shell casings (in 1975 fingerprints were about all there was for crime scene examiners). No credible ransom calls were reported to the museum or police, both of whom were anxiously monitoring phones. So, while there may have been whispers in Boston barrooms about who pulled off the caper, they remained just rumors to the investigators. Still, the promise of a reward got people talking. And that meant Al Dotoli—as the best friend of a known art thief—would be getting some visitors.

As time passed without any leads, conjecture that Al might know the whereabouts of the painting, or even that he was complicit in the heist, became widespread throughout Boston. Wannabe wise guys would invariably try to strike up a conversation with him about the heist and the painting's location, but Al remained mum. "Those in the know thought they knew more than they did," he recounted.[19] There were rumors spreading that he was holding the painting for Myles or otherwise abetting, which he was not. Such reckless speculation put Al at the center of an international crime story in which he had played—and wanted—no role.

Soon enough, the rumors led to phone calls to his home. The first was from someone claiming to be an insurance investigator looking to make a deal with Al. He never said how he came by Al's name or number, and Dotoli, unsure of the caller's true identity, brushed him off. Then the bounty hunter–types also started ringing his home, dollar signs in their eyes, hoping to serve as middlemen for a painting that Al genuinely didn't have. "Never in a thousand years would he think to give it to me," he said. "And there was no way in hell I'd ever take it!"[20] These contacts proved to be mere nuisances, however, and were part of being the closest friend of a legendary thief.

Myles had been on the run when the MFA heist took place, fleeing justice rather than facing a jury for another art theft. But he had just been apprehended and was now behind bars in the Charles Street Jail awaiting both state and federal prosecution. That meant he was out of the reach of people looking to get their hands on the valuable masterpiece. Al was the next best thing—the only option, really—and he understood this. But things soon escalated beyond the usual level of annoyance for Al.

One evening, while working in his home office, Al noticed through a window in his front door that a long black Cadillac limousine pulled into his driveway. It was an unusual sight in his quiet middle-class suburban neighborhood, but it didn't shock him. Perhaps it was Steven Tyler or one of the many rock stars he knew. But when he saw a shadowy figure emerge from the back seat, he thought, "Jesus Christ, that's the fucking Mafia."[21] He wasn't off by much. Doughy, bald, and bespectacled, it was local club owner Rudy Guarino, a man tightly connected to countless Mob figures, who stepped out of the vehicle. Al had known Rudy for years through their connections to live music. Guarino ran the Sugar Shack, a popular soul music club in Boston's infamous Combat Zone, where one could sit just feet from the stage and watch the O'Jays perform, rub elbows with the likes of football legend Jim Brown, score any of a variety of illicit drugs, or cut a deal with the pimps who called the place a second home. Given Guarino's business dealings in nightclubs in Boston, Miami, and Las Vegas, it would have been surprising if he hadn't connections with La Cosa Nostra. Typically, Guarino would call Al when he needed organs or amplifiers for the Sugar Shack, and Dotoli would deliver the items and the invoices personally. They'd hang out together, have a drink, and talk about the industry. But not on this night.

Guarino stood in Dotoli's living room and told him, "I just came from The Hill [Providence's Federal Hill]. Raymond and the guys would be really appreciative if you would ask your friend to consider giving this painting to us," he said. "And we'd show our appreciation." With those words, Guarino opened a briefcase flush with cash. "Al, there's sixty grand here, and that's a starter . . . there's a lot more available." With that, Guarino departed, leaving Dotoli speechless.[22] It wasn't merely the money that left him awed, nor the Mafia's certainty that that Myles was behind the heist. It was the mere mention of the name Raymond.

"Raymond" was Raymond L. S. Patriarca, the mafia don who ran all six New England states from his unassuming storefront in Providence, Rhode Island, housing his "legitimate" business—Coin-O-Matic, a vending machine company located on Federal Hill that doubled as Patriarca's headquarters and, thus, the seat of organized crime for the entire region. To gangsters throughout New England and beyond, it was known simply as "The Office." His reach was such that a New England mobster-turned-informant would testify that the CIA once turned to Patriarca to assassinate Cuban dictator Fidel Castro.[23] When the Kennedy brothers were in power, they targeted Patriarca. After all, he controlled the powerful Mafia gangs in their hometown of Boston, and Bobby Kennedy, ever the crusader against organized crime, vowed "we're going after that pig on the Hill."[24]

Patriarca was respected and feared by everyone, and he sat on the Mafia commission in New York alongside the likes of the Bonanno, Colombo, Lucchese, Genovese, and Gambino families. The mere mention of his first name made Dotoli suddenly, and understandably, very uneasy. This approach by Guarino now escalated the whole affair. Al plopped his six-foot-four lanky frame onto a sofa. He instinctively thought to grab a beer to relax, but he wasn't sure he could keep it down. Scattered emotions passed through him like a chill: irritation that he was now unwillingly irrevocably entwined in Myles's mess, relief that his daughters were not staying with him that evening, and dread that he was on Patriarca's radar screen. Patriarca's reach was vast, and his ruthlessness legendary. It was indisputably better to be in the cops' spotlight than Patriarca's. Just months earlier, Patriarca had been released by the Rhode Island Parole Board after completing a prison sentence for conspiring to kill two hoods. That followed a lengthy sentence in a federal penitentiary in Atlanta for his role in the shotgun killing of organized crime figure Willie Marfeo.[25]

Al wasn't leaving anything to chance. No sooner had Guarino's limo left his driveway than he made a decision. He could no longer simply brush off the nuisance phone calls and visits to his home from shady men. The situation had taken a sharp turn. "It's getting dangerous," he thought. "This shit has to stop. It's coming down on me now." Like it or not, he would have to be part of the solution.

In order put the matter of the stolen Rembrandt to rest and keep his family and himself out of serious trouble, it was now clear: "I've got to see Myles," Al decided.[26]

CHAPTER 2
1975: A VERY BUSY YEAR

Right from the onset, 1975 was an incredibly busy year for both Myles Connor and Al Dotoli. Not only would Connor steal a big-name painting from a major museum, but Dotoli was hard at work with a big name himself, consulting for megastar Dionne Warwick. She was fresh off her number one hit, "Then Came You," which she recorded with the Spinners, and she was now planning an international tour, and that meant Al had his hands full coordinating shows with production teams from multiple time zones, languages, and capabilities. It was still the early days of big concert tours, and not all locales were up to the task of providing the professional sound, lights, and technical support required to support a major act. Fortunately, Al is a born planner. Whether it be a show or his own recordkeeping, everything is organized, accurate, and greatly detailed. Myles, on the other hand, is a hoarder and usually has objects and assorted ephemera strewn everywhere. But when it comes to their work, they share an important quality that is central to their life stories: they are both fastidious tacticians.

As Al focused on Warwick's 1975 tour, Myles was busily engaged in a region-wide bank robbery spree that brought him and his small but fearsome gang of thieves the sorts of hauls that would be considered huge even half a century later. It was the norm—not the exception—for them to drive away from a bank job with more than a hundred thousand dollars. And the heists were numerous; Myles was nothing if not active. Having the stolen masterwork in his possession did not make him want to lay low at all. It made him even bolder—but not careless. He was methodical, carefully thinking through his approach to heists the way a football coach might plan for a big game. He knew well that the downfall of so many thieves was caused by a lack of careful planning. So, he put his greatest asset—his intellect—to work, mulling over the most effective methods to thefts that resulted in big money, smooth getaways, and no one getting hurt. This meant a great deal of research and reconnaissance, especially for his latest favored approach to hitting a bank: striking immediately after the staff bundled up money in anticipation of pickup by the armored car service. What could be better than ready-made bags of cash just sitting there waiting to be taken? But it required meticulous timing so that Myles and his crew weren't happened upon by armed guards. That might necessitate an ugly encounter that wouldn't end well for anyone. For a Myles Connor operation, this sort of planning required going far beyond merely getting an insider on board and "casing" a target. It meant truly studying it, making the effort to examine things like alternate escape routes, locations of police precincts, places to stash the cash, and a slew of other steps that few scriptwriters would conceive. It was this thorough approach that would prompt him to set out on a long weekend drive. And if he could sneak a little culture and romance in on the way, all the better.

Myles had pressing business in western Massachusetts, for he was determined to be productive in 1975. Banks were foremost on his agenda. No matter that he had recently been arrested yet again, this time for art theft and related crimes. After posting bail, he got off to a quick start, setting his sights on the Norfolk County Trust in East Milton, not more than three miles from the house in which he was born. It was a hard score to pass up, because he had an insider, Rona Prewitt, who just happened to be the bank's head teller. Rona was a fan of his, frequenting his rock and roll performances at the Beachcomber, an immensely popular South Shore club, and she was willing to do whatever Connor told her to do. In this case, just before she was due at the bank, she was grabbed at gunpoint. Myles's cohorts pretended to force her to open the door and, of course, the vault. One of the men would take things a step further and, to give the ruse a veneer of authenticity, struck her with his gun. Once inside the vault, they loaded $116,000 in cash into bags before making their getaway.

Later that day, Connor sped up onto the lawn of Sha Na Na leader Lennie Baker's home to see Al Dotoli, who was there visiting with his friend. As Baker fumed over his choice of a parking spot, Myles barged in the front door. With a big smile he said, "Surprise, surprise!" and tossed a brown paper bag to Al. Forever borrowing money from him, Myles repaid $600 he owed Al. The next day, Al deposited it into the very bank from which it was stolen, completely unaware of the heist. Once again, Myles's plan worked like a charm. Years later he would be indicted for the robbery. Prosecutors relied on fabricated testimony, falsely implicating a few of his friends, including Martha Ferrante and Steve Gorski, who was dragged before a federal grand jury by FBI Special Agent Bernie Murphy.[1] Despite Connor's guilt, and in what would prove to be a trend in his criminal career that would consistently infuriate police and prosecutors, Connor and his friends were all acquitted.

An inveterate risk-taker, only nine days after his big take at the Norfolk Trust Company, Myles turned his attention to a bank in South Hadley. Though quite a distance from his home, doing a bit of recon out in western Massachusetts was a good excuse for him to stop by to see Martha Ferrante, a pretty younger woman he met while he was imprisoned at Walpole State Prison and she was a college student volunteering at a halfway house. Eventually, the two began dating. She lived not far from South Hadley, so he could make a day of it. And, what's more, the art-loving thief could make a stop at the bucolic Mead Art Museum to take in some culture. He had never seen the collection before, and it was small enough that it wouldn't take too long to enjoy, so he decided to indulge his obsession with fine art.

That might seem strange. Few men with an arrest record an inch thick have been known for their connoisseurship. Myles Connor is hardly Thomas Crown. For one, though he didn't enjoy violence, he didn't think twice about employing it when he felt it necessary. Also, Myles's taste in women was more Bonnie Parker than Rene Russo. Though he enjoyed fancy cars and art, he had little interest in associating with high society or dabbling in finance. The riches he accumulated through his illicit activities were almost entirely dedicated toward the acquisition of antiques, particularly Japanese militaria. Crown could keep his fancy haberdashery; Connor's idea of an indulgent expenditure was more likely an Edo-period full set of armor, or as he would say with perfect pronunciation, *yoroi*.

With snow in the forecast on February 8, 1975, few Bostonians would choose to spend their Saturday trekking out to Amherst simply to visit an art gallery. That's not to say that the Mead Art Museum at Amherst College isn't worth the four-hour round trip, but merely that there are better days to see its collection than a blustery February afternoon that could very well extend into the evening should the Massachusetts

Turnpike get even a coating of precipitation. Perhaps it would be better on such a day to get your art fix at one of the bigger museums in or nearer to the city.

Those who know his name associate Myles with only two things: crime and rock and roll. Deep inside Myles Connor, however, lurks the heart of a cognoscente. The timing was excellent: just weeks earlier, the Mead Art Museum had opened two new exhibitions of British art. The larger of the two featured portraiture, with Sir Joshua Reynolds's portrait of Lord Jeffrey Amherst, a work considered the best of his paintings in New England, the headliner.[2] The second exhibition featured landscapes, including Edward Lear's *Pentedatilo* and Philip Jacques de Loutherberg's* *A Stormy Landscape*. It would make for a worthy departure from the nastiness associated with the pending South Hadley bank heist that he was concocting.

Though Amherst College, founded in 1821, is one of the oldest institutions of higher education in the United States, the Mead Art Museum is a relative newcomer to the vibrant world of cultural institutions in Massachusetts. Despite Amherst having received in 1855 Assyrian reliefs from the ninth-century palace at Nineveh from American missionaries—relics worthy of a serious museum—the small, neoclassical, marble-fronted building did not open to students until 1949 (its formal opening to the public was held on May 20, 1950). The architectural firm chosen to create the building, McKim, Mead & White of New York, was a perfect and uniquely apt choice. For one, they were the designers behind some of the most acclaimed and noteworthy institutions in the Northeast, including the original Pennsylvania Station, the Rhode Island State House, the Boston Public Library, the Brooklyn Museum, and the main campus of Columbia

---

* Sometimes referred to as Philip James de Loutherberg.

University. But perhaps just as important, the funds to build the museum were left by one of the firm's founders, William Rutherford Read, Amherst College class of 1867. Upon its opening, the Mead's collection was quickly identified as one of the finest smaller collections in the country.[3] Works by American and British artists like Gilbert Stuart, Rembrandt Peale, John Singleton Copley, Benjamin West, and Winslow Homer are joined by Claude Monet, William-Adolphe Bouguereau, and Peter Paul Rubens.

Yet more appealing to Myles, but, unfortunately for him, off view, was the Mead's impressive collection of 2,500 Japanese woodblock prints from the eighteenth and nineteenth centuries. The woodblocks include works by the great masters of the craft, including Hokusai, Utamaro, and Hiroshige. Myles's love for all things Asian and, in particular, Japanese, was decades old. He was an expert in karate (which he pronounced with a Japanese accent) and was by now amassing a formidable samurai sword collection, a pastime inspired by his maternal grandfather.

Myles arrived at Amherst College early in the afternoon under a dolphin-gray sky that heralded the impending snowfall. Though technically the spring semester, the campus was cold and quiet, with few students milling about. Winter had robbed the trees of foliage that in other seasons beautified the classic New England setting. The temperature was hovering right around freezing as he drove the small winding roads past the imposing bronze statue of Henry Ward Beecher to the center of campus where the museum is located. Parking his mid-1960s blue convertible Griffith sports car by the museum, he stopped before entering to take in the Mead's imposing exterior oddity: the Stearns Steeple located by the entrance. The 150-foot-tall stone steeple had been part of a Gothic revival church on campus, a testament to the religious origins of the college. With the school's steady move toward secularism and the move of devotional services to the college chapel, the church was razed to construct the museum. However, the steeple—complete with its bells—was spared.[4] Impressed, if not puzzled, Myles then stepped through the museum's marble-flanked main entrance. His first stop inside was another surprise: the stunning Rotherwas Room, a gallery constructed from a parlor that belonged to a seventeenth-century English knight, complete with the original fireplace and walnut paneling. Myles was awed by the craftsmanship, and he quickly realized that the Mead might just have more surprises in store for him.

Though the museum has a far more extensive collection of American art, Myles chose to devote his short visit to the European art gallery. He was instantly taken by Frans Snyders's *Larder with a Servant*. But then, who wasn't? The piece is six-and-a-half feet wide and more than four feet tall, dominating the room it occupies. Connor, a devoted animal lover, studied the still life carefully: a large table topped with an assortment of fare for a meal. It included a dead deer and boar, a multitude of deceased fowl, a large lobster, and fruits and vegetables. A servant with a tray stands ready to refill it, and two hungry dogs at bottom consider the pending feast. It was the sort of dramatic baroque work that he enjoyed. His interest in Asian art aside, Connor admired the Dutch and Flemish Masters, another taste acquired from his maternal grandfather. He moved onto much smaller works by far bigger names, like Rubens's oil sketch *Christ Enlightening the World* and Monet's *Morning on the Seine near Giverny*. The serenity of the latter, a beautiful hazy landscape in shades of pink and green, represented a stark juxtaposition to Snyders's work.

As he traversed the museum and studied the works, one painting in particular—a landscape—caught his eye. It appeared to him to be another Dutch baroque work, perhaps even a Rembrandt. But this piece was not hanging on the gallery's walls; rather, it was in what appeared to be an administrator's office. That made it unlikely to be a work by Rembrandt, but could it be by one of his students? Govert Flinck perhaps? The office's open door was to Myles an invitation to explore. Once in, he found that, unlike the rest of the collection, there was no label listing an attribution and title. He studied it intently for a few moments when, suddenly, Amherst professor and museum director Frank Trapp interrupted his gaze.

Trapp, an imposing bald man who favored large, thick, black-framed glasses, was surprised to find a short, strongly built man with flaming red hair standing within his workspace. The director had a reputation as an abrasive man who didn't suffer fools, and, true to form, he did not take kindly to this intrusion into his nonpublic space. Trapp had been with the Mead from its very inception, working alongside its founder, Charles Morgan, and serving as its first curator not long after returning to the United States after serving with the US Army in Guinea during World War II. He had played a major role in amassing the Mead's collection, having acquired more than 2,500 works during his tenure, and ultimately served as director for twenty years. With a specialty in older European art, Trapp's influence on the museum is indelible, especially the works that most attracted Connor.[5] But their shared appreciation of the painting Trapp selected for his office did not endear him to the interloper he encountered.

"What are you doing in here?" Trapp snapped, both surprised and annoyed by the intrusion.

Connor was unfazed by Trapp's indignant tone and remained calm and polite, his eyes fixed on the canvas. He explained that he had noticed the landscape as he was exploring the museum.

"Is it a Flinck?" he asked, in his clipped Boston accent that had the distinct air of an intellectual. This apparent pedigree, however, mattered not to Trapp. He ignored the question and barked at Connor. "I will kindly ask you to leave. Now!"[6]

Perhaps it was Trapp's experience as a soldier that led him to reflexively address Connor with a command rather than a request. Moreover, the museum was his life—as much a home as a workplace. In his view, Connor had violated his personal and sacred space.

Despite Trapp's tactlessness, Connor took one last look around the office before departing calmly and without incident. Clearly, the director didn't know that he had just encountered a notorious thief. He returned to his work as Connor resumed his browsing in the public areas for a short time before leaving.

That evening, as the snow continued to fall, Myles drove home in his little Griffith and summoned his henchmen Tommy Sperrazza and John Stokes to a meeting. Naturally, they assumed it was to go over the plans for the imminent heist at the South Hadley bank that Myles had scouted earlier in the day. The two were young but had already spent all their adult lives—and some of their adolescence, too—either committing crimes or serving time for them. They were tough, fearless, and serious trouble. They had been introduced to Myles by his longtime criminal cohort, Ralph Petrozziello, a man with a penchant for violence who had participated in the murder a Boston Police officer with Sperrazza in 1974 during an armed robbery of a supermarket manager. Whether separate or apart, these men were as dangerous as any in Massachusetts; so much so that Al Dotoli banned them from attending Myles's concerts for fear that they might do something that would make him a pariah to booking agents and venue owners.

Connor told Sperrazza and Stokes that he had another, more urgent job that needed attention. Without explaining why, he told them they were going to rob the Mead Art Museum, and they were going to do it *tonight*. "I was seriously insulted," he later said of Trapp's behavior toward him. "And so I went back with the boys."[7] The two young criminals were always game for anything that Connor had concocted, and they quickly agreed to abet him.

The motive for most art heists is simple and obvious: money. Thieves who are used to getting pennies on the dollar for moderately valuable items like cars and jewelry see giant dollar signs when they look at masterpieces. Earnings on even a tiny percentage of the value of multimillion-dollar objects can be irresistible to criminals. So, they sometimes set out to steal them. Unlike other highly valuable items like diamonds and cash, paintings in museums are meant to be enjoyed by the public, who are expected and welcomed to linger and gaze deeply at them. The whole point of a museum, in fact, is to provide people from all walks of life with access to these precious items, encouraging quiet interaction with them. While such accessibility is the cornerstone of public art institutions, it also often proves irresistible to the nefarious. But once the masterpiece is stolen, thieves learn that the obverse to such easy access is the inability to fence the work once it's taken. Most art stolen from museums is just too valuable and highly recognizable to offload.

A noteworthy example is the theft in 1978 of a painting attributed to Rembrandt titled *Portrait of a Rabbi* from the de Young Museum in San Francisco. It and three other Dutch works were stolen in an overnight heist that, though somewhat elaborate in that it included what appears to have been thieves rappelling through a skylight, was primarily the result of poor security at the facility. As was typical until relatively recently, the experts of the day attributed the heist to the classic

Dr. No scenario in which a sinister collector commissions a masterpiece heist so that he can enjoy it on his own. Noted "art cop" Robert Volpe of the New York Police Department said at the time that "it's obvious there was prior knowledge as to the target, and the Rembrandt was probably contracted for. That was the motive; a customer waiting." Art insurance adjuster Arnold Miller posited, "My hunch is that it was a contract job, ordered by some guy in a foreign country who would go to any length to possess 'The Rabbi.'"[8] These theories, in reality, are nearly never the case. In the case of *Portrait of a Rabbi*, there appears to have been no such buyer. Instead, the thieves handed it and others off to a third party. On the evening of November 2, 1999, during a weekly open house, a crate was left at Doyle Galleries in New York City. Once the contents of the crate were deemed safe, authorities found within it three of the works stolen from the de Young, including the Rembrandt.[9] In an unfortunate twist, the painting was ultimately determined to be neither painted by Rembrandt nor depicting a rabbi. It is now referred to as *Portrait of a Man with Red Cap and Gold Chain*.[10]

It is this difficulty, if not downright impossibility, of fencing stolen masterworks that makes repeat offenders uncommon. Having learned that this particular crime does not pay, the thief classifies it as a one-off and moves on, or back, to other illicit activities and abandons dishonest forays into museums. Though paintings are still stolen on a rather frequent basis by criminals with visions of a huge score who have not yet learned the folly of stealing masterworks, it's rarely a recidivist crime.

Myles Connor, however, is a unique man with no interest in the lessons learned by lesser crooks. He has no time for rules, either. When it comes to repeat performances, it's difficult to match his prolific work when it comes to the stealing of high-value paintings. Perhaps more interestingly, no thief in criminal history has stolen art with the motives that compelled Connor. While money certainly attracted him to all manner of criminality, riches were not the impetus for his art thefts. Instead, the motives ran much deeper. So, on that snowy winter's night in 1975, Connor commandeered a van and headed back to Amherst not with riches on his mind, but revenge for the disdain and discourteousness with which Trapp had treated him. He would break into the Mead and steal paintings from it—from them—to exact vengeance against the elitist who had dared to literally look down his nose and scold him.

The men arrived back in Amherst under cover of darkness and snowfall. The inhospitable weather held an advantage in that there were no students walking about in the shadows of the early morning hours. Gaining entry into the now-closed Mead Art Museum was no great challenge for a thief of Connor's skill. Purely by habit, he had earlier noted that the windows in the museum were neither alarmed nor particularly robust before he even contemplated a heist. It was instinct. Tradecraft. It didn't matter if he was in a museum, a bank, or a church (though his presence in the latter was rather unlikely). Details like the integrity of security hardware stood out to Connor the way a shark, even when sated, will notice its natural prey. So, while the idea of a master thief in a balaclava making the moves of a yogi around an array of red laser beams to get his hands on a Fabergé egg springs to mind, Connor merely broke a window and climbed through. Stokes and Sperrazza followed him in. Connor knew well that the methods of burgling a museum are many, but the path of least resistance was always the best. Besides, the simplicity of this job added to the personal satisfaction he felt in exacting vengeance for the affront.

Once back inside the Mead, Connor immediately set his sights on the work in Trapp's office that he had mistaken for a Flinck. It was, instead, painted by the great master Pieter Lastman. One can understand his mistake: Lastman had taught Rembrandt; Rembrandt had taught Flinck. Further, the painting was a portrait depicting a young and, curiously, clean-shaven St. John the Baptist seated with a lamb by a tree in a setting and tone not dissimilar to Flinck's *Jesus and the Samaritan Woman* (1634). An oil on canvas about three-and-a-half feet tall and just shy of three feet wide, *St. John the Baptist* was easily taken from the wall. And now it was no longer Frank Trapp's. It was his.

A few antiques in the museum collection caught the eyes of Stokes and Sperrazza. Neither knew a lick about art, but they were experienced enough in stolen objects to know that there was a bustling market for antiques that could be easily fenced. Ironically, their shared ignorance of fine art spared them the wasted effort of trying to guess which of the other paintings would be worth stealing. Meanwhile, Myles decided to treat himself to another painting in the European section. Choosing what appealed to him rather than what might be worth the most money, he grabbed Hendrick van Vliet's *Interior of the Nieuwe Kerk, Delft*.

Van Vliet devoted a good portion of his oeuvre to church interiors and architecture. The painting of New Church was completed in 1661, right in the heart of the Dutch Golden Age both in terms of date and location. Delft during this period was where greats such as Johannes Vermeer and Pieter de Hooch created some of the period's most important works. The painting's perspective attracted Connor as he quickly gazed into the church toward the apse before removing the frame to make for a much lighter item to carry.

Less cultured thieves wouldn't know van Vliet, or even Lastman for that matter, especially in the United States. But Connor knew them both well. Taking the van Vliet—which is a bit smaller than the Lastman—was no hard task for Connor. Perhaps due to his unfamiliarity with the museum's collection and layout, he made no effort to steal its collection of Japanese prints. He had not, after all, set out to commit a major heist. This was an act of retribution. In mere minutes, he and his two brutish cohorts were out of the Mead Art Museum and headed back to Boston. They left behind no clues, save for footprints in the fresh snow that continued to fall in Amherst.

Once home, Myles traded his Griffith for a big roomy Cadillac before returning to Amherst. He wrapped the paintings in blankets to keep them from being damaged and then put the stolen art, valued at about $250,000, in the trunk of his car.[11] Vengeance had been served.

Early the next morning, the phone rang at the Massachusetts State Police barracks in Northampton, about twenty miles southwest of Amherst. An anonymous caller tipped off the police that a theft had occurred at the museum. The state police contacted the college's police department, which responded immediately to the Mead. There they discovered a flurry of footprints in the snow and a broken window. Upon entering the building, they found the empty frames on the floor. Fingerprints were lifted, but in 1975 there were little other forensics to be done—not even video recordings to review. With no useful evidence and no apparent leads, recovery was not imminent.

Surprisingly, news of the theft did not carry far. It received almost no notice in major media outlets. In a later press release issued by Amherst College, officials would say that the "Dutch canvases had been savagely removed the frames and stolen."[12] This was hyperbole. Connor never treated fine art roughly. He was relatively unique in that regard, as in so many others. For instance, any other thief who had just breezily stolen two Dutch Masters basically on a whim would celebrate the score. He'd probably instantly go to work trying to fence them, putting out feelers to trusted sources. But not Myles. While he certainly wouldn't turn away a payday, money wasn't the object of this crime. So, after dropping off Stokes and Sperrazza, he drove to his sister's home in Hanover, Massachusetts, to store the paintings in her large garage. He opened the Cadillac's ample trunk and gently unwrapped the blankets wrapped around each painting. He stopped and took his time to enjoy each work by the dim lightbulb in the compartment. While revenge was his motive, that didn't mean Connor didn't revere the works. Even in this setting, they glowed, the mastery of the artists evident in a suburban driveway under the cover of darkness. Finally, after having experienced the paintings in his own way and on his terms, Connor gently filed them away with the other pieces of art and antiques that he had acquired, licitly and otherwise.

There was, of course, still the matter of the bank heist that begged attention. Weeks later, Connor returned yet again to the area, this time with Ralph Petrozziello and another trusted accomplice, Billy Oikle, whom he had met at Walpole, and successfully pulled off an armed bank robbery in South Hadley. A bank job in a sleepy rural town was child's play for seasoned stick-up men like this crew. Unlike today, where bank robberies rarely result in big dollar figures, Myles and his gang regularly walked away from them with scores over $100,000. South Hadley was no different. After making a safe getaway, the trio hid the money in the woods to avoid any problems at the roadblocks the police would surely establish. Later, when the commotion died down, they'd go back to the woods and retrieve their loot.

As with so many of Connor's art capers, the tale doesn't end there, tidily wrapped up in a blanket. When the police entered the Mead Art Museum after the heist, they didn't find two empty frames on the gallery floor—they found three. A painting by Jan Baptist Lambrechts, a minor Dutch artist, titled *Interior with Figures Smoking and Drinking*, was also missing. But who had taken it? Years later, Myles would be arrested in a sting operation in a Bloomington, Illinois, hotel by the

FBI while trying to establish a cocaine distribution network. The feds seized his collateral, including the two Dutch paintings—the Lastman and the van Vliet—but not Lambrechts.[13] Myles insists these were the only two works he took. To be sure, the Lambrechts does not fit his style. The Mead Art Museum still awaits its return.

CHAPTER 3
OPENING ACTS

A rt theft is what Myles Connor did best, and committing those crimes brought him to more museums than many have visited. He estimates that he robbed about thirty museums, but he can't be certain. But to those divining his future upon his birth in 1943, a career as a cop rather than a crook seemed the likeliest path. His father, Myles Joseph "Joe" Connor Sr., was a ranking police officer in their hometown of Milton, Massachusetts, and at one point was a finalist for the chief's job. An honest cop who cared about his town and his family, Joe Connor was the sort of police officer who would stop to help an elderly person carry in their groceries or answer a neighbor's call in the middle of the night, even when off duty. Later in life, after he retired from the Milton Police Department, he was hired as a security guard at a public high school in Marshfield, Massachusetts. While authority figures aren't usually the most popular people among high schoolers, Joe was so beloved that when he retired from that job the students dedicated their yearbook to him, and a scholarship fund in his name for Braintree High School graduates was established.[1] Such was the influence of the service-minded elder Connor that one of his three sons joined the Massachusetts State Police while another entered the priesthood and served as the chaplain for the Boston Police Department. Only the son who bore his name strayed from the straight and narrow. For years, Myles Jr.'s favorite response to the many who would question how he and his siblings' paths were so divergent was a deadpanned, "I don't know where they all went wrong."

A brilliant young man, Myles Connor could have been just about anything he dreamt. He excelled in medical science, art history, Asian culture, and more. As a teen, he was attracted to herpetology, collecting venomous snakes and even an alligator—somewhat odd pets for an adolescent living in a Boston suburb. He even worked at an exotic pet store for a short time. His weakness for dangerous animals was an early indicator of his penchant for veering from the mainstream and toward the extreme and the concomitant headlines he had a knack for attracting.

In 1960, when he was but seventeen years old, he drew the interest of *Boston Globe* columnist Ted Ashby, who visited Myles at home to interview him about his pets and his music. Prompting the exit of a "murderous-looking tarantula" from its box, Myles offered to hold it in the palm of his hand to show the reporter and photographer from the *Globe*. The newsmen recoiled in horror and pleaded with him to put the creature back in its box. This surely brought the young, blue-eyed redhead amusement. He also introduced the reporters to his dear friend Albert, a young alligator dwelling in his attic, many miles from its natural habitat. Ashby described Albert as "affable" in comparison to the tarantula, though adding that the reptile "hates everyone except [Myles]." The gator and the spider were but two of his exotic pets. "I don't have too many other species at the moment. Just a few reptiles, one seven feet long. Some other things. I've had a fox, a skunk. Had four boa constrictors. Three piranhas." Asked if she ever visits the pets in the attic, his mother Lucy told the *Globe*, "I never go up there."[2] Her only son would remain an animal lover throughout his life, favoring

Marlin Perkins's *Wild Kingdom* and National Geographic specials over sports and sitcoms.

Myles also had a passion for music. A rebel by nature, he took to the electric guitar and formed a rock band when the genre was still in its nascent stages and scaring suburban moms and dads around the country. In other words, it was just the sort of thing he loved. He studied guitar, paying three dollars per lesson to a neighbor, Red Hart, an early rockabilly guitarist who performed at a country western bar in Boston called the Hillbilly Ranch.[3] Traditional scales and triads weren't part of the lessons. Instead, Hart just taught him "the cool stuff." In turn, Myles taught neighborhood beginners what he was learning for fifty cents each. It was at this time that fourteen-year-old Alfred Dotoli, also growing up in Milton, made a decision that would change the course of his life forever.

Too young to drive, Al often walked the neighborhoods of Milton, and on occasion he would traverse Oak Road. As he passed number 12, he'd hear the roaring and unmistakable twang of an electric guitar backed by an amateurish rhythm section blasting from a home located beneath a canopy of oak trees. It was 1961, and the Beatles were on their second stint in Hamburg, two years away from leading the British invasion of America. So, the music Al heard coming from the house didn't have the pop sensibility that the Fab Four would bring. Nor were the musicians inside the home—Myles's aptly named backing band the Wild Ones—interested in Chesterfield suits and their velvet collars. Rather, what he heard was raw. It was black leather jackets and switchblades rock—the sort of songs with lyrics about outlaws and fighting authority. It appealed to Al. No matter who was playing it, nor what it took to learn how, he wanted in.

Al had already developed a love for the guitar. He was barely ten years old when he took the money he had saved up from birthdays and errands and bought his first: an acoustic Silvertone guitar that he furiously worked to teach himself to play. He later bought a Harmony electric guitar and even formed a small band with his eighth-grade school friends. But it was what he heard coming from the Oak Road house that really moved him. It wasn't difficult for him to find out that was the domicile of Myles J. Connor Jr. and his parents. Even at his young age, Myles had already earned a reputation as a rebel in the town. But Al was determined to learn to play like him. In his blue jeans and T-shirt, the tall, lanky adolescent approached the oversized front door and could hear the band playing in the living room with a passion that he wished for himself. He turned the old-fashioned twist doorbell and heard the band come to a stop. Seconds later, the front door swung open. Before him stood the much shorter Connor, his fiery red hair almost matching his dismay at being interrupted.

The tall, brown-haired string bean standing on his stoop spoke in an almost surprised manner. "You're Myles Connor!"

The older teen replied, "I know that. Who the fuck are you?"

"I'm Al Dotoli. I want to learn to play guitar like you."

Myles warmed to him in an instant. Al possessed an uncanny likeability that won him friends from a wide demographic and across all social strata, and not even Myles was immune.

"Come on in. We'll be done pretty soon," Myles said.[4]

Al watched as Myles and the Wild Ones ran through a few more songs, sitting there listening to the older boys, impressed with everything he heard and badly wanting to graduate from novice guitarist to what they were doing. He was amazed at Myles's vocal range and command of his instrument. As soon as the rehearsal ended, Myles turned to Al and handed him his guitar. "Show me what you know," he instructed. Al played him a few basic songs and then described what he wanted to learn. "Show me the boogie-woogie," he said.

Myles took him through it, step by step, like a sensei with his *senpai*. Immediately, Myles took Al under his wing. He would be his guitar teacher, but unlike the others, he didn't charge Al for the lessons. They'd practice in the living rooms of both of their homes, with Al attaching an electric pickup to his acoustic guitar's sound hole.

Standing next to each other, the newly inseparable friends presented an interesting contrast. In one photo, the two are dressed for a major event: Myles was opening for the Dave Clark Five, a huge act from England famous for knocking "I Want to Hold Your Hand" out of the number one spot a year earlier. Myles is wearing a flashy gold dinner jacket with a black collar and gold lapels, black pants, and tuxedo shirt. His flaming red hair matches the fire in his eyes. His build is slight, though later he would develop into powerful spark plug of a man. To his left is Al, his teenage manager, in a smart charcoal jacket with a white shirt, skinny black tie, and silver tie clip. His hair is wavy and brown, and though he is smiling, he appears just slightly more reserved than his friend, even though the photo was taken at his mother's home. Al has not yet developed the signature look of surprise he often bears, his eyebrows arched high as if in a constant state of delighted surprise. One suspects that a lifetime of watching the endless exploits of his friend fixed them that way. As Al describes it, "Myles did ten things at one time. And he gave 10 percent to all of them. And he did all of them as good as we would if we did each of them at 100 percent. Music. Robbery. Academics. He'd excel at all of it."[5]

One other thing about them stands out: Al is a full nine inches taller than Myles. Myles never shied away at making light of his own stature, sometimes remarking with a grin, "I might be a small potato, but I'm hard to peel." Despite the disparity in height, Myles served as sort of an older brother. Al's own brother, Joe, was also an excellent student and a bit of a rebel. It was said that "Joe only crosses the street on red or yellow. Al waits for green."[6] The same sort of contrast applied to his relationship with Myles, though in the latter's case, it might be said that streetlights represent authority, so he paid them no heed whatsoever. Al's relationship with Myles caused no rivalry with Joe, who at first doubted his brother's raves about his new friend's ability and intelligence, until the day Myles sat with Joe while he waited for Al. Joe, who was studying premed at the time and aspired to be a veterinarian, was taken aback by Myles's knowledge of science and medicine. He later told Al, "Boy, that guy is smart!"[7]

Al would produce his first concert in 1964. Myles, who was already famous among the youth in Milton, would headline. It took place in Saint Agatha School's gym. Born for the business, Al set it up like an old pro. He printed fliers, made posters, and sold one thousand tickets. He also arranged for security, because he knew that a group of teens from Milton were likely to fight another from Dorchester's Savin Hill. Myles entered the show with his 160-pound Doberman, Gunner, and wearing a black cape with a blood red lining. Despite the size of the crowd, he wasn't the least bit nervous and opened with Chuck Berry's "Johnny B. Goode." As feared, a fight soon broke out in the crowd. The Milton police were called, and none other than Myles's father, Sergeant Joe Connor, responded. He stormed onstage and warned, "If there is any more violence or any more fights, I'm shutting this down!" After just one more song, the melee broke out again. Joe went back onstage and interrupted his son's set, taking the microphone, and saying, "I warned you people, the show is over!" Myles put his arm around his father, took the microphone back, and said with a smile, "Aww, dad!"[8]

Barely out of his teens, for Myles, rock and roll stardom wasn't the only thing for which he was preparing. His parents had recently split, and his father had moved out of the family home on Oak Road. Father and son, though, remained very close, and Myles suffered none of the alienation that sometimes besets the children of divorce. Soon thereafter, Myles's girlfriend, Victoria "Vicky" Laws, had moved in with him and his mother, Lucy. She had little choice—her mother had ordered her out of her home. It wasn't Vicky's teenage pregnancy that enraged her mother; rather, it was her daughter's steadfast refusal to end things with her troublemaking boyfriend. In December 1961, she and Myles, age eighteen, married in a small ceremony. His best man was the drummer for his band, Ronald Castriano. It couldn't be Dotoli, who was still just fourteen years old at the time. Eight months later, Myles J. Connor III was born. Lucy, concerned about her son's station in life and ability to support his sudden family, told Myles it was time to find real work. The young rebel was soon employed as an Electrolux vacuum cleaner door-to-door salesman. His first demo was at a friend's house, and he ruined his pal's mother's floor. He quit right away, moving on to encyclopedias. After taking umbrage with a man's attitude at one house and flinging what was supposed to be an enticing free gift at the homeowner, he quit on his third day. His adolescent stints working at an exotic pet store and at a bottling plant (where he punched his boss) aside, these were the only real jobs Myles Connor ever held.

Fortunately, though the Wild Ones had disbanded, Myles landed a regular gig playing his brand of rock music at a popular stop known as the Lewis Room at Revere Beach Plaza, Massachusetts's answer to the Jersey Shore. He performed alone with his electric guitar, taking the stage six nights per week at 8:00 P.M. and performing five exhausting forty-five-minute sets in which he covered songs by Elvis Presley, Roy Orbison, Jan and Dean, the Everly Brothers, and others. He quickly gained a following due to his combination of raw talent and unbridled enthusiasm from the first set to the last every single night. Before long, he told the owner of the Lewis Room that he needed a drummer, and the wish was granted. But Myles wanted a proper rhythm section. So, he told Al Dotoli to buy a bass guitar.

"But Myles, I don't know how to play the bass," said Al, now eighteen years old.

"That's okay, I'll teach you," Myles replied. He proceeded to give Al lessons, advising him that whenever he came to a part of a song he didn't know, he could simply pretend to play it. Myles's furious guitar would mask any flubs. The gigs were a lifesaver for Al. His father had told him that unless he got a job making at least seventy-five dollars a week, he would have to start washing dishes at the family restaurant beginning at 6:00 A.M. every day. Myles was again able to convince the venue owner that he needed a bass player—at a salary of seventy-five dollars a week. A band was born.

When they weren't performing, Connor and Dotoli spent nearly all their time together. They were most often seen speeding around Milton and its neighboring towns with the significantly taller Dotoli riding on the back of Connor's motorcycle, the two smiling and laughing. They cut an unusual image but enjoyed every minute of it. A vignette: the pair was speeding along the expressway, ostensibly minding their own business en route to Laconia, New Hampshire, for a massive assemblage of motorcycle enthusiasts called Bike Week. Suddenly, a car sped up and pulled close enough beside them to cause Myles to swerve to avoid being struck. Then the driver did it again. These were no mistakes. Not one to let a slight go unrequited, he directed Al to reach into one of his saddlebags and retrieve his flare gun. Exactly why he had a flare gun never entered Al's mind. Myles then caught up to the car and fired into the open driver's side window and struck the inside of the windshield. The driver struggled to control the car as it filled with smoke, skidding to left and right until it came to rest in the breakdown lane, as Connor and Dotoli roared in laughter.

That Myles wasn't cut out for domestic life surprised no one, and before long he and Vicky were no longer living together. Conveniently, there were two spaces above the Lewis Room available, and since he was performing there nightly, he turned one into a makeshift studio apartment and used the other as a dressing room. Despite the separation, Myles and Vicky remained friends and even had a second child together, a daughter, Kim, who was born in 1965 (they didn't officially divorce until 1967).

In the summer of 1965, Myles and Vicky made the five-hour drive to the home of his mother's uncle in Sullivan, Maine, just southeast of Bangor on the Atlantic coast. The town was familiar to the Connors; Myles's mother, née Lucy Conant Johnson, had many family connections there, which meant he had spent every summer of his youth in Sullivan with them enjoying a break from the city heat. While there, he heard tell of a very old, very wealthy woman who had recently passed away. Soon the talk turned to antiques.

"I was at the dinner table at my granduncle's house, and I remember them talking about how sad it was that Mrs. so-and-so had passed on and her children were going to get everything that she had and she despised her [daughter]," Connor said. "Being aware there was this house filled with antiques and stuff, I decided to take a look."[9]

Like his father, who accumulated hundreds of guns in his lifetime, Myles had an affinity for firearms. But unlike his father, whom he described as "perhaps the only truly honorable person that I have ever known in law enforcement,"[10] many of those that he kept were either acquired illegally or were illegal to own. In fact, in the trunk of the Cadillac he had driven to Maine was a bevy of guns purchased from one of the many crooked men he met at Revere Beach. In short order, he had acquired a reputation there among the criminal element as a tough young man who could be trusted, and many notorious Mob figures frequented his act. They took a liking to this rock and roller who didn't shy away from anyone. One story in particular made its rounds through the various beach clubs and bars.

While Myles, Al, and his drummer were performing, a surly and tough older man at the bar was annoyed with the modern rock music they played. Soon, he started yelling at the band, repeatedly demanding they play Patti Page's 1950 hit "The Tennessee Waltz." Angry that he was being ignored, he hurled a beer bottle at the band that somehow passed just between both Myles's and Al's heads, crashing into the wall behind them and exploding. Myles took off his guitar, jumped off the stage, and beat the much bigger man into submission. When he felt he had taught him a lesson in manners, Connor climbed back up onstage, put his guitar back on, and began singing again. *I was dancing with my darling to the Tennessee Waltz . . .* He played the song and, later, he and the man became friends.

In Maine, Myles took Vicky out for a drive in the Cadillac and, by no coincidence at all, happened upon the large, now-unoccupied home of the recently deceased antique-collecting woman. Committing crimes with the mother of his young children in tow wasn't something he intended. Instead, he'd just have a look around. As Vicky waited in the car, Myles surveyed the condition of the window and door locks securing the house. They were no match for him, and the treasures he saw through the windows proved too tempting to resist. Besides, in his mind, there would be no victim. The dead woman and her daughter did not get along, so "there was a sense of justice, if you will, by going down there and relieving some of the antiques that the woman had and not letting the daughter have them."[11] For most, this would be purely rationalization—the sort of fodder a desperate defense attorney would throw out to a skeptical jury. But not to Myles Connor, who would spend his life living by a very strict code. One of history's greatest thieves, he'd steal from just about any place but wouldn't dream of pilfering from a friend, family, or the needy.

Myles entered the house stealthily and with little effort. Once inside, he helped himself to a grandmother clock he knew he could fit in the giant trunk of his Cadillac. He placed it gingerly in the vehicle, moving aside the cache of weaponry within. As he went to reenter the home, a sheriff's deputy, alerted by a suspicious neighbor, pulled into the driveway behind him. The two men knew each other, and the deputy began to question Connor. He attempted to sell him a line about being interested in buying the home, but the officer knew better and made a move to arrest him. Myles, concerned more about the machine guns in his car than the antique clock, put up a fight. The deputy drew his weapon, but, using his martial arts skills, Connor relieved him of it and fired random shots at the ground and into the air. After a couple of punches to his jaw, the officer fled. The son of a cop, Myles called after him asking if he was okay, but the deputy kept running. Then he jumped into the abandoned patrol car and moved it so that he could get the Cadillac out of the drive, shooting the police radio so that the deputy couldn't immediately summon assistance after the getaway. Then he and Vicky drove off, with the latter no doubt shaken—but not surprised—by the whole matter. He had avoided arrest, but only temporarily. Myles Connor was now a wanted man.

Despite Myles's reputation, and though he was a gentle young man, Al Dotoli was drawn to Myles like a mouse to a glue trap. In this case, music was the bait. For the next sixty-plus years, the pair would be inseparable, except for Myles's periodic lengthy sentences. But that was part of being friends with him. "That's Myles," Al would say with a shrug each time he'd go to prison. Sometimes he'd say it with sadness, others with frustration, because from the moment he first heard him play in that Oak Road living room, Al knew he was listening to something special. Myles had a unique gift—the ability to shift from the operatic countertenor of Roy Orbison to the gravelly bass-baritone of Johnny Cash with ease. A natural showman, onstage he was electric, pouring limitless passion into every song, including the ballads. His musical act was no act at all. It was an external display that mirrored Myles's internal fire for collecting fine art and antiques. When he belted out the apropos "Riot in Cell Block #9," one could imagine the feeling he had when he would behold a fourteenth-century samurai sword. That was at the root of his incessant thievery—an insatiable need to obtain what he coveted. As C. S. Lewis wrote, "In order to be bad, one must have good things to want and then to pursue in the wrong way."[12] The money obtained from his crimes, whether it be museum and bank jobs or, as Myles described it, "dabbling in the importation of cocaine from South America to the United States," was enormous, and it was all to buy Japanese swords and antiques. Not to show it off or boast about it, but to collect it, to treasure it. Even when money was short, there was never a thought of selling off any of these prized possessions to hold him over until the next score. Myles could always count on Al for a loan or a gig. But finding a fourteenth-century katana? Now that wasn't something that came along every day.

It can be argued that Myles's addiction to acquiring antique treasures was genetic. His maternal grandfather, Charles Johnson, was an avid collector, and Myles and his parents lived in his grandfather's home for the first thirteen years of the young man's life. The two were close, and "Gramps," as his grandson called him, left an indelible impression on him. Myles fondly recalls the time when he was ten years old and received a coveted BB gun for Christmas. True to his endless youthful impishness, he fired the gun in the direction of a house four doors down, taking out a garage window. Understandably upset, the neighbor marched over to the Johnson house and, finding young Myles in the yard, manhandled him. Grabbing him by the ear, he pulled him to the back door and knocked. When the door opened, Myles would recall, "He said something derogatory to my grandfather." The neighbor confronted Gramps, saying, "'He just took out the window to my garage. I want you to do something about it.' Gramps hit the guy with one shot and he knocked the guy right out. He called the police, but they knew my father and grandfather. 'As far as I can see you put your hands on a ten-year-old kid, you had no business doing that. I suggest you put the whole thing to rest,' and he did."[13]

On his mother's side, Myles could boast a *Mayflower* pedigree dating back to William Brewster. His mother's great-great-grandfather, William Gregory Cole, was a New England arts patron and cousin of Hudson River School founder Thomas Cole. His ancestry also includes the Revolutionary pamphleteer Thomas Paine, from whom Myles says he likely inherited his "rebellious and anarchistic streak." Lucy was also related to suffragist Julia Ward Howe.[14] But it was through his grandfather Charles his great passion for all things Japanese and artistic was born.

Together, they made countless visits to the Museum of Fine Arts, Boston. They'd travel the Fenway neighborhood often to see the vast and impressive collection there, and Johnson would use it to teach his grandson about the Old Masters, the great artists of the early American republic, and, of course, the collection of Japanese swords and other Asian art. Though a working man, Charles Johnson had a great many connections with the intelligentsia, including trustees of the MFA. One with whom he was particularly close was the curator William Sturgis Bigelow. Bigelow was perhaps the greatest American expert of Japanese culture and artifacts of his era. In 1881, he grew disenchanted with life in Boston and traveled to Japan, remaining there for seven years. It was during this time that Japan was rushing toward Westernization, discarding a massive amount of treasures that Bigelow eagerly scooped up.[15] In time, he would donate tens of thousands of Japanese artifacts to the MFA, helping it to create what the museum describes as "one of the most comprehensive collections of Japanese art in the world, including paintings, sculptures, decorative arts, and vast holdings of ukiyo-e woodblock prints."[16]

At the turn of the twentieth century, Myles's grandfather accompanied Bigelow on one of his trips to Japan and purchased a great number of artifacts of his own, including a large cache of samurai swords. According to Myles, his grandfather "had a collection of Japanese swords just as good as the MFA or the Met." Because of the new opportunities in Japan, his grandfather obtained approximately two hundred high-end swords that he would leave to his beloved Myles. It would be the start of an insatiable lifelong thirst for *daisho*: the katana and *wakizashi* swords and all related items, including precious sword guards. There would never be too many. There would never be enough.

Police officers throughout Maine were on the hunt for Myles Connor after his escape from the sheriff's deputy. Word went out to all points that he was on the run and that he was armed with a weapon stolen from the officer. What's more, he had fired shots. No matter that in his view they were meant as warnings—tell that to the officer who had been punched and had his gun taken. This was serious business, and Myles knew it. He fled south on Route 1, no doubt hoping to escape back to Massachusetts, where he had a better chance of blending in than he did in sparsely populated rural Maine. But an alert Maine State Police trooper soon identified his Cadillac, took Connor and Vicky into custody, and transported them to the county lockup in Hancock. Vicky was quickly released.

In 1965, the Hancock County Jail, run by Sheriff Merritt Fitch, was like many other mid-century county jails in rural America. Relatively small and simple (the sheriff's wife cooked dinner for the inmates), it lacked the fortresslike security one sees in modern jails. Nevertheless, Myles found that the hardware encaging him was too sturdy to enable an escape. So he devised another way out.

While he certainly inherited his taste for Japanese antiques from his Gramps, it was from his paternal grandfather that he inherited his wild side. William Joseph Connor was born in Galway, Ireland, and immigrated to the United States in 1911. According to Myles, Grandpa Connor didn't simply leave Ireland for a better life—he fled after shooting two constables, most likely related to his activities on behalf of the Nationalists and Republicans in Ireland. In the United States, he met and married Catherine Halloran, and the pair settled in the heavily Irish neighborhood of South Boston. He worked as a teamster, and the couple raised three sons and a daughter. His eldest boy was Joe Connor, Myles's father. His second son was named William, who chose to use the last name Connors. Bill Connors would go on to be a trusted advisor and friend to John F. Kennedy. Siblings Mary and Thomas Connor would come later. Though a born rebel and fighter, even William Connor couldn't have imagined the exploits of his grandson Myles.

Stuck inside his jail cell, Myles Connor decided to use his formidable wiles to get out of the lockup. Well aware of the exploits—both real and mythical—of a kindred spirit, John Dillinger, the infamous leader of a notorious bank-robbing crew, Myles decided that he, too, would fashion a phony gun to force the guard to open his cell at the Hancock County Jail. Familiar with all manner of handguns due to the collecting habits of his father and grandfather, he methodically sculpted a small gun from a bar of soap, to which he then he applied black shoe polish. By his fifth day of incarceration, Myles was ready to make his move. When the jailhouse trustee and a deputy sheriff appeared, he pulled his soap gun on them. Neither was armed, and neither was willing to take a chance with the man wielding what appeared to be a gun. After all, he had fired shots when apprehended just days before. The cell was opened, as demanded. Connor struck them both with forceful karate blows not meant to injure but to enable his getaway. He fled the area, running through the Maine woods, swimming through rivers, and hiding out in the cold and unforgiving unsettled land abutting Route 1.

The police spared no resource to track him down. Light aircraft circled the area. K9 officers were led through the woods by bloodhounds. Small boats patrolled the nearby bodies of water. Roadblocks were set up along the highway. None of it worked. On his third day as a fugitive from justice, Myles was surprised to hear his mother's voice over a megaphone imploring him to surrender. It was a clever ploy by the police, but ineffective; he wasn't about to surrender. Then another voice over the bullhorn proved even less helpful to the authorities. Al Dotoli warned him, "There are more cops out here than Heinz has pickles!" he cautioned. "They'll shoot you!"[17] Myles heeded the helpful information his loyal teenage friend relayed. But as was inevitable considering the breadth of the operation to capture him, Myles ran out of real estate and was captured.

Connor was convicted rather quickly on the charges related to both the attempted robbery of the abandoned home in Sullivan as well as the escape from the jail. However, his attorney filed an appeal and soon he was back in Massachusetts, where he would resume his music career. But now, at just twenty-three years old, Connor's reputation as an outlaw spread throughout the nightclubs at which he performed.

His adventures in Maine had made headlines from Bangor to Boston. This figured in his forming his reputation back home in two disparate ways: while the criminal element was impressed with his fearlessness and willingness to fight the law, area police knew that they were facing a major challenge with the bold, slippery, and clever crook. It would be the start of a decades-long Machiavellian effort to put Myles Connor behind bars, no matter the tactics or ethics employed.

CHAPTER 4
VENGEANCE

It was a quiet evening at the home of Sergeant Joe Connor. It was early March 1965, and he had just finished a long and, frankly, troubling shift on the job with the Milton Police Department. Joe was a very highly regarded police officer in the town. Just two years earlier, he was on a short list of three officers under consideration to be the department's chief. When he arrived home on this night, his son Myles was on the couch toying around with his guitar. As usual, Joe hung up his hat, took off his gun belt, and went upstairs to change out of his uniform and into civilian clothes. But something was amiss. He didn't say hello to Myles when he came in, and his son could sense a pall in the house as soon as soon as his dad entered. That was unusual. Joe Connor was a kind man with a gentle spirit and rarely brought his work home with him. Myles, now twenty-two years old, knew something wasn't right, but decided to let his father be.

Later, as the two men ate a simple dinner together at their modest dining room table, his father remained uncharacteristically sullen. Myles hated seeing his father down and finally asked him what was wrong. Joe explained: there had been a theft of a few antique guns at the Forbes House Museum in Milton. He had been called in to see the chief—not unusual, since Joe was a ranking officer on the force. But he had not been summoned to seek his help on the case. Rather, the leadership at the museum demanded that Sergeant Connor be questioned about his possible complicity in the heist. After all, the higher-ups at the Forbes knew well that he had a large collection of antique guns, some of which were not unlike those taken in the robbery. The chief defended his man and tried to push back, but the wealthy and powerful backers of the Forbes House insisted. The chief was left with little choice, and Joe was questioned about his whereabouts.

Of course, Sergeant Connor hadn't stolen the weapons. It wasn't in him to do so. Sure, Joe was a gun enthusiast. He had even been selected by the Milton Police Department to serve as a firearms instructor and was sponsored by the FBI to attend an instructor's course. But as much as he enjoyed guns, he valued his honor far more. The interrogation was a severe humiliation. Joe was serious about public service, having been with the department since 1943. A decorated officer respected by his colleagues and fellow townspeople alike throughout the entirety of his twenty-two years of service, he was revered by his son, who asked in a soft, caring tone tinged with empathy and disbelief, "They did that to you, Dad?"

Utterly deflated, his father simply replied, "Yes, son," as he quietly picked at his dinner.

Myles was incensed but did not let it show. Instead, he remained at the dinner table with his father in silent solidarity. He could abide being accused of a crime himself, but he knew his father was beyond reproach. The insult to his beloved dad not only ached but also triggered the class warrior within him. Myles was acutely aware that though his maternal lineage was *Mayflower*, his paternal ancestors were Irish immigrants of the generation that suffered discrimination for their religion and ethnicity. The thought that the bluebloods running the Forbes House

Museum would impugn the character of his thoroughly honest father roiled him. And the vicarious affront meant action was necessary.

The Forbes House Museum, located on Milton Hill, is just a short seven-minute drive from the Connor household. An historic building overlooking the Boston skyline, it was constructed in 1833 and, until 1962, was the home of four generations of the Forbes family. By 1964, the twenty-room mansion had opened to the public as a museum and immediately made headlines when a rare and unknown letter to a Forbes ancestor written by a twenty-one-year-old Ralph Waldo Emerson was discovered in the attic.[1] It was just one of the many nineteenth-century treasures within. The museum was and remains chockablock with art and artifacts, especially items from China, where the Forbes family gained great wealth via the China trade—the risky yet highly profitable era of commerce between the Qing dynasty and the United States. It also boasts a substantial holding of objects of interest from Ireland, collected by Captain Robert Bennet Forbes while he carried out humanitarian efforts during the Great Famine.[2]

The famous mansion on the hill was something of a curiosity for Milton residents, so when it opened its doors to the public as a museum, a steady stream of visitors came to see what was within. A home inhabited by a family with an iconic name associated exclusively with wealth and upper-crust social sensibilities was a great draw for the working class. For some, it provided the opportunity to put themselves in the scene, not unlike the way the ladies of Boston stood in interminable lines in white gloves and their Sunday best to have tea with the Kennedy women during the congressional campaigns of John F. Kennedy just a few years before. Today, it can best be likened to the large audiences transfixed by the world depicted in the hit television show *Downton Abbey*.

Myles, too, was quick to visit upon its opening, and was a repeat customer, returning often to admire the treasures amassed by the Forbes family. It was not lost on him, of course, that the items were not secured in any way. Many just lay untethered to tables or pedestals. Others, like large Chinese porcelain vases, sat on the floor with nothing to keep visitors from touching them, or worse, accidentally kicking them or knocking them over. And while Myles had no nefarious intentions while conducting his self-guided tours of the collection, these sorts of vulnerabilities always registered with him, like a tailor noticing an ill-fitting suit. It was intel he would file away in a memory palace filled with countless collections of art and antiques. He never knew when, or why, he might need it. But it was there.

Despite his frequent visits, Myles never felt welcome at the Forbes House Museum. There was something about the way the staff looked at him. He suspected it was partly due to his station in life. He certainly did not present as a Brahmin, as it was his preference to sport Levi's and leather. Admittedly, he had a chip on his shoulder that dared the patrician to knock it off. But no matter the cause, he already possessed a burgeoning dislike of the people at the museum prior to the slander of his father.

For these reasons, before he had finished that last bite of his dinner with his dad, Myles decided he would visit the museum again. This time, he would leave his Cadillac and take the van that he used to lug his musical equipment from gig to gig. And his visit would occur after visiting hours had ended. In fact, long after.

Revenge was in the air when Myles pulled up to the Forbes House. The museum is situated on a relatively large plot of land, and though its address is officially Adams Street, it is set back quite far from the street. Its smallish parking lot is shrouded in trees, obscuring any view of it from the surrounding roads, and Myles took advantage of the arboreal cover, conveniently parking right outside the front door of the building. In preparation for the heist, he observed the night watchman's schedule and waited until he left the house for a few hours.[3] Myles had his entry route already in mind and easily popped open a basement window before wiggling his agile frame through it. From there it was a simple heist. He helped himself to everything and anything that appealed to him. Myles's frequent visits to the Forbes House Museum made his illicit shopping spree a snap. Vases, paintings, antique rifles, lamps, tapestries, fine china, old coins, and even some items that belonged to Abraham Lincoln—he took as much as he could and loaded it into the van. The most valuable item he lifted proved to be an historic silver tray presented to Captain Forbes in 1847 by the people of Cork, Ireland, in gratitude for his charitable delivery of clothes and food during the famine.[4] Once everything was loaded, he drove off with the valuables. No alarms sounded, no witnesses were in sight, and no sirens were nearing.

It was Myles's rookie outing, and it was wildly successful. He had exacted vengeance, obtained items he loved, and gotten away with it with great ease. There was no violence, and, better still, the victim deserved their loss—at least in his view. His only slipup was a touch of shortsightedness. He hadn't fully thought through his plan for stashing all that he had taken. Bringing it to his father's house where he lived was completely out of the question—he'd never store stolen goods where they could land his father in hot water. Especially *these* stolen goods. Al Dotoli would never agree to risk his blossoming future by holding the loot, especially considering that every cop in Milton would be looking for it come morning. Instead, Myles brought it all to the home Vicky and their children, Myles III and Kim, shared with her new boyfriend. It was conveniently located on Adams Street in Quincy, not far from the Forbes. The local police knew the pair was no longer together. And Myles felt that he could still trust her, despite their split. After all, a reliable hide for one's stolen goods is an essential part of any post-heist plan. It's one that proved both extremely valuable and, later in life, extremely costly for Myles.

The next morning, staff at the Forbes were shocked to see that their collection had been meticulously robbed of many of its finest pieces. Investigators found no clues that pointed at any specific suspects. This was the age before ubiquitous video surveillance and, given the relative seclusion of the site immediately surrounding the museum, there were no definitive eyewitness reports to provide detectives with a start. All they knew was that the thief had an eye for the better objects. Starved for viable leads, the Forbes House Museum announced a $1,000 reward for the return of the silver tray from Ireland. They told the media that, in total, the loot was valued at up to $100,000 (the equivalent of about $1 million today).[5]

It's doubtful that Vicky and her boyfriend would have known the value of the items that Myles had stowed away with them. But when the news hit and broadcasted the high estimate and a reward for information, they both became nervous. Panicked at the prospect of being arrested again because of Myles's adventures, Vicky decided she wanted the art out of the house immediately. Though she hastily accepted the stolen goods when he appeared at her door with them, she and Myles happened to be going through one of their argumentative spells at the time. She was in no mood to do him any favors, let alone abet his criminal activity. So concerned was she about the trouble that the stolen goods might bring her, Vicky took many of the smaller stolen items and left them on the lawn of the Forbes House under the cover of darkness. She called Myles and angrily demanded he get rid of the bigger items. But he was out of town, having taken advantage of his one night off from the stage at the Lewis Room to travel to New Jersey with a pair of brothers who shared his affinity for samurai swords. Worried about what else Vicky might do, he decided to turn to the person he trusted most in the world: Al Dotoli. Though he detested involving Al in his darker pursuits, Myles had little choice. Even if he convinced Vicky to wait just one more day for his return to the area, Myles feared that he might be tailed right to the goods. In Al he had someone no one suspected of stealing anything. And he knew Al would never rip him off. As Dotoli put it, "You can ask a criminal to come help you steal something, but you don't say, 'Now that we've stolen this, will you give it back?'" Thus, Dotoli was the natural choice.[6] Besides, he had always maintained a good relationship with Vicky, one that extended beyond her and Myles's separation, transcending the many tiffs she might have with her ex at any given moment. Such was the type of friend Al was—the kind, understanding sort who didn't often hold grudges or let little things intrude on friendships.

Myles called Al and asked him to pick up the remaining art and antiques from Vicky's home and deliver it all to his own makeshift hiding place in his mother's garage. Al agreed. He never asked if the works were stolen. He just accepted Myles's plea for help. It was not unlike the time when Myles asked him to hide something dangerous for him at his home during Al's first marriage. The former Mrs. Dotoli, a cynical woman on her best day, wanted nothing to do with Myles and was very suspicious of Al's actions. Nearing the end of their marriage, he arrived home one day to find her unusually pleasant to him—until she unleashed on a tirade about a machine gun she had found secreted in a pile of old clothes in the basement. In her defense, it must have been a startling find, but when you marry Myles Connor's best friend, nothing should really surprise you. That tale, illustrative of Al's no-questions-asked willingness to help his oldest friend, is but one of many. Indeed, there are more than either can recount from their half century together. Dotoli always simply assumed an "I don't want to know" attitude and did what he was asked, not because he was taking marching orders but because of his loyalty and affection for his best friend. Yes, he had heard some news about a local theft somewhere and wondered if Myles was the culprit. But no words needed to be exchanged on the matter, especially over the phone. What was important was that Myles needed his help, and the only answer Al knew was "yes." He didn't know the provenance of what he was asked to pick up—and he didn't want to know.

Al borrowed his sister's funky two-door Nash Rambler convertible, put the top down, and drove to Vicky's home in the cool March air. He was no stranger there; he would often pick up a six-pack and stop by to shoot the breeze with her. Today, though, there would be no time for small talk. Vicky led him to Myles's things and helped Al carry them out to the car. He squeezed two large Chinese vases into the back, sliding smaller items and antique rifles neatly into them. The rest of the art and antiques he loaded into the trunk or put on the floor for safe travels, but still the sheer volume caused some of the items to jut high out of the little automobile, reminiscent of a scene from a slapstick film. Traversing Adams Street on his way to Myles's mother's home, Al passed two traffic cops at an intersection with all the Forbes treasures clearly visible in the open convertible. Even with notice of the stolen objects spread across the department, the two officers, who had a reputation for tossing back a few drinks at lunch, noticed nothing, no doubt due to their somewhat dulled senses. Al safely delivered all the valuables to the garage with Lucy Connor none the wiser. Later, even the daring hellion Myles Connor was astounded to know that Al had paraded down Adams Street with the pilfered loot in plain view, taking a route that led him right past the Forbes House Museum.

Moving the stolen artifacts was unquestionably a big ask from Myles, regardless of how close he and Dotoli had become. But the two shared a closeness that meant favors didn't require negotiation. And there was no quid pro quo. The friendship would take priority over careers, girlfriends, and sometimes even their better senses.

The success of the Forbes House Museum heist left Myles with a taste for art crime. He was taken by how easy it was to steal things that he loved. In mere minutes, he became the owner of the sorts of objects about which he learned at his grandfather's knee and read about with endless fascination. Those things he didn't love could be sold for cash that could be converted into swords. The lure was impossible for him to resist. He wouldn't wait long to do it again.

Connor soon visited the Boston Children's Museum. Many are familiar with today's famous and vast modern facility on Boston's waterfront, but in the mid-1960s the museum was in a stately, repurposed mansion in the Jamaica Plain neighborhood, a residential setting that is a nothing like the setting of today with its views and high visibility. The institution, the second oldest of its kind in the nation, was at the time headed by Dr. Michael Spock, the son of the famed activist and pediatrician Dr. Benjamin Spock. The younger Dr. Spock worked determinedly to expand the museum's collection and its "hands-on learning" opportunities for its visitors. In a *Time* magazine feature, it was described as "a very different kind of museum. It has no collections behind glass, no bored guards, no admonitions to be quiet or keep hands off. In fact, the staff is frankly put out when a child is reluctant to try on an Indian sari, scrape the stretched deer hide with an Algonquin stone tool, or try on the Boston Celtics' Tom Sanders's size seventeen basketball shoes." Dr. Spock, it mentions, oversaw this "permissive atmosphere" where the children's energy and enthusiasm was visceral.[7]

While a museum for kids doesn't exactly resonate as target for theft, the Boston Children's Museum drew Myles's attention because of its focus on Japanese culture and the impressive collection it built around it. The institution houses thousands of Japanese items and artifacts and its connection dates back to the earliest years of the twentieth century and the travels east by collectors like the aforementioned William Sturgis Bigelow and other Boston luminaries such as Isabella Stewart Gardner and Edward Sylvester Morse,[8] considered the father of Japanese archaeology.

Not long before Connor decided to pay a visit to the Children's Museum, it launched the MATCH program, which provided multimedia kits including actual objects from Japan for use in the classroom. MATCH kits were even made available for museum visitors to rent and take home for further study.[9] It was just another indication of the strong effort that the museum made to educate not just children but whole families about the rich culture of Japan. For the dedicated Japanophile Myles, the museum's collection was like a siren song luring him to visit. But he wasn't content to simply see what the public could observe or take home a kit. He wanted access to everything.

To get a view behind the scenes, Myles decided to create a persona that would guarantee him access. He approached the museum with a request for a private tour of the collection, including its storage. But rather than identifying himself by his real name, he shed his rock and roll appearance and adopted the dress and air of an academic. It was a plan to which he had given much thought. It was essential to pose as a PhD of some sort, though "psychology is the easiest," he said. "And you're always a graduate of one of the more prestigious Ivy

League colleges," he added.[10] Bringing along impressive pieces from his own collection would also help establish his status and expertise.

Myles introduced himself to Children's Museum staff as Dr. Michael Joseph, an expert in Asian artifacts. This was only half a falsehood—while he did not hold a doctorate, nor had he graduated from any formal university program, his knowledge on the subject was extensive and could rival that of area academics. Such was his acumen that he easily convinced the staff and was taken to see the Japanese treasures the museum held off-view. Once inside the museum storage area, he held lengthy and in-depth conversations with his guides, flashing his impressive expertise on the subject. Ultimately, Myles asked when they would be on display to the public. That's when he learned, to his shock, that most of the items would remain in storage forever. He instantly reasoned that he would liberate them from the indignity of steerage in dark, seldom visited back rooms waiting years or even decades for another researcher to enjoy them.

Connor began by casing the exterior of the museum for an easy route in. It didn't take him long to find one. Wishing to enter through the attic, where the bulk of what he coveted was stored, he formulated a plan straight out of an action novel. A few nights later, he drove his van to the Children's Museum and climbed to the roof by scaling a sturdy drainpipe. It was the sort of athletic prowess that he would often display, whether in the dojo practicing karate or in the weight rooms of prisons where the 135-pounder once bench pressed 445 pounds in a competition. Once on the roof, he secured a rope around a chimney and rappelled down the side of the building to an attic window. Confident that it was not alarmed based on his observations during his tour, he broke open the window and set about selecting items that appealed to him. Unlike his illicit shopping spree at the Forbes House Museum, this time Connor was limited in his choices to those things that he could fit into his shoulder bag. No matter, though; there were plenty of things that caught his eye.

While many thieves will describe their fight-or-flight instinct shifting into overdrive while perpetrating a burglary, Myles never experienced such anxiety. Instead, he remained calm—insouciant even—in the environment, taking neither more nor less time than necessary to get his targets in hand. He moved about the Children's Museum just as if he were on a tour. His only surprise came when he went to the lower floors to take more items for his collection, only to find that the old-fashioned laser beam motion sensors were turned on. He decided against trying to two-step through them and went back upstairs and out the window, exiting and descending the building in the same way he had entered it. Another easy and profitable heist. He could get used to this.

In the annals of crime, few, if any, were cleverer than Myles Connor, and his nascent career as an art thief impressed his criminal contemporaries with its unique combination of cunning and deeply seated refined tastes. What's more, his exploits seem to have played a major role in inspiring an era of art crime in Massachusetts that was nothing short of breathtaking. Aside from the looting of archeological sites and wartime looting, few places anywhere in the world would experience the flurry of major art theft that ensued in the Bay State during the decade or so after his first heists in 1965. Some were massive. All were noteworthy. A sampling illustrates the point.

In December 1966, forty-two paintings were stolen from the Provincetown home of the late and famed artist Hans Hoffman when a thief unscrewed a storm window on Hoffman's summer home. The works were collectively estimated to be valued at $250,000 and consisted mainly of Hoffman's own creations. The director and founder of the nearby Chrysler Museum,* Walter P. Chrysler, called that estimate low, and the curator of the Chrysler described the works as well-known and "saleable."[11]

---

*   The Chrysler Museum relocated to Norfolk, Virginia, in 1971.

In 1970 the Chrysler Museum itself suffered a major theft when a painting titled *The Temptation of St. Anthony* by Hieronymus Bosch was taken. The work, valued at up to $500,000 (around $3.85 million in today's dollars), was stolen in an entirely stealthy manner, with no clues left behind. Such was the skill of the perpetrator that no one could determine exactly how or when the painting was stolen. Only an empty space on a gallery wall and a discarded frame on the floor, found two hours after the museum opened, indicated that a theft had occurred. The painting was later left on the porch of the museum director just shy of a month and a half after its ordeal began. No one was ever arrested for the heist. Years later, Myles, a great fan of Bosch's work, was asked if he had taken the painting. He said he had not. When asked why, he replied, "Because I didn't know it was there!"[12]

In 1972 two men entered the Worcester Art Museum as visitors, proceeded to the second floor, and removed four paintings from the walls before sliding them into bags specially made for the occasion. Works by Rembrandt, Pablo Picasso, and Paul Gauguin, valued at the time at more than a million dollars, were taken by criminal underlings of local thief Florian "Al" Monday. Despite Monday's admonitions, his henchmen used a handgun he provided to shoot an elderly guard who attempted to intervene as they made their getaway out of the main entrance. The paintings were later recovered when two men waiting to be sentenced for a violent crime forced Monday to take them to the Rhode Island pig farm where he had hidden the works in a hayloft. They in turn exchanged the masterworks for a small measure of leniency from the judge. The heist gave the institution the unfortunate distinction of being the first museum in history to be robbed at gunpoint.[13]

Harvard University was victimized several times during this period. The most noteworthy was history's largest antique coin heist, which occurred at the university's Fogg Museum in 1973. Using a clever ruse involving a left-behind shopping bag said to be containing an important birthday gift, armed thieves gained overnight entry into the building and took millions in gold coins. Many of the coins were later recovered buried in the woods by Massachusetts State Police detective John Regan, a longtime close friend of Myles's father.[14] The coin heist came less than a month after the home of a professor at Harvard's Graduate School of Design was raided by thieves who took three paintings by Jackson Pollock while the academic was rowing on the Charles River. The most valuable of the three large paintings was said to be worth half a million dollars.[15]

Two and a half years later, Harvard was again the victim of an art heist. Harvard president Derek Bok and his family were sound asleep when thieves broke into his home and took six paintings then valued at $385,000. The burglars clearly knew Bok's home, as they quietly lifted the works from three different rooms without waking anyone.

Such was the flurry of thefts that by 1976, *The Boston Globe* published a story titled "A Growing Concern over the Theft of Art." It opened by referencing the theft at the Harvard president's home and went on to cite other recent art crimes, including the theft of an Edvard Munch painting and twenty other artworks from a home in Newton, a $100,000 oil painting by Andrew Wyeth from a home in Wenham, and a "hoard of objects" from the Hammond Castle in Gloucester. It added that the region "enjoys an unhappy distinction as one of the American centers of art thefts."[16] Homes, museums, colleges, churches, and galleries, like the Pucker-Safrai Gallery, robbed in 1974 of fifteen works, including a Georges Braque and a Henri Matisse, were all fair game.[17]

To be sure, art theft was happening throughout this decade around the country and the world, and on a massive scale, with works by virtually every famous artist falling victim. In fact, just days before Connor struck at the Forbes House, a painting by the Old Dutch Master Bartholomeus

Breenbergh titled *The Finding of Moses* was stolen from the Centraal Museum in Utrecht, the Netherlands.[18] And less than a week later, Vincent van Gogh's *Cypress and Flowering Trees* was lifted from a mansion in Hillsborough, California.[19] But Massachusetts was, and in some ways remains, a most parochial place, and what went on in the country and the world outside of the Bay State had little influence over what the criminal mind there conceived. In fact, Myles's foray into Sullivan, Maine, was merely a crime of opportunity, born of the fact that he summered there. But that isn't to say he was hesitant to stray from the confines of his home state to steal art and antiques. He certainly victimized museums outside of the Commonwealth, including, he says, the Metropolitan Museum of Art in New York City, though exactly what he took and from whom eventually became a haze due in large measure to the sheer volume of items he acquired, either via theft or through purchases made with ill-gotten gains. His unique motives were matched only by his inventive methods for stealing the items he coveted.

Perhaps his most successful and oft-used modus operandi was the Asian art specialist ruse he first employed at the Children's Museum. Connor's extreme level of intelligence would later earn him membership in the high IQ society Mensa and allowed him to pull off the role with great aplomb. He could talk about his specialty with curators from any museum without betraying the fact that he had never attended university. So, when he presented himself as Dr. Michael Joseph, institutions were happy to show Connor the unique treasures they had in storage. Once he earned their confidence, he would sometimes be left alone with the sorts of things that he had spent so many years reading about. With no one watching, innumerable items were there for the taking.

When not incarcerated, Connor would steal from more museums than he can recall. This is attributable to not just his prolificacy but also the passage of time and a heart attack he suffered in 1988 while incarcerated. The episode impacted his ability to recall so that at times he must be prompted with the name of an artist or location to remember his escapades. The best he can offer is an estimate of about thirty. But one thing is certain—a large number of museums throughout the Northeast were looted by Dr. Michael Joseph. To this day, many may not even be aware of it. One need only look at the thefts that have occurred from various museums' storage areas to understand the difficulties they have securing their inventories. "The advantage of taking something from storage," Myles noted, "is that it is never missed . . . they truly, rarely, check inventory."[20] Most illustrative is the discovery in 2023 that about two thousand items—mostly jewelry—had been stolen from storage at the British Museum in London. Months later, the museum sued a longtime curator for the losses, claiming he took the pieces over several years and sold them through various venues, including eBay.[21] The episode illustrates the vulnerability that exists at museums around the world, including the most esteemed among them, and even in the modern age with technological means available for cataloguing and inventorying the items. Add to this that the FBI's Art Crime Team estimates that more than 80 percent of all museum thefts involve the complicity of an insider, and the difficulty of securing a collection increases exponentially. All this is to say that prior to the advent of modern techniques in the decades between the mid-1960s and mid-1980s, museums were at the mercy of a master thief with a genius-level IQ who could make himself a trusted insider and steal an almost endless supply of art and antiques based on nothing more than his emotions, which ranged from deep passion to mere whim.

CHAPTER 5
THE FUGITIVE

At the very onset of 1966, investigators working for Gabriel Byrne, the Suffolk County district attorney, received a startling tip. Myles Connor and an associate, Thomas Cericola, were prepping for a major art theft at Harvard University's Fogg Museum. The museum director, John Coolidge, confirmed reports that one of three Rembrandts in their collection was being targeted. Acting with urgency, Byrne sent Sergeant John Regan of the Massachusetts State Police to swear out warrants for Connor's and Cericola's apartments in Revere, Massachusetts. The judge granted the police warrants, giving them wide latitude, enabling them to search for everything from guns and counterfeit money to stolen antiques and other valuables.[1]

On January 12, officers from the Massachusetts District Commission and the Revere Police Department conducted raids at both residences. The effort was not in vain. Inside the dwellings police officers discovered stockpiles of stolen property that required four police vehicles, including a wagon, to transport. Guns, silencers, television sets, Oriental carpets, Chinese vases, lamps, and even a full suit of armor were found. They also recovered an obvious Connor calling card: thirty-nine swords. One thing the police didn't expect to find was particularly difficult to handle: a box with a handwritten sign placed on top that read HOT: IF BITTEN BY SNAKE, DEATH IN FIVE MINUTES. Inside was a five-foot-long cobra. Myles commonly kept exotic lethal pets: two weeks earlier, thieves attempting to break into Myles's girlfriend's apartment fled in panic when they were met by his pet wildcat.[2] Asked about the cobra, Myles replied, "I had it for protection."[3] Between the swords and the serpent, investigators couldn't have hoped to find better indications of Connor's involvement with the giant stash of stolen wares.[4]

The swords that were seized presented a special problem for Connor, as many were not stolen but from his own collection, inherited from his grandfather or legitimately purchased by Connor over the years (with illicitly obtained money, of course). But they were gathered up as if they were also taken from homes or museums on the North Shore. Seven were said to have been stolen from the Peabody Museum in Salem.*[5] They were not. Nevertheless, police officers brought those to the office of the District Attorney and sent for a curator from the museum to assist in identifying them. Everything else was stored in a vault on the tenth floor of the Suffolk County courthouse pending identification.[6]

While officers gathered the hoard of stolen goods, Myles had just finished a show not far from the raids at the Lewis Room on Revere's Beach Plaza. Police officers were waiting for him and Cericola outside the club where they were arrested without incident. They were released on $50,000 bail each. Myles, only six days removed from the chaos in Maine, was in trouble yet again.

Though Myles Connor would eventually become perhaps too familiar with the things he coveted in the collections of most every museum in

---

* Now the Peabody Essex Museum, and not to be confused with Harvard's Peabody Museum of Archaeology and Ethnology.

the New England area, by 1966 he was not yet fully acquainted with the Fogg Museum. Truth is, it was never one of his favorites. The Fogg had just a handful of Japanese swords. Nevertheless, police officers hoping to collar him created an allegation that Connor was plotting a theft there. While it might have made some sense to allege he had his eye on a sword or two, or even the few dozen Japanese woodblock prints in their holdings, they clumsily created a pretext that Connor was plotting to steal a Rembrandt painting from the Fogg. Perhaps one of the investigators had learned that just a couple of years earlier, the Fogg had been gifted a beautiful *Head of Christ* by Rembrandt and assumed it would be a worthy, albeit fabricated, target.

In truth, Myles had no such plan. Stealing a Rembrandt was nowhere on his agenda, at least at this stage. Collecting Asiatic antiquities, particularly swords that he had inherited or procured—legally and otherwise—was his sole focus when he wasn't onstage or with a girlfriend. But better to add a sense of urgency to the pursuit of Connor by claiming to be working not only to solve a crime, but also to preempt one.

When word of this accusation made its way to him, Myles was unsurprised. Speaking of law enforcement, he said, "They lie for any number of reasons, but lie they do, and on a rather regular basis." He went on, "To make it all the more obnoxious . . . they invariably utilize their well-scrubbed wholesome image for the platform as to why they should be believed."[7] John Doyle, who led district attorney Byrne's team of cops in Suffolk County, was one of the officers at the top of Connor's mind when he contemptuously recalls this episode. Both Regan and Doyle would play major roles in Connor's future.

Though the Fogg Museum plot was pure fiction, the Forbes House Museum burglary was not, and in the winter of 1966 the police and prosecutors were finally able to win an indictment against Connor for that crime. Many valuable Asian pieces from the Forbes were recovered during the search warrants in Revere, and though Cericola wasn't involved in the Forbes job, he was also indicted by virtue of the cache of items recovered in his possession, too. Armed with the indictment, the police were eager to arrest Connor yet again.

Police officers went to Myles's place in Revere well aware that taking in the elusive thief was no easy task. When they knocked on the door, a warrant in hand, his twenty-two-year-old girlfriend, Bonnie Sue Garian, spoke to them through the door to delay them. Finally, they barged in. Though Myles had a slight head start, they had him at a disadvantage—he and Bonnie were in various stages of undress. Nevertheless, Myles again made a run for it, grabbing his recently removed jeans and bolting to the bathroom where he jumped out of a window and ran off into the freezing February night shirtless and shoeless.[8] In what was becoming an almost monthly occurrence, he was again on the run, refusing to acquiesce to the commands of pursuing police officers to halt. It was no use. They wouldn't be able to catch him. Myles ran off into the night, grabbing spare clothes pinched from clotheslines in the backyards of houses he passed along the way.

In his apartment, investigators found no dangerous exotic pets, but they did recover a loaded gun on his bedside table, as well as a cherished Japanese Luger. The police issued a thirteen-state alarm for his capture. The all-points bulletin relayed Connor's description which, by now, was becoming very well-known to area police. Two nights later, Revere police officers Nick Melchionno and Joe Moretti was doing their usual patrols of North Shore Road when they noted a car that had been implicated in Connor's escape. Pulling behind it, they noted his unmistakable flaming red duck-tailed hair in the rear of the vehicle. "Connor has red hair—so red he looked on fire in the darkness," Moretti said.[9] The chase was on. Suddenly, Connor jumped out the back door of the moving vehicle and fled again on foot. While Melchionno called for backup, Moretti fired a shot at Connor but missed. A swarm of twenty-five responding officers searched the area, including abandoned houses, but again came up empty.[10]

A fugitive once more, Myles didn't really have a plan. He couldn't very well go onstage and perform. He had to stay away from the homes of both his parents. He couldn't go to Al Dotoli's family's house. He would stay on the run for as long as it took to figure out a way out of the big jam he was in, occasionally checking in with his attorney to see if he had yet conjured up a way to alleviate the certainty of a long prison term.

As usual, Myles leaned on Al's loyal friendship. Al would be careful not to be followed and, when he was sure he hadn't a tail, he would meet up with a heavily disguised Myles. He was Myles's source for contact with trusted friends, money, and sustenance. Al's mother, who was very fond of Myles, never asked her son where his friend might be hiding out. Officially, Al hadn't the slightest idea where he was—at least that is what he told his parents out of a sense of respect for them. Al's mother Mary—a tall, lean, pretty woman from whom Al inherited his looks—would make extra meals that she knew Myles liked and put them aside in containers for Al. She never said who exactly they were for, but it wouldn't have been more obvious to her grateful son had she left a sticky note with Myles's name on it.

Massachusetts State Police detective John Regan paid a visit to the Dotoli household, where they encountered Mary and asked to speak to her son. Mary assured the police that young Al had no idea where his renegade mate was. Al confirmed this. Just then, Regan's partner walked into the kitchen from the garage carrying a smallish pair of dungarees. "Really?" he said. "Well, there's no way your son is fitting into these."[11] Despite the obvious evidence that Al had been with

Myles, there was nothing the frustrated police officers could do but leave. After all, the pants could have made their way there in a myriad of ways at any time prior to Connor's run.

While Mary Dotoli was the picture of composure in the face of the police regarding the young fugitive's whereabouts, Myles's mother Lucy was understandably anxious. Referring to the Revere police officer firing at her fleeing son, she said, "Somebody should have helped him. They shouldn't be shooting at him. He needs psychiatric help." She recalled that he never ran away from home when "getting in Dutch" with his parents. "He was a homebody" she recalled. "He was doing so well with the band," she said, her voice breaking into a despondent whisper.[12]

In the meantime, Myles was up to his usual hijinks. He and Al ventured into downtown Boston to meet some hippie friends in a third-floor apartment. Myles was heavily disguised in a Scottish tam-o'-shanter to cover his telltale red hair and wore a long coat. He mimicked the hunched-over posture of the elderly, and he carried with him a violin case. As if appearing in an old episode of *The Untouchables*, inside was a Thompson submachine gun. It would be almost too cliché for anyone to suspect him of being armed in such a manner. He and Al went up to see the group and, as they climbed the stairs, they could smell that the occupants were smoking marijuana in the apartment. The two friends had visited only for a short time when Myles's sixth sense kicked in. Always one to rely on his gut instincts, he told Al that they should leave. The two were headed back down the stairs when they were encountered by police officers racing toward them. Myles, still performing as an old man, said to the cops, "Hurry! They're smoking marijuana up there!" The police continued upstairs and raced into the apartment while Connor and Dotoli fled the area. Another narrow escape was made. But narrow escapes are not often repeated.

During a furtive meeting with his father, the elder Connor warned his son that police were planning to shoot him on sight.[13]

For many young women in the Boston area, Myles had certain qualities that made him irresistible: he was an intelligent and charismatic young man with a guitar and a well-earned reputation as a bad boy. That meant even though he was still legally married to Vicky until 1967, there was no shortage of girlfriends. His relationship with the paramour of the moment, Bonnie Sue Garian, would be his downfall.

The police had gone more than two months without a reliable sighting when officers, who were tracing Myles's estranged wife Vicky's calls, determined that Myles could be found in Boston's Back Bay at Garian's apartment. Officers quickly began staking out her neighborhood. On April 27, 1966, they identified their target walking to a Beacon Street phone booth. Connor, sensing the police closing in, dipped into a doorway of one of the street's famous brownstones. But it was too late. Massachusetts State Police corporal Jack O'Donovan, accompanied by two Boston police detectives, confronted him. Knowing he was armed and extremely dangerous, the three plainclothesmen drew their weapons as Myles responded in kind. O'Donovan ordered him to drop the gun. Myles, recalling his father's warning, yelled back, "Drop yours!"[14]

What exactly happened next is a matter of dispute. The media reports at the time, which conflict greatly on many important facts, state that Connor fired first at O'Donovan immediately after telling the police to drop their weapons. Connor swears that he only fired when one of the two detectives shot at him first. While it is likely that the police would have understandably fired first in response to

Connor's refusal to drop his gun, it's impossible to know exactly what occurred. Connor was not one to fire first at anyone, let alone a police officer. History shows that his previous encounters included warning shots fired into the air and never at an officer. Moreover, as evidenced by Officer Moretti, who freely admitted to firing at the fleeing felon, shooting the notorious criminal was neither forbidden nor criticized.

Connor's shot struck Corporal O'Donovan in the lower abdomen, sending him to the ground, from which he returned fire. Later, he would acknowledge that Connor intentionally aimed low as to avoid a mortal wound.[15] Detectives returned fire, striking Myles in the left shoulder as he turned and fled on foot to nearby Marlborough Street with the two detectives giving chase. The sound of sirens drew near as more police officers sped to the scene in response to radio calls announcing, "Shots fired, officer down." Myles climbed up a fire escape to the roof of another of the area's brownstones with officers following a trail of blood he left behind. Once they found him on the roof crouched behind a chimney they opened fire, hitting him two more times. Still, he summoned the strength to run and jump over a ten-foot gap between buildings, making it onto a neighboring rooftop. But Myles's run was over. Detective Arthur Linsky tackled him, and Officer Everett Blais helped pry his gun from Myles's hand.[16]

Blais described Connor as "soaked with blood both from the gunshots and from glass littering the rooftops." Nevertheless, Blais said, "Connor kept kicking and writhing but we finally got the cuffs on him." Linsky stated that at that point Connor was "pretty far gone."[17] Myles asked Blais, "How's the cop I shot?" Blais told him O'Donovan was being transported to the hospital and asked if Connor had been hit by shots on the rooftop. "You got me twice," Connor said.[18]

Blais's comments about Myles kicking and writhing were a vast understatement. He had been, in his words, "shot to hell,"[19] especially by the bullets that struck him on the roof. He had also been beaten severely by police officers. He recalled them poking at his wounds and punching and kicking him in the genitals.[20] With a bevy of angry officers surrounding him, Myles was certain that he would be killed. One spoke of throwing him off of the roof. Finally, when fire department officials had made their way to the building's roof to organize transport for the arrestee down to an ambulance, the fire captain ordered the police to stop pummeling Myles. He was put onto a stretcher and carried down the ladder of a fire truck. Connor is certain that fire department captain saved his life.

At the hospital, Myles's prognosis was grim. He had a "shattered spleen, transected kidney, perforated intestines, hits to the spine, elbow, leg, hand, liver, and stomach."[21] Fortunately, he was taken to Massachusetts General Hospital, one of the best hospitals in the state if not the nation. Doctors there did yeoman's work to save him. In just a matter of weeks, Myles's condition would be so grave that he would drop from 135 pounds to just 66 pounds. But given the indomitability of the man, it surprised none of his friends that he pulled through. And as he grew stronger, he became friendly with an impressive state police officer who had been his father's friend since youth, John Regan. Regan stood watch over Connor, well aware that there was an element on the side of law enforcement that wished him ill if not dead.

Myles's mother stood vigil at the Boston City Hospital, to which Myles had been transferred, watching over her boy, not sure if he would survive. Lucy was brought there each day by the ever reliable Al Dotoli, who, Myles remembers, "would stand there and stare at me in worry and wonder at my condition."[22]

Meanwhile, Corporal O'Donovan was resting peacefully in the hospital. O'Donovan, known to his friends as "OD," was described as "an extraordinary trooper whose reputation for tenacity and toughness drew respect from colleagues and even some criminals." O'Donovan had served in the US Marine Corps during the Korean War and had made a major impact in the fight against organized crime by taking down the infamous gangland murderer Vincent "The Bear" Flemmi just months prior to the shootout with Connor. He received a State Police Medal of Merit for that effort. As tough as they came, "He was the first one to kick in the door and last one to leave the scene," said Bob Long, who served with O'Donovan in the state police. As O'Donovan lay in his hospital bed after being shot by Connor, he called over to a fellow detective and showed him the bullet wound. "Hey Mickey," he said, "ain't that a beaut?"[23]

In February 1967, almost a year after the drama on the rooftops, Myles Connor pleaded guilty to seventeen of the twenty-five indictments he faced. A state judge sentenced him to twelve to twenty years with his various terms to run concurrently at Walpole State Prison, where he would be elected to a leadership position by his fellow inmates and make criminal connections that he would utilize for decades to come. As had been true when he returned from his problems in Maine, Myles entered Walpole with a reputation that would serve him poorly in polite society but extremely well among the toughest prisoners in the Commonwealth of Massachusetts.

Despite being a fugitive from justice, stealing more than an estimated $1 million in antiques in multiple burglaries, and shooting a state trooper, Myles ended up being paroled after serving just six years. He quickly returned to his music career. Ever the loyal friend, Al Dotoli had arranged shows for him almost from the moment he stepped out from behind the prison's walls. Resuming his role as "the President of

Rock and Roll," Myles played to capacity crowds at the Beachcomber at Wollaston Beach and on Cape Cod. His time in prison behind him, Myles seemed to be finally ready to fulfill Al's vision for him. He even sat down for an interview with Jim Morse of the *Boston Herald*, Boston's tabloid newspaper, to discuss his freedom and his future. Myles remembered Morse from his reporting a few years earlier at Walpole during the unrest between prisoners and guards and thought him to be an honest journalist. Morse began by asking Connor about his past.

"It's not easy to explain what happened to me," he told Morse. "I'm not even going to try. Maybe if things had been a little different it wouldn't have happened. I don't want to talk about it. Errors have been made. There's no doubt about that."

Myles went on to express his opinion about those who might close the book on him based on his crimes. "I've learned not to make closed or final judgments of people. I hope that others will do the same in respect to me."

The sentiment was pure Myles Connor. He was being truthful about his hesitancy to judge people. Perhaps it was what helped him to quickly become a leader among his fellow convicts. He refused to pass judgment on others, and he believed in redemption. Of Walpole, he said, "When you leave a place like that, you can't be a defeatist. Returning to the 'wrong way' isn't the answer. If you go the 'right way,' you'll end up far richer—morally and materialistically." He added that one key to success after incarceration is that "a fellow must have a goal."[24]

Myles's goal, however, was a familiar one—collecting, by any means necessary. He was soon back thieving, employing and perfecting the ruse he had used at the Boston Children's Museum, posing as Dr. Michael Joseph. One museum was especially accommodating to the learned Dr. Joseph. The Peabody Museum in Salem, Massachusetts, lays claim to the world's largest and most impressive collection of artistic and other cultural treasures from the Far East, a result the sixteenth-century European merchants who journeyed to Asia's port cities and returned with a mother lode of items created by craftsmen eager to exploit the growing markets in the West. With Salem serving as a key port in colonial America, tens of thousands of works made their way to New England. Ultimately, nine thousand of them ended up in the possession of the China Trade Museum (coincidentally, located in Milton, Connor and Dotoli's hometown) before they were transferred to the Peabody Museum. This drastically bolstered their collection, which has also benefitted from decades' worth of work to bring Asian culture to the American people.[25] Today, the Peabody boasts many thousands of such artifacts and, like the Children's Museum, profited from the legendary Edward Sylvester Morse's work. Morse would serve as the museum's third director.

The Peabody Museum's holdings, especially its impressive array of Japanese porcelain, greatly appealed to Myles. The relatively minuscule percentage of works on public display did little to quench his curiosity, and a young emerging rock star with a criminal history had little hope to access what was filed away on endless rows of shelving in storage. But the scholar Dr. Michael Joseph might be afforded the courtesy. Just as he did at the Children's Museum, Myles used the pseudonym to make a formal request to see what was being held backstage. To solidify his bona fides, he even brought some of his own impressive pieces to the Peabody—the sorts of things that only a serious connoisseur would own and appreciate. The ploy worked. He was granted his wish and was escorted to the nonpublic areas to see those items to which very few would ever be privy. He spent innumerable hours examining the stored items over the course of many visits. So frequent were his trips there that he eventually struck up a working friendship with a kind and knowledgeable curator named Peter Fetchko who, impressed with his guest's deep knowledge, spent hours talking with him. Over time, he became comfortable enough with the purported Dr. Joseph that he allowed him to remain alone in storage to study whatever he chose.

Fetchko remained unaware of the true identity of this kindred spirit with whom he had developed a mutual respect. He treated the disguised Connor like an equal and without condescension, bonding over their shared passion. The curator's collegial manner paid dividends for his museum. Myles Connor never stole anything from the Peabody Museum. He just couldn't bring himself to take advantage of the people who had treated him so well and who clearly loved their objects so much.

Ironically, during his time as an ostensive researcher, Connor noticed that some items had gone missing and deduced that they were stolen by janitors. He advised staff members, and the suspects were transferred away from the area.[*]

Years later, when Connor was arrested for another of his crimes, he was shown on a local news broadcast being led into court as the television reporter mentioned his name. One Peabody staff member is said to have exclaimed, "That's not Myles Connor, that's Dr. Michael Joseph!"[26]

Myles's decision to not steal from the Peabody Museum may seem incompatible with his long history of thievery, but a closer study of the man reveals that throughout his life he adhered to a strict code that made such an act unthinkable. In a handwritten missive he wrote while imprisoned, he described it in fine detail, explaining his personal

---

[*] Incredibly, years later, an actual academic, Dr. John Quentin Feller, would be arrested for stealing artifacts from museum storage at a wide array of museums. In one instance, he stole a rare Chinese tea and coffee service from the Rhode Island School of Design and later donated it to the Peabody Museum in Salem, earning him a seat as a trustee at the grateful museum.

ethos related to friendship. "There is no cheating, no grifting, no back biting, no gossiping, no hurting the weak, the old, the infirm, or the innocent. Your word is your bond and you do your best to carry out every promise that you make and you make no promise lightly. You'll go to the wall for a friend, you'd die for a friend, and you expect the same in return. Loyalty is the one factor you value above all else. Loyalty to your family, friends, and beliefs. If you think you see true loyalty in a person's makeup, you will overlook a whole lot."[27]

Clearly, the museums he considered "friends" were a select few. Most others weren't as lucky. Myles decided to rob the George Walter Vincent Smith Art Museum in Springfield, Massachusetts, this time via a clever hybrid approach. He used the Dr. Joseph guise to see what the museum held that was to his liking. With a good sense of what he'd take, he came back another day out of disguise and with a partner. The pair employed the stay-behind approach. Entering as visitors during open hours, they hid within the building just before closing and emerged later when the only other occupant was an overnight watchman. Myles easily subdued the guard at gunpoint, but the theft was interrupted when a friend of the guard showed up to visit him. Connor decided to abandon the heist.

There was only one other robbery that Myles called off and left empty-handed. In the early 1970s, he and two accomplices broke into a large home near Harvard Square close to the residence of famed Harvard art historian Seymour Slive. Myles had learned that the house was "filled with valuable art." He went up to the second floor and there found a young woman who was apparently housesitting fast asleep. "My conscience got the best of me," he would later say, adding that he didn't have the heart to steal anything and get the house sitter in trouble.[28]

No matter, though. There would be many more heists to come, and many millions of dollars in art still to steal.

CHAPTER 6
THE BOOST EFFECT

In 1969, Coe Kerr, president of the M. Knoedler & Co. art gallery in New York City, abruptly stepped down from his position after a successful thirty-one years with the esteemed company. The departure sent shockwaves through the elite world of art dealers, in which Kerr was a big name. His decision was his own and was not without controversy. Asked by the culture reporter for *The New York Times* why he had decided to move on, Kerr replied that the reasons were "too complicated to explain." Clearly, something was afoot at the Knoedler, as Kerr wasn't the only high-ranking figure to make a sudden departure. One of their directors, Harry Brooks, also elected to separate from the gallery, joining Wildenstein & Co., a major rival.[1]

Kerr did not leave without a plan. He immediately established his own gallery, trading on the renown he had established over the decades at the Knoedler. The venture required the help of a few game-changing allies. First, in order to open his concern in the costly art realm, he needed the sort of financial backing that he alone could not provide. So, he established a partnership with a wealthy benefactor who would serve as the gallery's owner: R. Frederick Woolworth, the son of Norman B. Woolworth, whose family brought the world the famous five-and-dime stores. Norman and his wife Pauline Woolworth were noted art collectors, populating an estate in Monmouth, Maine, with a large collection of well-known art, including 174 paintings depicting the nation's early history.

Kerr's second big alliance was with the legendary father and son artists Andrew and Jamie Wyeth. His connection to the Wyeths extended back to a chance encounter in 1948. Kerr was at the Chadds Ford Inn in Pennsylvania when he noticed two men looking into his car. Understandably concerned, Kerr approached them to see who they were and why they were looking at the cache of valuable paintings contained within the vehicle, which included a Vincent van Gogh. The gawking pair were the Wyeths. A conversation was struck, and a friendship was born. The serendipitous encounter must have made for a most memorable moment for Kerr, as he had purchased an Andrew Wyeth nine years earlier at a sellout show in New York. For the next seventeen years, they were a trio. Kerr became their representative, and the Wyeths repaid his exceptional service by following him away from Knoedler to his new eponymous gallery. "There was never any question we'd stay with Coe Kerr," Andrew Wyeth's wife said.[2]

It's no wonder, then, given the tight relationship between the Wyeths and the ownership of the gallery, that Mrs. Woolworth's collection would include many works by the Wyeths. It didn't hurt, of course, that the Woolworths' home in Monmouth, Maine, was but fifty miles away from Cushing, the Wyeths' summer home, and the setting for Andrew's best-known painting, *Christina's World*. So famous is that painting, which today hangs in the Museum of Modern Art in New York, that the colonial farmhouse depicted in it was designated a National Historic Landmark in 2011.[3]

The Wyeth paintings owned by Mrs. Woolworth were hardly the only works of note in her vast summer estate. In fact, her collection was considered "one of the finest private collections assembled during this century," according to William Gerdts, who authored a catalog for a special exhibition of her works held to benefit the Girl Scouts in New York City in 1970.[4] A sampling of her works, collected along with her husband primarily in the 1940s and 1950s, shows that this was no overstatement: Winslow Homer's *The Unruly Calf*; Childe Hassam's *Lannion, 1900*; Rembrandt Peale's *Rubens Peale with a First Geranium*; Henry Inman's *The Artist's Daughter, Mary*; Eastman Johnson's *In the Fields*; Alfred Bierstadt's *Deer Crossing*; Fitz Hugh Lane's *Gloucester, Massachusetts, 1856*; John Singer Sargent's *Carolus Durand*; and Mary Cassatt's *Portrait of Mrs. Harrison*, among others. Amherst College art historian Professor Carl Schmalz Jr., a noted watercolorist and a Mainer, wrote of the Woolworth collection, "In the high quality of these paintings, their concern with craftsmanship, their animation and variety, we are permitted to retrieve something of the wonderful excitement of the burgeoning new nation on whose achievements our own generation rests."[5]

Life at the Woolworth homestead provides a view of wealth—American style—of the era. Pauline Woolworth, Frederick's mother and herself a sculptor and painter, had a studio at the homestead for her use during the summers. Frederick's children would wake each day to the smell of bacon and eggs cooking, eating breakfast alongside their father before embarking on active days utilizing the amenities on the estate. There were tennis courts, a bowling alley, a thirty-two-horse stable, a racetrack, children's playhouses, and chicken coops to keep everyone busy. But at the estate, known collectively as Clearview Farm, gathering for meals was what united the clan. A later *Town & Country* feature on the all-important Sunday lunch reported that "the meal began at noon sharp. Lime daiquiris were served at 12:15, with a feast of cold lobsters, roast beef, and Yorkshire pudding directly following at 12:45. Whoever was in residence (and had reached the age of 10) attended in proper dress. 'You were always on your best behavior for Sunday lunch,' [Frederick's daughter said]. 'We were expected to act like ladies and gentlemen.' Right after the meal the luncheon party would go swimming or water-skiing or go catch frogs—the adults too."[6]

The Woolworth collection gained much attention in the late 1960s and early 1970s, and selections from it were frequently loaned for various exhibitions, especially within the state of Maine. In March and April 1972, thirty-six of the family's paintings and drawings were on loan for an exhibition at Colby College in Waterville, just forty-five minutes away. Pauline, known as "Gaga" to her family and "Bobbie" to her friends,[7] was a member of the college's Friends of the Arts, and Frederick was an adviser to the group as well as a trustee of the school, so they were both happy to lend some of their finest pieces to Colby's art museum.[8] The decision to loan the pieces turned out to be rather unintentionally well-timed.

In late April 1972, the family homestead was unoccupied. Frederick was busy working in his New York City office, and his mother was still at her home in Miami, having not yet moved north to Monmouth for the summer. Though the estate had caretakers in its employ, they did not live in the family home but rather in separate quarters on the thousand-acre estate. Sometime over the weekend of April 22, disaster struck. When staff entered the home on Monday morning, they found that it had been victimized by thieves who entered by smashing an exterior glass door. The police and Frederick Woolworth were notified immediately, and the latter immediately flew home.[9]

An inventory of the collection found that fifty paintings had been taken, their frames neatly left behind. Frederick reported that he could tell the thieves were professionals by the way they removed the works from their frames. "It was all very carefully done," he told the press.

His mother was bereft. "There was a tremendous sadness . . . they were very important to her," he reported.[10]

Interestingly, the thieves did not make off with any of the family's several Wyeth paintings. One was away on loan, and they overlooked or didn't recognize the others, including a watercolor that had been painted specially for Frederick. The thieves also oddly concentrated most of their efforts on only one room on the second floor. Fortunately, high-value works by Winslow Homer, John Singer Sargent, and Gilbert Stuart had also been lent to a museum at the time and were not on the walls. But given the size of the collection, several very important works were in the house and taken. Frederick Woolworth estimated that the most valuable was Thomas Waterman Wood's *Yankee Peddler*, which he said was worth $50,000.[11] There was also a Grandma Moses work, *The Mail Is Here*, as well as works by Samuel Morse, George B. Miller, George Catlin, and many others. Sheriff Stanley Jordan told the media that the total haul was valued at $477,000, a peculiarly specific number given that Frederick Woolworth estimated the loss at over $250,000.[12] Regardless of the amount, the loss of nearly a third of their paintings was devastating. Mr. Woolworth said, "Losing this many paintings take a bit of the of the heart and soul out of the collection." Still, he remained optimistic, positing that the art would likely be recovered due to its recognizability to dealers and collectors. Here, his experience in the art world was evident. He knew that highly valuable and recognizable works were, and remain, notoriously difficult to fence. With the attention that the heist would draw, offering them for sale on the legitimate market where they might fetch their actual value would be an enormously risky endeavor. And besides, much of what was taken was at least partially insured.[13]

Still, the theft struck a severe blow to the Woolworth family. It must have resurrected stories about the famous theft suffered nearly a half century before when another Woolworth heiress, Mrs. James P. Donahue, was quietly robbed of $750,000 in gems from her six-room suite at the Plaza Hotel in New York as she bathed. The take, equivalent to $13.5 million today, was front-page news and took place within twenty-four hours of her receipt of two strings of valuable pearls from Paris.[14]

Though not quite as valuable as Mrs. Donahue's jewels, the paintings were perhaps more singular. Pearls, it can be argued, are much more replaceable than a Grandma Moses. But from the perspective of the thief, pearls are more easily fenced. A long string of pearls can even be turned into multiple sets. To the untrained eye, gemstones are hardly as distinguishable as Morse's *Reverend McKinstry*. Nevertheless, the gems were soon recovered after a controversial private detective who specialized in the recovery of stolen jewelry produced them for a payment of $65,000 to the thief. The whole matter involved such shady circumstances that the detective was later indicted.*[15]

Though state, federal, and local officials were all hunting for the thieves and the fifty stolen Woolworth paintings, there was little to go on, and no suspect sleuth emerged to help the cause. Sheriff Jordan stated, without explanation, that because the paintings were carefully removed from their frames, he didn't believe the thieves were known criminals from the area.[16] As for repeat offenders, there had been no significant thefts at the Monmouth estate in the past, but for the occasional pilfering of what Mr. Woolworth described as "petty things." Further, the family had made the home accessible to many members of the public who wished to visit and see what his mother and father had amassed. The number of people who might know about the second-floor room that had been raided was therefore somewhat vast

---

* The detective, Noel C. Scaffa, was tried twice before being acquitted.

and completely unknown.[17] Monmouth, a town of about two thousand people, was remarkably safe, and burglaries were rare. Rounding up the usual suspects just wasn't an option.

There exist in the field of criminology two general explanations for the repeat victimization of certain targets: the flag effect and the boost effect. Both are suitable for consideration when it comes to art heists. The first, in this context, is the flag effect (sometimes referred to by the less euphonious term *risk heterogeneity*) which refers to targets that stand out as more suitable or attractive to criminals. For instance, a home might present as less secure than others, with weak, antiquated locks and windows, poor lighting, and other signals to thieves that penetrating the perimeter would be easy to accomplish. Or a neighborhood might be known to be ripe for crime because of a dearth of police patrols. The second, the boost effect, can refer to a target that is struck because it is known to have been successfully targeted in the past. It could explain why one criminal repeats his victimization of a single establishment, or why a separate thief decides to target it after learning of a successful heist. Of course, when it comes to fine art, the boost effect can dissipate over time and after repeat break-ins because of the diminishing number of items known to still be available to steal.[18]

It's the latter that prolific thief Allison Williams referred to in an interview with *The Philadelphia Inquirer* from prison. Williams, who with his brother, Cliff, had in 1966 robbed the Saratoga Springs home of Cornelius Vanderbilt Whitney of $781,000 in jewels, told the *Inquirer* that years later they were scanning the society pages seeking ideas for another score when they read of the Woolworth Estate heist in Maine. That summer, they traveled to Monmouth and stole a half dozen paintings from the house, revictimizing the Woolworths. "I knew if they were hanging in there they must be worth something," he said. "Woolworth was no dummy."[19] Indeed, he was not. Woolworth had temporarily moved most of the remaining paintings in the home for safekeeping, just in case the likes of the Williams brothers came.[20] It's a testament to the size of the collection that the pair was still able to walk away with six pieces.

In June 1973, there was a break in the first Woolworth Estate burglary. Three men—Charles Hahn, James Lloyd, and James Thompson—were arrested by the FBI on charges related to the interstate transportation and attempted sale of most of the paintings stolen the year before. The three had attempted to sell them for a $30,000 advance to two undercover federal agents. Hahn had brought one of the paintings, a Howard Helmick painting, as proof of life, and it was recovered during the arrest.[21] Frederick Woolworth's educated guess about the difficulty selling the works was correct. Now the hunt was on for the rest.

Despite their access to the paintings, none of the three men were charged with the theft. At Thompson's sentencing in March 1974, federal judge Charles R. Weiner said, "I believe [Thompson] knows the people who stole the paintings." He continued, "I believe he is part of a ring."[22] Though that ring was not discovered, a separate one would soon form.

Charlie Crafts hailed from Everett, Massachusetts, a hardscrabble Boston suburb. Crafts was a convicted felon with a lengthy arrest record and served time at Walpole State Prison until being paroled in 1966. The experience did not warn him off from consorting with criminals. In 1968 he paid a steep price for it. He and a friend, Arthur Pearson—a gangland figure who had nearly been killed two years earlier by Mafia hitman Joe "The Animal" Barboza—were stabbed in Boston's North End. Crafts, badly injured with multiple stab wounds to his abdomen, managed to make his way to a nearby firehouse where he was treated and rushed to the hospital. Pearson wasn't so lucky. He was stabbed seventeen times and found slumped over in the front seat of his car, dead.[23]

Crafts's father was a World War II veteran and a community leader, and in 1954 he and his wife Eleanor purchased a campsite in Winthrop, Maine, on a piece of land, abutting the west line of the Woolworth land. Each summer they could trade the fast pace of city life for the peace of scenic lakes for themselves and their children. The younger Charlie visited as often as he could. During one of his visits, he caught word that the Woolworths had been robbed. Charlie had spent a good amount of time traversing the area over the years and knew the landscape well. It was poles apart from the life he knew so well back in Greater Boston. Here, the odds of being brutally stabbed in the stomach by Mob associates were nil. There was no need for a big police presence. Relatively speaking, there was no crime in this part of Kennebec County, even when the population doubled each summer. Except, of course, for the big art heist.

Newspaper reports of that theft and the subsequent arrests and prosecutions of the three men who tried to sell the works remained fresh in Crafts's mind. It wasn't lost on him that the stories spoke of the magnitude of the Woolworth collection. Though fifty paintings had been taken two years earlier, the media reported that equated to less than a third of their paintings. The media made mention that the house was unoccupied when it was robbed, and that Frederick Woolworth had to fly in to survey the damage, and that many valuable works had been overlooked by the thieves. All this got him to thinking.

One of Charlie Crafts's friends from back home in Everett was a man named Richard Donati, known as Dickie to friends and family. Dickie and his identical twin brother Bobby were well-known in Greater Boston as habitual thieves, dabbling in the theft of everything from furs to jewels to Oriental rugs. Despite this, the twins were well liked by just about everyone. Myles Connor knew them both and became close friends with them, and when he was imprisoned in the 1960s, it was the twins who looked in on his mother. He fondly remembers that the Donati boys would "fight like cats and dogs," but quickly added, "they had a warm heart. They were just very warm-hearted people."[24] Many remember the brothers fondly for their congeniality. "They were kind souls," remembers a family member.[25]

Charlie knew that his friend from the old neighborhood was interested in antiques. A few years earlier, Dickie had been arrested in New York with three other men when they transported $1 million in silver and antiques stolen in the Boston area. The artifacts ranged from chalices and paperweights to an antique Bible and a valuable stamp collection. They also were carrying one thousand counterfeit Massachusetts driver's licenses.[26] Surely, if Dickie was willing to traffic in these items, then he'd likely want in on whatever was left at the Woolworth home.

Indeed, he did. And Dickie knew just the guy to help ensure the heist went off without a snag: Myles Connor. Dickie knew that this was exactly the sort of score Myles would enjoy, and that if anyone could get in and out of that house without detection, it was his rock and rolling friend. So, Dickie reached out to Myles and pitched him the score. Myles, never one to pass on an opportunity to steal from the rich or disappoint a friend, agreed to take a look at the estate.

The pair traveled to Monmouth to survey the target. Dickie and Myles checked out the house on the land known to be Frederick's. It was perfect—out of the sight line of any possible witnesses and set back and obscured some by woods. Even better, they found that despite the previous heist, the Woolworths hadn't bothered to install security on the property. What they could see through the windows excited both men. Dickie, an expert in Oriental rugs, was pleased with what he saw as he shone the flashlight through the windows. Myles, too, was enthusiastic. He was acutely aware that the paintings and antiques in the home were not fakes. The Woolworth family did not need to purchase cheap imitations. Content with their survey, they returned to the Crafts's camp to discuss their findings and to finalize a plan for the weekend break-in. Then they met with two trusted flunkies they brought along to help lug all that they could fit into the van that Myles had borrowed from back home.

The quartet of thieves drove to the estate under the cover of darkness and parked the van nearby.[27] Using a Stanley Wonder Bar, they went to work prying open the rear door on the east side of the house. In short order, the door latch broke, and the bandits were inside. One of the men ran upstairs to a bedroom on the west side with a balcony that overlooked the road to the house and kept a lookout just in case any silent alarms they had overlooked had been triggered. The others moved through the house like game-show contestants trying to quickly find and gather everything that appeared valuable before the buzzer rang. Myles, however, remained calm, as was his wont. The most experienced of the thieves when it came to cultural property, the first things that caught his eye were not paintings but two Simon Willard grandfather clocks. They were the sorts of things that ordinary thieves would pass by without a second look, but Myles knew their value. Willard had been perhaps the nation's best clockmaker, creating pieces in the late eighteenth century that today can retail for upward of $60,000. Though they were large, measuring about seven feet in height, Myles was committed to taking them. He and Dickie hoisted them in the van and went back to taking art and antiques. It was Dickie who noticed attractive paintings on the wall, shining a flashlight on them for Myles to inspect. He knew instantly that they were by the Wyeths and directed the others to grab them. They did as they were told, removing small lights that were attached to the frames to illuminate the artistry held within. From a small third-floor bedroom they took a sheet and a blanket to wrap the delicate works. There were three works by N. C. Wyeth with an estimated value of $140,000: *Cover of Treasure Island*, *Pennsylvania Farmer*, and *Dark Harbor Fisherman*. Two were by his son, Andrew: *Lost Balloon* (valued at $25,000) and a reproduction of *Distant Thunder*. Interestingly, not even Myles realized that they were taking a reproduction. The Woolworths were famous for their collection of paintings, not copies. But given the darkness, the presumption of what was on the walls, and the natural urgency inherent to a heist, it's understandable that none of them knew that *Distant Thunder* wasn't the original masterpiece. By flashlight, Myles could see Andrew Wyeth's wife Betsy lying in the grass with a storm brewing, and he ordered it taken. After all, the original was so well regarded that it was the favorite painting of First Lady Pat Nixon and had been exhibited at the White House in 1970.[28] But not this one. It was, in fact, merely a print valued at just $150. Still, the four genuine Wyeth paintings were worth $165,000 (more than $1.3 million in today's dollars). The Wyeths and all the rest of the loot were loaded into the green van and the quartet of thieves drove off undetected. The plan had gone off without a single obstacle.

In all, they made off with twenty-two paintings, two grandfather clocks, and a considerable collection of smaller antiques. Not everything they pilfered was a high-value item. From the master bedroom they stole trays filled with jewelry that they would later find were merely costume pieces and not the valuable gems they'd expected to find in the home of a Woolworth heir. They even broke open a large plastic bottle that held spare change and a $20 bill. Those minor items aside, the burglary in total resulted in a huge take. And much of what they stole, save for the Wyeths, would be easy to fence back in Massachusetts, which is where they went to store the stolen goods, once again turning to Myles's none-the-wiser girlfriend Martha Ferrante to borrow space in her barn in western Massachusetts for safekeeping.

At around 9:00 A.M. on May 28, 1974, the housekeeper responsible for the Woolworths' house entered the home after a weeklong vacation. The time off proved to be opportune, providing her with the relaxation she would need before entering a scene she never expected.

She immediately noticed that one of the large grandfather clocks on the first floor was gone. That was curious. No one had mentioned anything about the stately piece going off for repair. As she progressed through the house, she noted another missing clock—this one, a beautiful banjo-shaped piece that hung from the wall. Proceeding further, she was aghast at the mess she found on the floor, especially the small lamps strewn about and the pennies emptied from the plastic bottle that held loose change. She looked up and found empty spaces where the paintings had been. There was no doubt now—she had to tell her boss. She quickly walked down to the property manager's residence, and together they returned to the house and surveyed the damage. At 9:15 A.M., the property manager called the local police to report a burglary.

Investigators noticed immediately that the pry bar used to break open the rear door left blue paint on the white doorjamb. An inspection of the premises resulted in just two other clues: a black police-type flashlight was accidentally forgotten in the master bedroom, and the culprits appeared to have left behind a box that had contained fried clams from Howard Johnson's. Though no useful tire tracks had been left behind by the thieves, the housekeeper remembered seeing an old green van parked on the road near the estate. And she remembered that it had Massachusetts plates. Police officers interviewed a laborer at the estate who also recalled the van and had made a note of the Massachusetts license plates.

The green van proved to be a very useful lead in the case. It was key to perhaps the biggest break in the investigation, which came when detectives canvassing the area spoke with a witness who told them that on the weekend when the theft occurred, he noticed that same green van with Massachusetts plates parked at his neighbor's camp. That neighbor was Charlie Crafts. FBI agents promptly went to the Crafts's camp and found two important items: a blue Stanley Wonder Bar with remnants of white paint on the business end of it, and a nine-millimeter handgun. Both meant big trouble for Crafts. The tool tied him to the heist and, as a convicted felon, possession of the gun was a criminal offense. The walls were closing in on Charlie Crafts.

Back in Massachusetts, Myles Connor had picked up where he had left off before his adventures up North. With the painting and antiques safely hidden, he returned to the stage. Al Dotoli was staying on course trying to turn this rock and roll rebel into something more than just a local headliner. But what he needed from Myles were two things: consistency and dedication. Without them, there was no way Al could cultivate the raw energy and talent that his friend had in spades into an act that agents and promoters would get behind.

Connor was cognizant of the fact that highly valuable works by well-known artists such as the Wyeths were nearly impossible to sell on the legitimate market. He also knew that there was little by way of a black market for them either, at least not for any sort of money that would make the heist worthwhile. But throughout his life—whether it be handling venomous snakes, singing his heart out into a microphone, fighting a guy twice his size, or scaling a building to steal a few swords—Myles Connor was nothing if not a risk-taker. Sure, he could end up in a jam with the police chomping at the bit to put him behind bars, but he wasn't about to shrink from a challenge out of fear of reprisal. In fact, it seemed that he welcomed, even preferred, danger. Perhaps that is why he took the Wyeth paintings, knowing from experience that not only would they bring extra heat into the hunt for the Woolworth thieves but would be extraordinarily difficult to monetize. It was "fortune favors the bold" sort of behavior.

Dickie Donati was also back in Massachusetts, quietly putting out feelers to his network of those interested in the commerce of nice things with questionable provenance. He and Myles were eager to make some money from their ill-gotten gains. After all, they hadn't stolen twenty-two paintings to hang on their walls, and the Simon Willard clocks weren't taken so that they each could have a statement piece in their living rooms. This was business. Dickie needed to support a wife and baby at home whom he adored, and Myles, as ever, needed money for more samurai swords and other Japanese fascinations.

Dickie was no novice at moving stolen goods. He and his twin brother had a long history of thievery, earning the nicknames "Spot and Steal" (one would spot something, and the other would steal it). Despite his chosen vocation, Dickie was an endearing sort. Al Dotoli described him as "a jovial, friendly guy" who was kind and generous. Dotoli recalled once returning home from work and finding Dickie and Myles sitting in his kitchen (Myles, of course, had a key to the house). Dickie thanked Al for letting him and Myles use his home to meet and asked him to go outside with him to his van. As he was opening the back doors of it, he asked Al, "What size jacket do you wear?" Al told him that his very tall and lanky frame made him difficult to fit. Dickie sized him up, searched through what seemed like a small boutique of fine leather jackets, and pulled out one that him perfectly—a gift for Al's hospitality.[29]

It took Dickie a surprisingly short time—a matter of weeks, in fact—to find someone interested in the Wyeths and, perhaps, a grandfather clock. An antique dealer from New York with a loose understanding of professional ethics was interested in buying them, and Myles was pleased to learn that they were looking at a payday. He volunteered to pick up the art and meet the prospective buyer with the goods. They agreed to meet in Mashpee, Massachusetts, on Cape Cod. It was a matter of convenience for Myles, as he was in the midst of a major multi-night concert event there organized by Al. He could sell the works and make it in time for his set. It couldn't have been more perfect.

CHAPTER 7
ON THE ROCKS

By 1974, Al Dotoli's career was in full swing. He was working on shows of all sizes, from jam-packed clubs featuring local acts in Boston to sold-out concerts throughout the United States and Europe featuring true A-listers. The gambit that saw him jump from renting out equipment to overseeing concert production had paid off, and he was busily bouncing from show to show, refusing to turn down any opportunity that came his way. Though still a young man, Al had an innate mind for business and an ethic of hard work that he learned from watching his father labor tirelessly at the family restaurant, with regard to neither the clock nor fatigue.

The lineup of performers Al supported read like a who's who of the era. Just three months earlier, he worked for Frank Sinatra at his first appearance at the new Providence Civic Center. He was in his fifth year working with superstar Dionne Warwick. Kris Kristofferson, the Grateful Dead, José Feliciano, Sha Na Na, and others also demanded his time and skills. He was also serving as manager to bluesmen James Cotton and James Montgomery. And, of course, there was Myles Connor.

Al handled every aspect of Myles's career—even his banking. "I don't think he ever had a bank account in his life," Al said.[1] Myles was gaining attention as a performer, and Al lined him up with big acts, opening for Chuck Berry and, on many occasions, Roy Orbison. Orbison, who frequently traveled to shows in a motor home, was said to prefer solitude in the vehicle, but Myles was welcome to visit him anytime. Some of the bigger acts were taken by his growing legend, especially amused by his jailbreak courtesy of a carved bar of soap. His real-life outlaw image didn't inhibit anyone's desire to perform with him, and it might have even helped.

Al was closely monitoring Myles's following, which had grown beyond the Lewis Room in Revere on the North Shore all the way down south to Cape Cod and indeed throughout New England. His popularity was booming. He was performing his own compositions in between dead-on covers of hits by Orbison and Berry as well as Elvis Presley and Johnny Cash. Audiences were wild for his brash and daring performances, which included driving onto the stage revving his Harley-Davidson some nights and hopping out of a coffin on others. Connor's residency at the popular South Shore club the Beachcomber provided him with a steady source of income and was so popular that the shows are still talked about half a century later. He poured every ounce of himself into his performances. And his relationship with the audience was symbiotic, with both ending the night hoarse and drenched in sweat. The President of Rock and Roll, as Connor was now widely known, was a great draw, and clubs loved to book him. His shows guaranteed a big audience and even bigger tabs at the bar.

Dotoli remained eager to elevate his friend's career beyond the club scene and into a national act, and his work with other artists gave him the tools to make it happen. He was coming to know some of the most powerful people in the industry, and he saw what it took to perform at a high level in front of demanding audiences. Moreover, Dotoli was at the forefront of putting together major concerts, which was no small feat. The era of the arena tour was still in its infancy, and Dotoli had been there from the very beginning, which made him a hot commodity in the touring business. Everyone wanted his services and his ability to produce first-rate sound, which was Dotoli's forte. "Most people don't realize it, but when someone like Kristofferson is alone on stage with just a guitar, the need for the sound to be perfect is even more important," he said.[2] Performers, agents, booking companies, venue owners—they were all on a first-name basis with the amiable and able young Dotoli. Access is everything in the entertainment industry, and he now had it. The trick was getting Myles to stay focused so that they could take advantage of it.

Al made several efforts to try to get Myles to record a full album. Both had already gained experience in the recording studio. Dotoli wasn't yet seventeen years old when he arranged and conducted Myles's songs "Someone Somewhere" and "Hey Little Schoolgirl," joining forces with Boston businessman Ralph Ranzo to create RCD (for Ranzo, Connor, Dotoli) Records and produce a 45 RPM.* Ranzo was another strong believer in Myles's promise as a musician. His 2018 obituary sums up his career as a music producer this way: "[Ranzo] managed up-and-coming local singers and bands. He wasn't quite so shrewd in this endeavor. He once had the chance to represent Led Zeppelin in Boston but he didn't think they were very good and so passed on it, and his top singing prospect was more adept at robbing museums, so he decided to become a business owner instead."[3]

---

* Connor's first 45 RPM, which featured the songs "A Lover's Prayer" and "I Don't Need You Anymore," was recorded in 1962 by Wink Records in New York. The label incorrectly lists him as "Miles Connor."

Ranzo's frustrations were nothing compared to those of Dotoli. Al estimates that he and Myles began recording at least five albums that were never completed, because with each attempt the latter ended up in jail before the project was completed. "It wasn't a matter of money," Dotoli said. "The musicians were all more than happy to perform for free, and so was the engineer. I produced the music, and the studio time was provided free by my contacts. The only expense was the tape, which was practically nothing."[4] Rather, it was the opportunity cost that nagged at Dotoli. Still, he forged ahead undaunted and as committed to his best friend as ever, confident Myles was on the brim of stardom.

Despite his best intentions and desire to please Al, however, Myles Connor just couldn't stop breaking the law. "You see, there's this passion called 'collecting,'" he will sometimes say. Or he'll laugh and jokingly reply, "I guess I'm just evil." His criminal exploits continued as steady as a drumbeat. Not merely petty crimes, either—major heists, some cocaine dealing, bail jumping, and other outrageous deeds that kept Myles in the headlines and the police ever more committed to putting him away, no matter what it might take.

Myles's obsession with collecting valuable items aside, there was a dark force pulling at him to commit more and more crimes—a notorious Massachusetts hood by the name of Ralph Petrozziello, whom he had met at Walpole State Prison. Petrozziello was a key part of his crew there, loyally acting as Connor's eyes and ears in that cutthroat environment. He was a valuable ally, respected for his toughness and feared for his capacity for violence. When they were both back out on the streets, they joined forces, coupling Petrozziello's pitilessness with Connor's cunning. No bank—whether it was in their neighborhood or as far away as Vermont—was safe.

Though they formed a formidable pair, they were starkly different men. Whereas Myles was a complex character who lived by a strict code and combined a genius-level intellect with a talent for daring, large-scale crimes, Petrozziello was quick to anger and had little interest in art and antiques beyond what he could pocket by taking them. He was attracted to money, plain and simple, and was quick to use force to get it. One anecdote illustrates his disposition. Myles and Petrozziello were meeting at Al's house, where the presence of listening devices and other methods of snooping was less likely than in either of their own homes. The two thieves discussed plans for a robbery, and when Al overheard the date they set, he interrupted. "Myles, you have a show that night. You can't miss it. You know you have to be there." Petrozziello was incensed that Dotoli would dare to intrude. He pulled a gun from his waistband and held it to Dotoli's head, saying, "I never fucking liked this guy. I'm going to shut him up right now." Without hesitation, Myles calmly drew his own gun and pointed it at Petrozziello. "If you shoot him, Ralph, I'm going to kill you right here." Petrozziello put the gun away, knowing that while he and Myles were close, the bond between his friend and Dotoli was impenetrable.[5]

It was the totality of the relationship in one vignette: Al trying to steer Myles toward music and a legitimate career and Petrozziello tugging him toward crime with a heavy dose of danger mixed in. Both men knew Myles had a love for both the songs and the swag, and at any minute one wrong move could mean the end of all of it. But one thing was abundantly clear: Myles would kill for his best friend.

The closeness of the relationship they had developed over the years formed in Al an almost otherworldly intuition about his musical mate. He could sense wicked winds blowing based on the shortest gaps in communication. He could pick up on the slightest variances in Myles's words or the twinkle in his eye. On one summer evening in 1974, it was mere background noise that led Al to believe that Myles was in deep trouble.

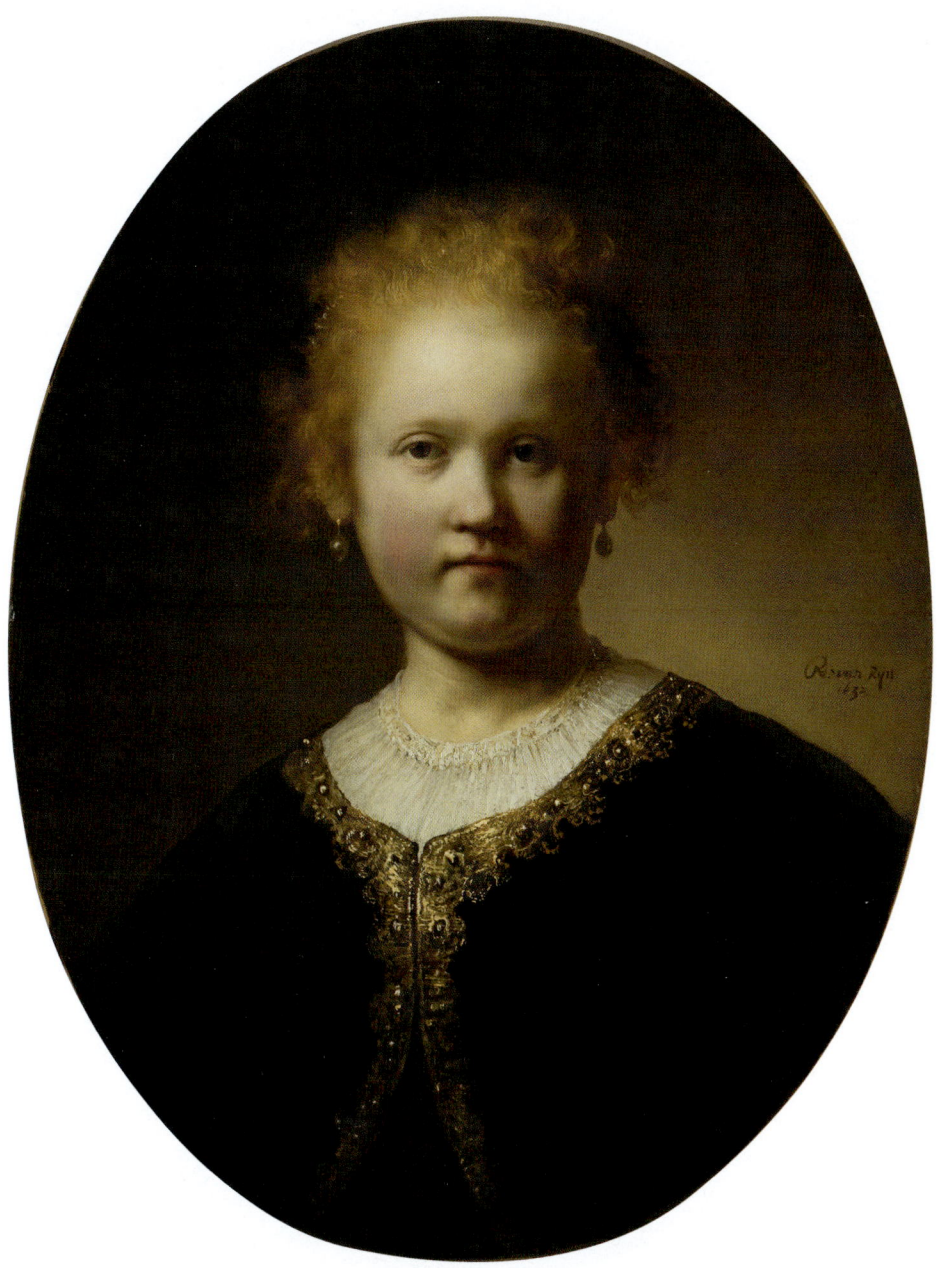

Rembrandt van Rijn's *Portrait of a Girl Wearing a Gold-Trimmed Cloak* (1632). The painting was known as *Portrait of Elsbeth van Rijn* when it was stolen by Myles Connor from the Museum of Fine Arts, Boston, in 1975. *Courtesy of the Leiden Collection.*

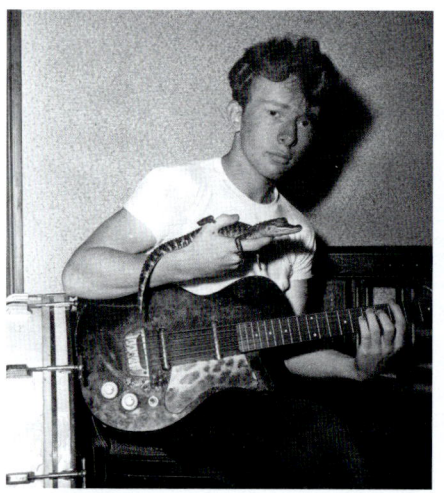
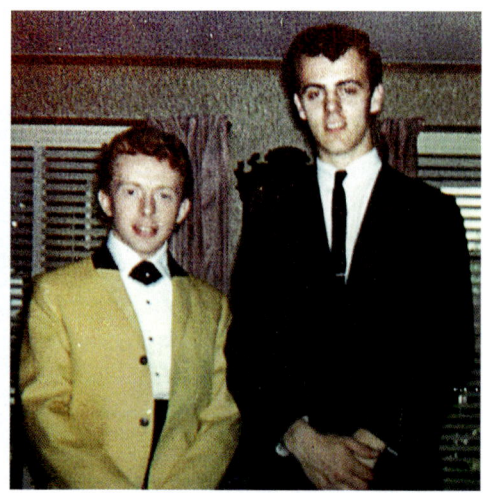
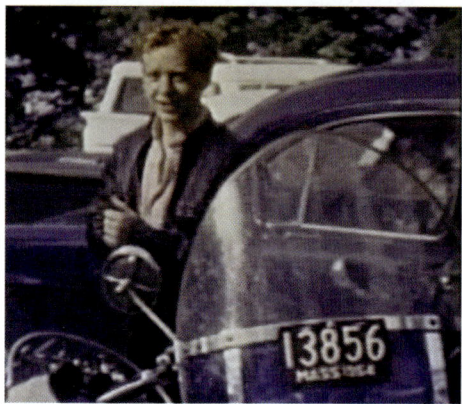

TOP LEFT: Myles Connor, age 17, with two of his great loves at the time: his electric guitar and Albert, his pet alligator. *Photo by Hugh E. O'Donnell/The Boston Globe via Getty Images.* TOP RIGHT: Connor and his best friend and manager, Al Dotoli, shortly before opening for the Dave Clark Five. *Courtesy of Al Dotoli.* CENTER: Connor and one of his early motorcycles. *Courtesy of Al Dotoli.* BOTTOM: Joe Gioiosa (left) with Myles's wife Victoria "Vicky" Laws and Dotoli, who is holding Myles J. Connor III. *Courtesy of Al Dotoli.*

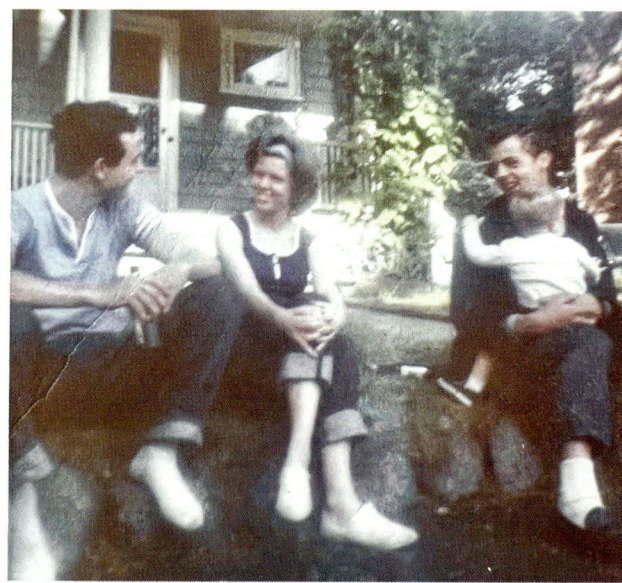

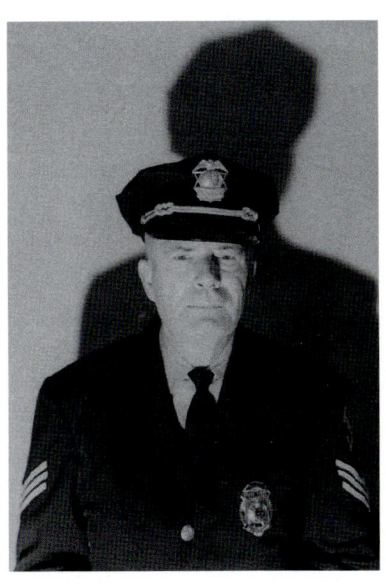
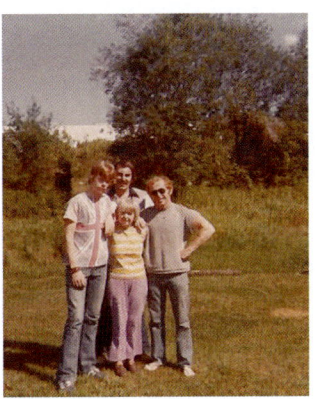

TOP LEFT: Myles's father, Sgt. Joe Connor of the Milton Police Department. *Courtesy of Myles Connor.* TOP RIGHT: Lucy Conant Johnson Connor, Myles's mother, (center) is flanked by her grandson Myles III to her right and her son Myles Jr. to her left. *Courtesy of Al Dotoli.* BOTTOM: An early handbill for an appearance by Myles, who by now was being billed as the "President of Rock & Roll." *Courtesy of Al Dotoli.*

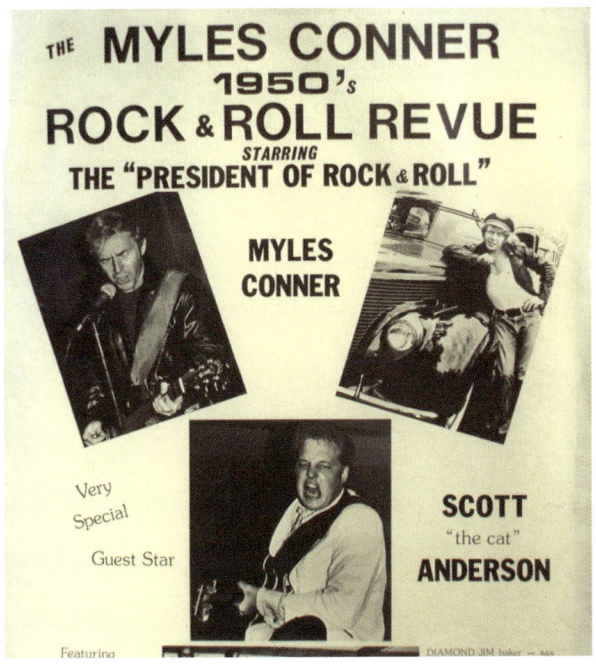

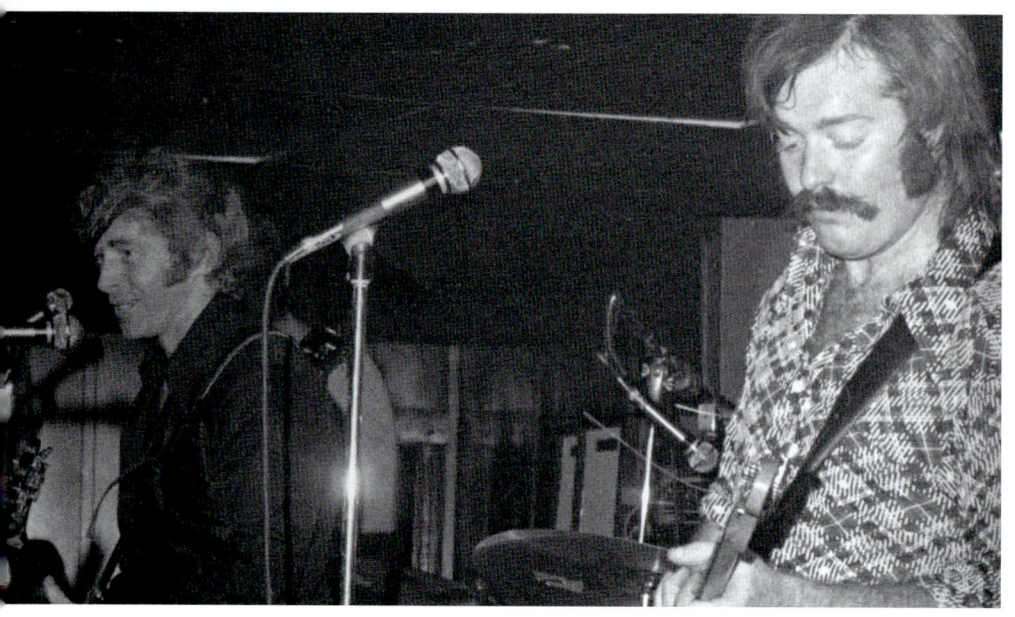

ABOVE: Myles (left) with bandmate Bean Lefebvre on bass. *Courtesy of Al Dotoli.* BELOW: Myles, in his leather biker's jacket and cap, posing for a publicity photo. *Courtesy of Al Dotoli.*

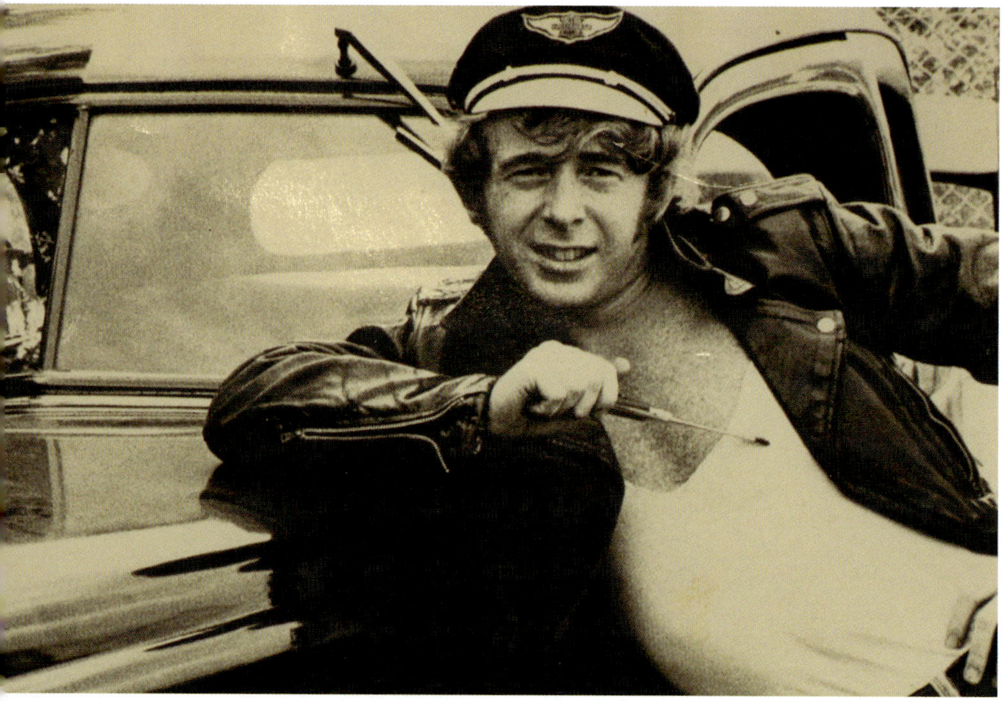

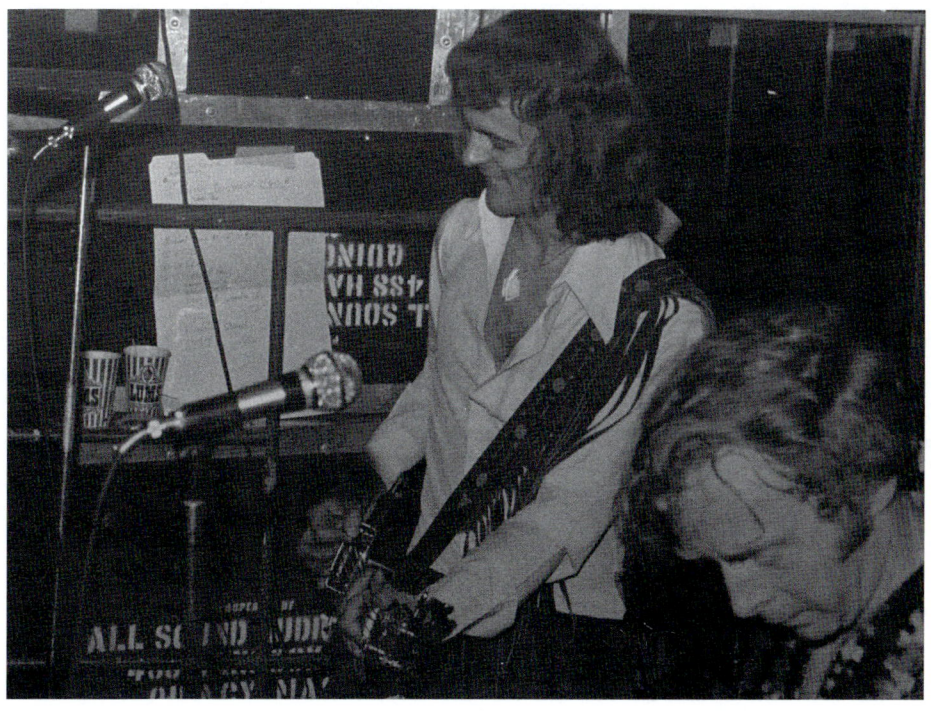

ABOVE: Myles and Al Dotoli jamming on stage. Next to Al are components of his famous sound system belonging to his company All Sound Audio. *Courtesy of Al Dotoli.* BELOW: Myles flexing some muscle. *Courtesy of Al Dotoli.*

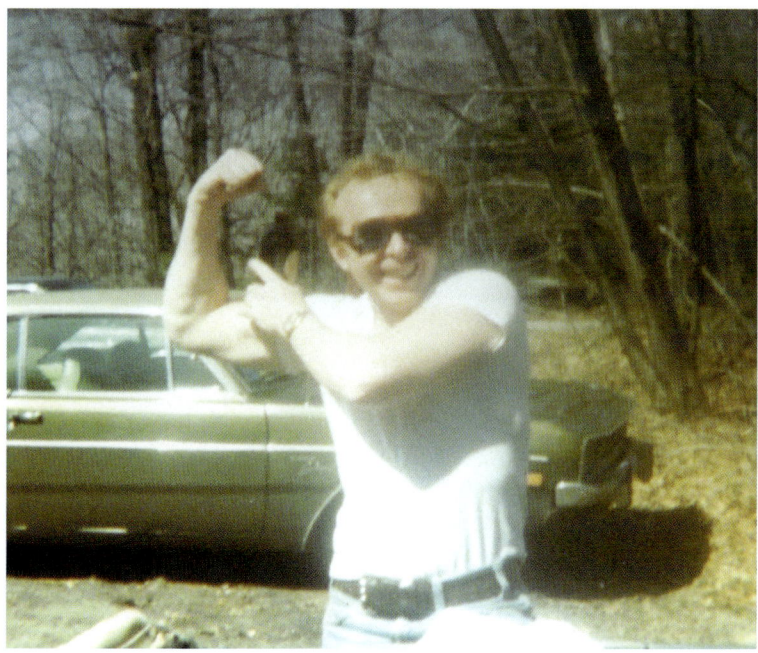

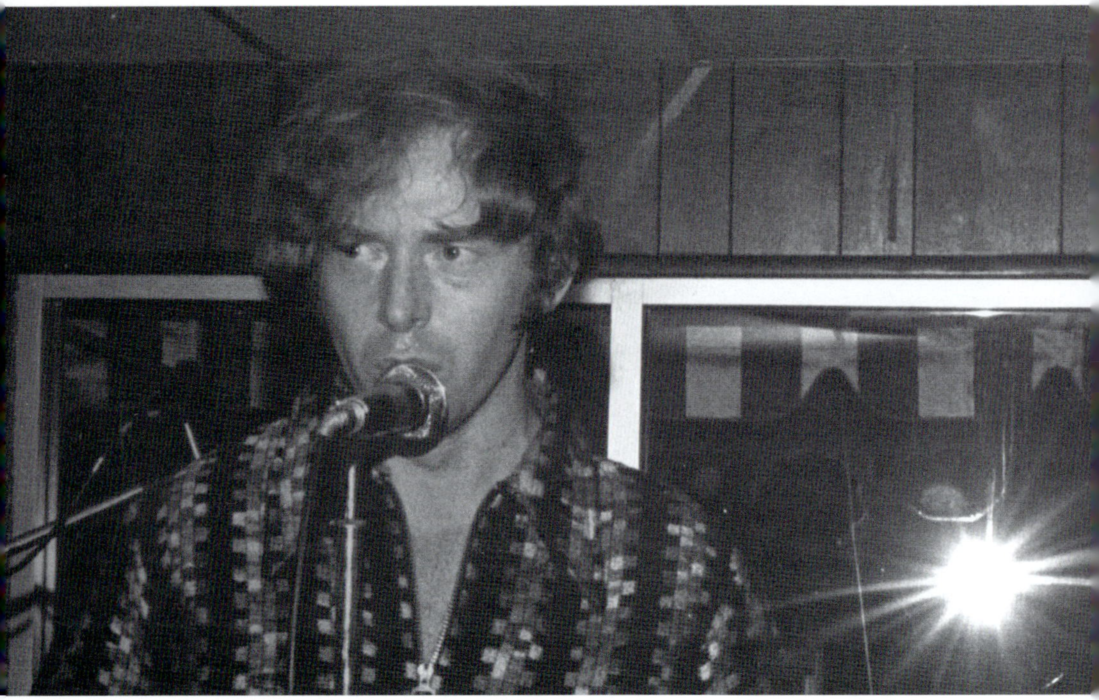

ABOVE: Myles singing a ballad. *Courtesy of Al Dotoli.* BELOW: The bar of soap sculpted into a gun that was used by Connor to break out of the Hancock County Jail. *Courtesy of the author.*

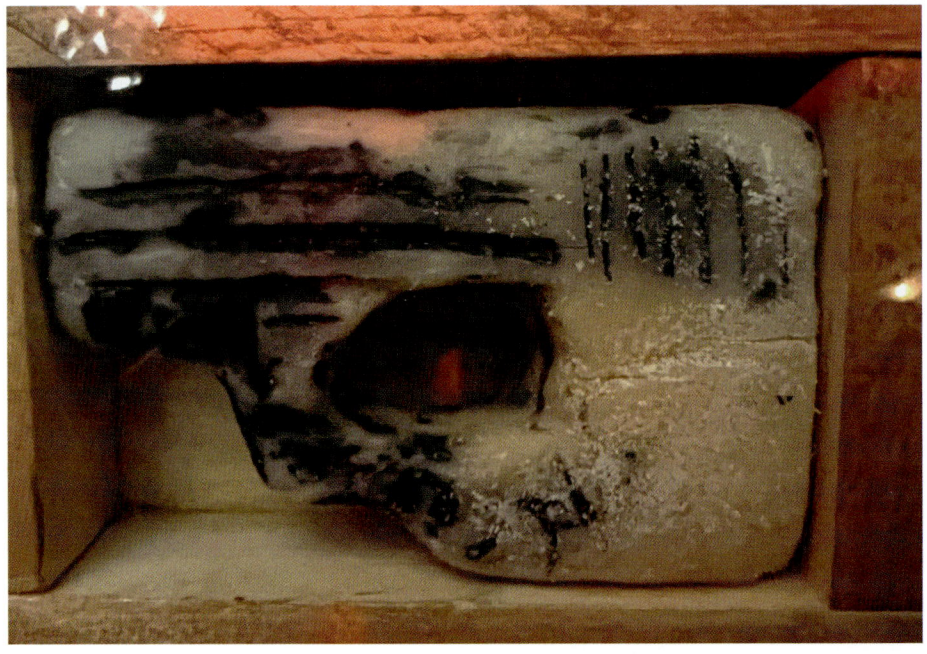

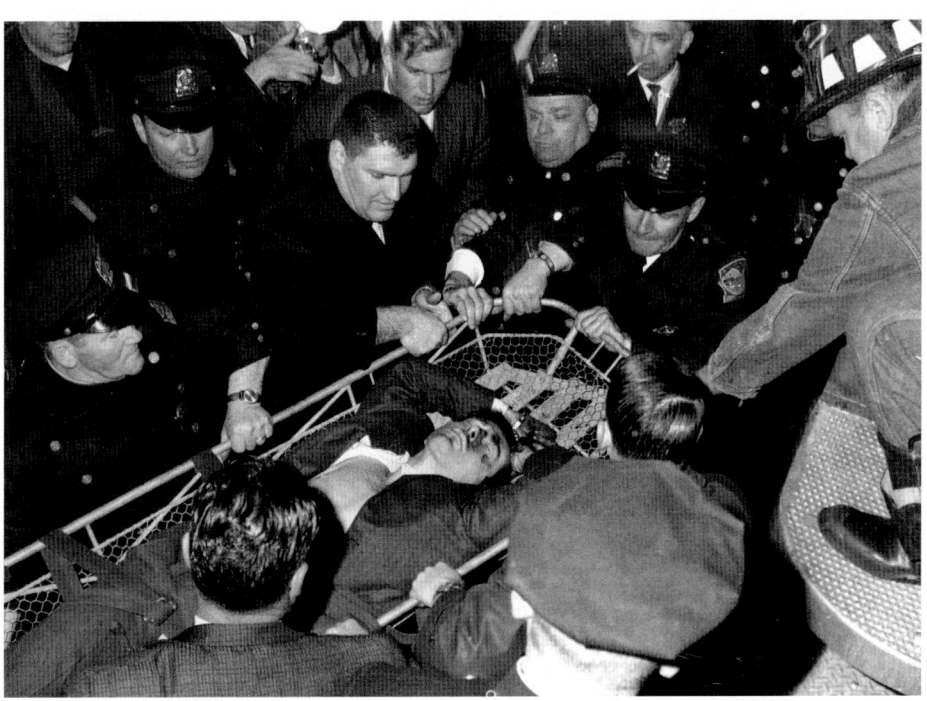

Myles Connor is lifted from a rooftop after a shootout with the police that left one officer injured. Connor suffered bullet injuries to a kidney, shoulder, spine, elbow, leg, hand, liver, and stomach. *Photo by Dan Sheehan/The Boston Globe via Getty Images.*

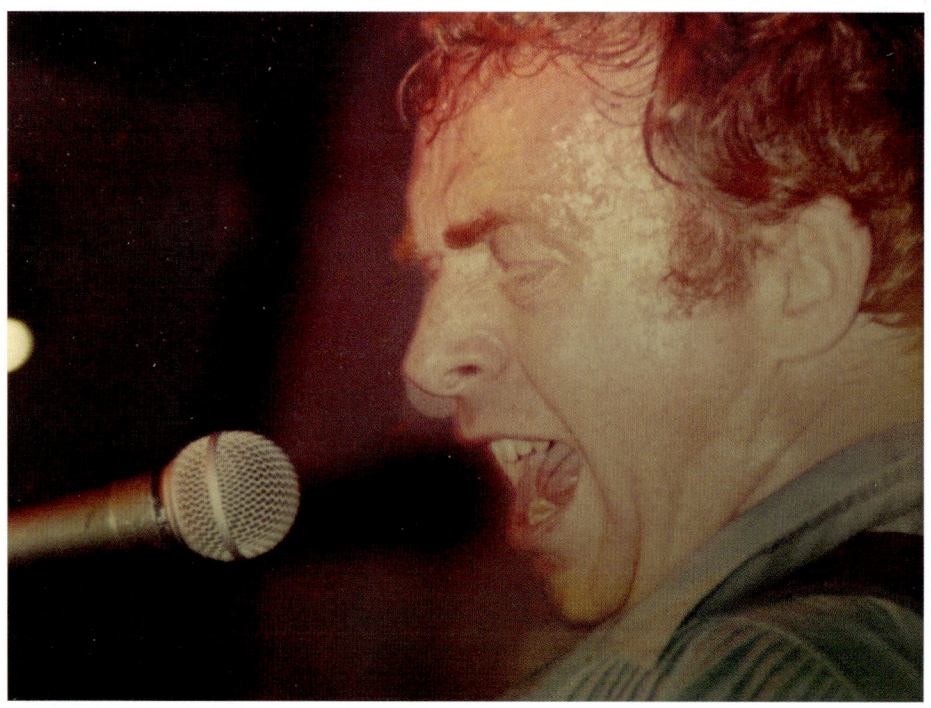

ABOVE AND BELOW: Connor was famous for his hard rocking shows and dynamic stage presence, packing clubs up and down the Atlantic coast. He left everything on the stage every night he performed. *Courtesy of Al Dotoli.*

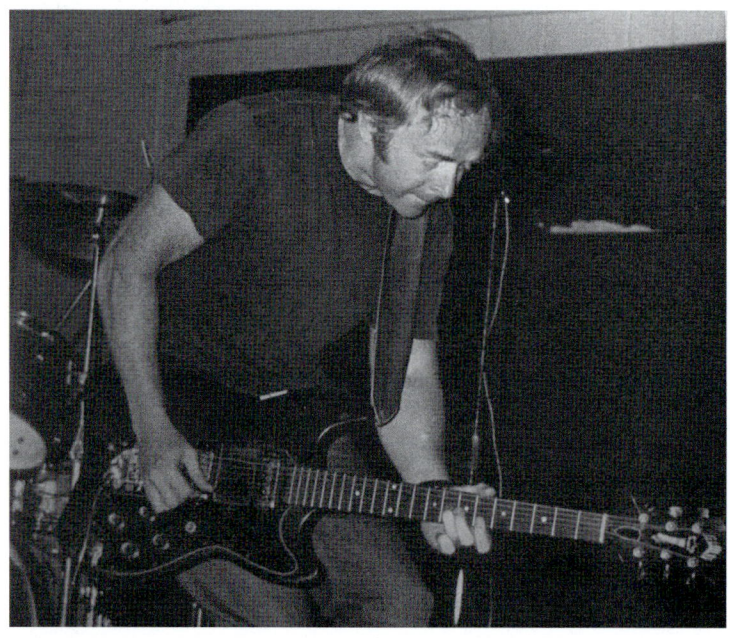

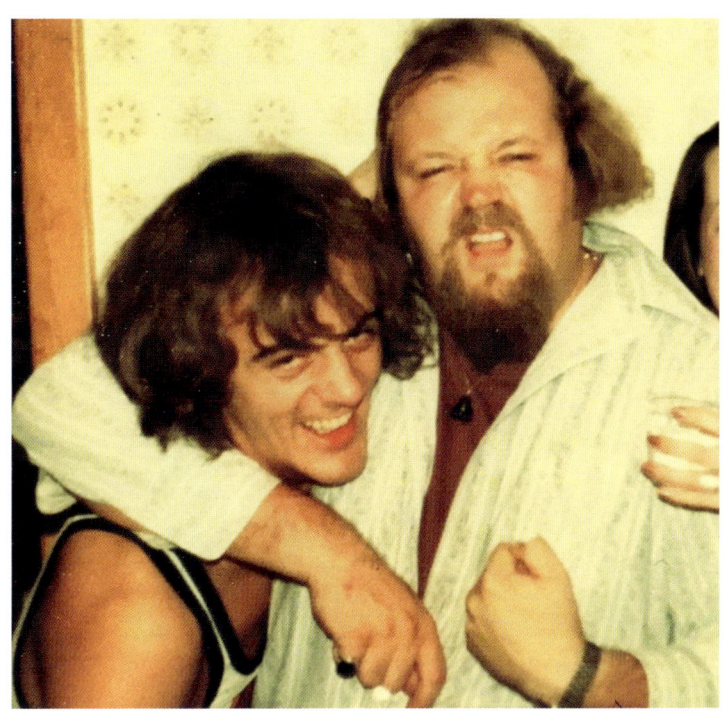

ABOVE: Al Dotoli with his close friend Lennie Baker of Sha Na Na. *Courtesy of Al Dotoli*. BELOW: Dotoli with his friend Dionne Warwick. Al handled tour and production management for Dionne's concerts throughout the world. *Courtesy of Al Dotoli*.

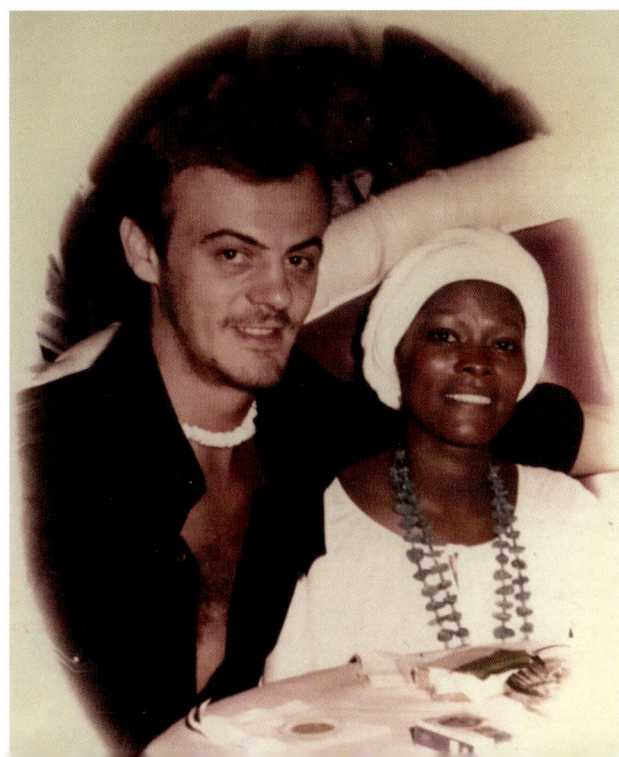

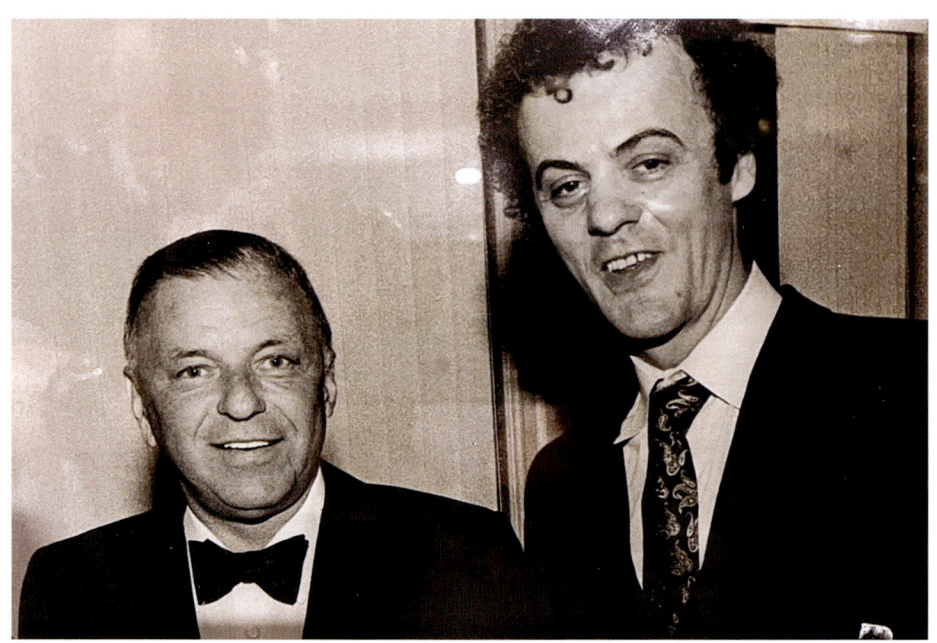

ABOVE: Al Dotoli with Frank Sinatra, for whom he served on the production touring staff dating back to the earliest of Ol' Blue Eyes's arena concerts. *Courtesy of Al Dotoli*. BELOW: FBI agents pose with the Woolworth's Wyeth paintings they recovered upon the arrest of Myles Connor in Mashpee, MA, in 1974. At right is Special Agent Bernie Murphy who led the operation. Also pictured are Butch Luker, Jim Buleigh, Paul Dembnicki, and Bill Baumgardner. *Courtesy of Bernie Murphy*.

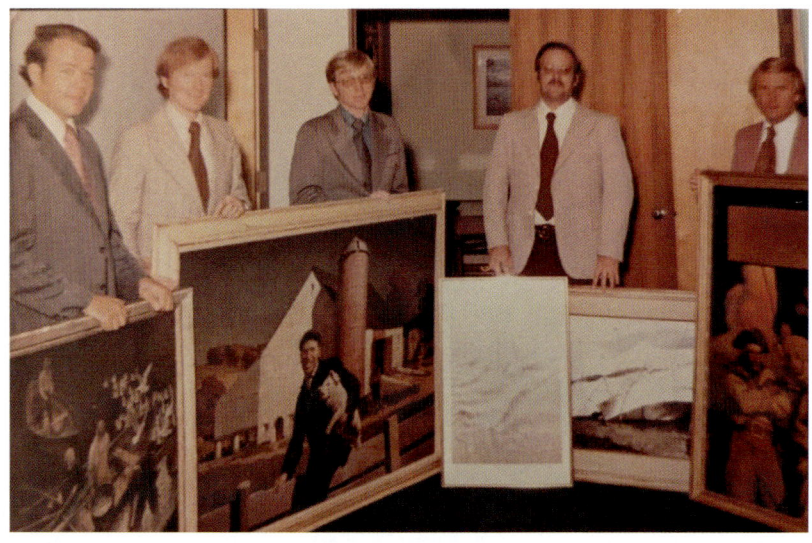

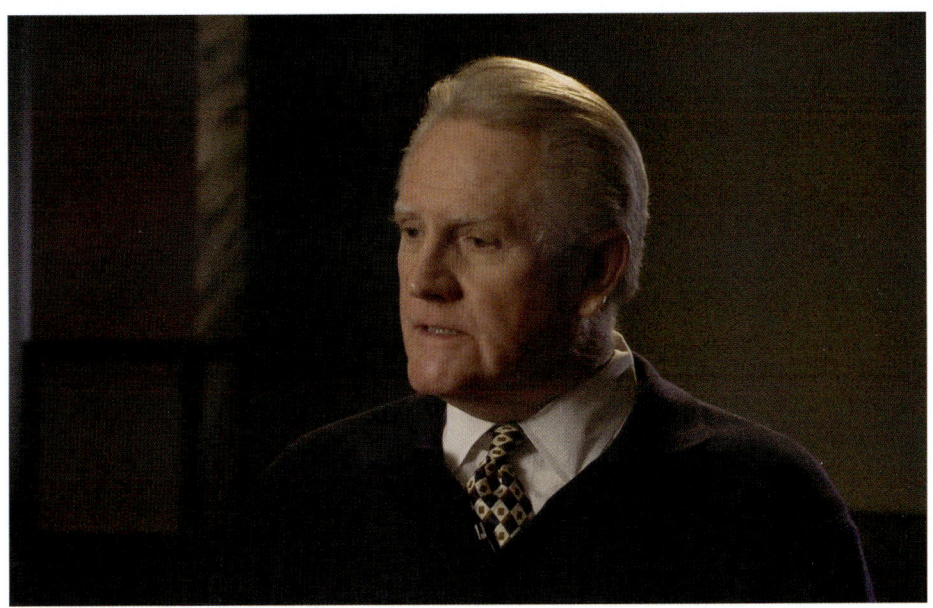

ABOVE: Bernie Murphy in a recent interview discussing the arrest of Myles Connor. *Courtesy of Al Dotoli*. BELOW: Major John Regan of the Massachusetts State Police (left) poses with District Attorney William Delahunt to his right upon the recovery of ancient gold coins stolen from Harvard's Fogg Museum in 1973. Regan would be instrumental in the recovery of the Rembrandt stolen by Connor from the MFA Boston. Middlesex County investigator Lawrence McCormick and attorney Robert Collins are also pictured. *Photo by Rachel Ritchie/The Boston Globe via Getty Images.*

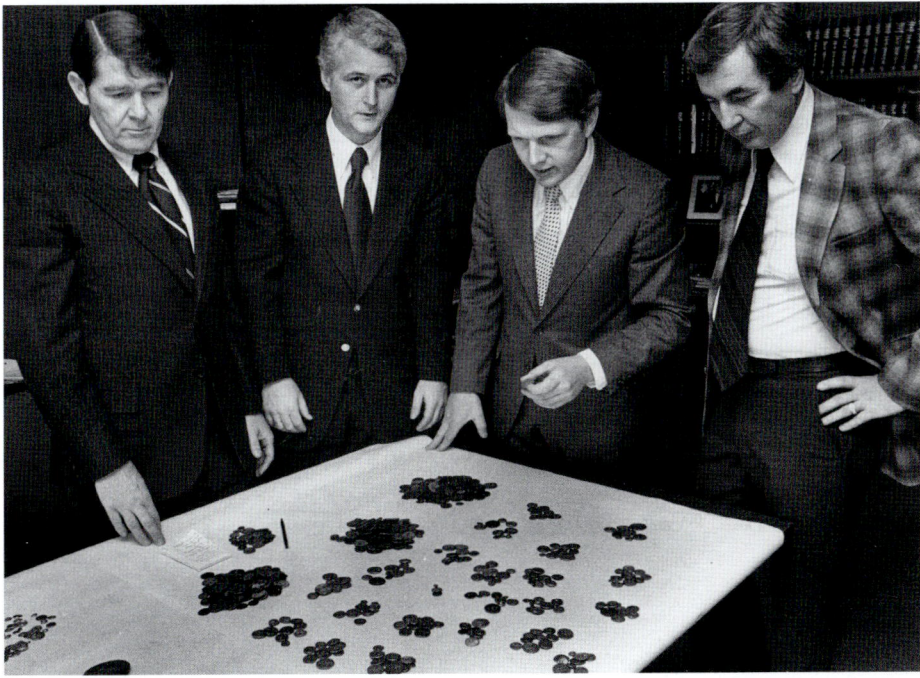

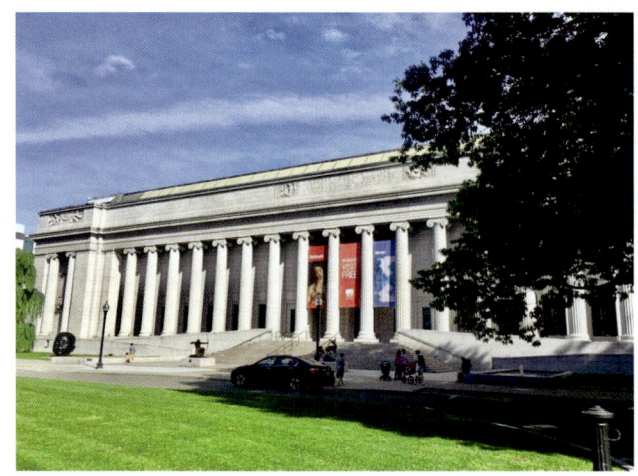

ABOVE: The Fenway Entrance to the Museum of Fine Arts, Boston. *Courtesy of the author.*
BELOW: The turnstiles in place in 1975 inside the MFA's Fenway Entrance. It was here that Connor and his partner, Billy Skinner, encountered guard John Monkouski and struck him on the head. As Connor fled from the museum with the Rembrandt in his arms, the painting was temporarily jammed against the narrow posts. *Photograph © 2025 Museum of Fine Arts, Boston.*

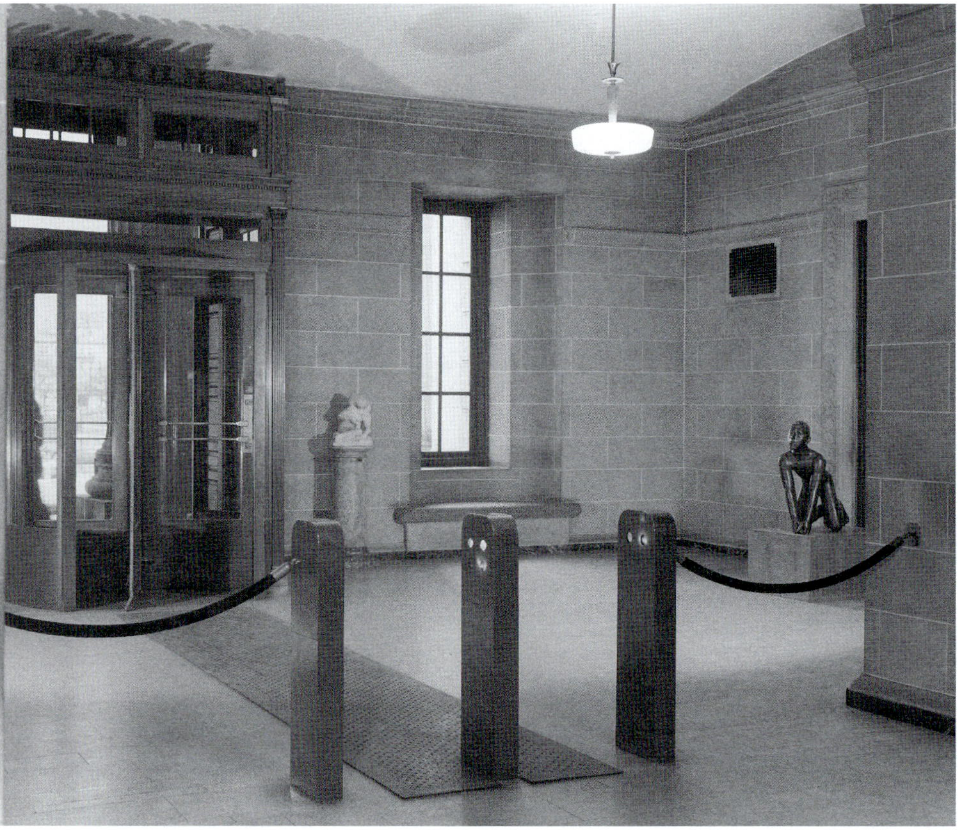

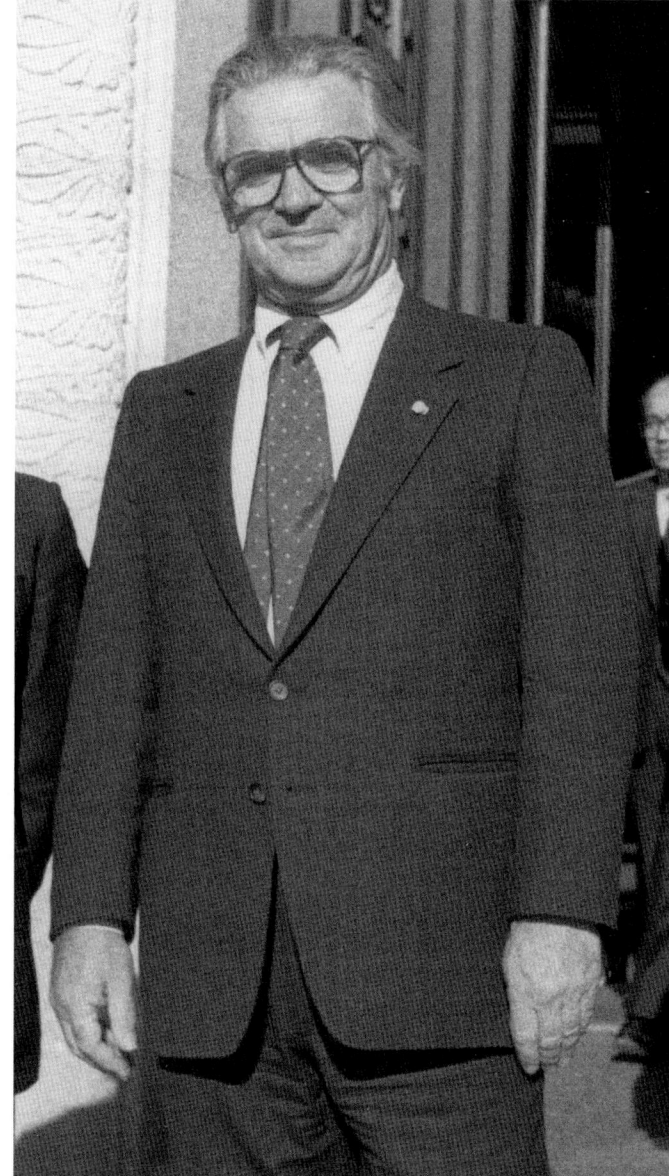

The reward notice posted in *The Boston Globe* soon after the heist. The notice set the criminal world abuzz which, in turn, led to pressure on Dotoli from many angles to produce a painting that he didn't have. *Courtesy of the author.*

Asian art scholar and director of the MFA Jan Fontein. Fontein took the helm of the museum while the Rembrandt painting was still missing and restored order in a time of some chaos at the famous institution. *Photograph © 2025 Museum of Fine Arts, Boston.*

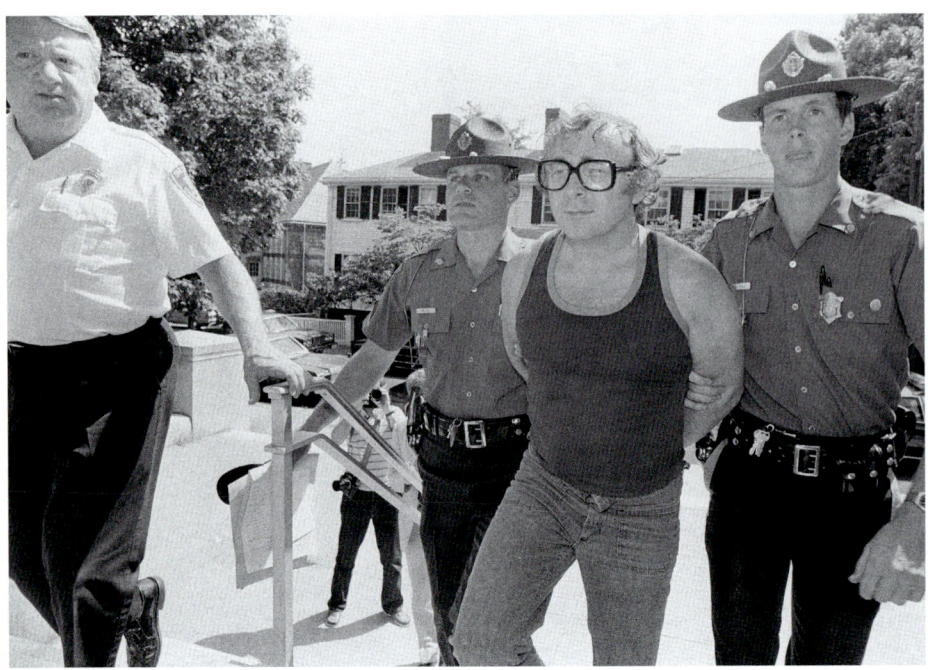

ABOVE: Myles Connor, cuffed and escorted by the Massachusetts State Police, after one of his many arrests. *Courtesy of the Associated Press*. BELOW: Myles and Al play an outdoor concert in the yard at Walpole State Prison. Such was Connor's fame and favor with prison officials—and Dotoli's ability to pull off a show—that he was allowed to perform at the notorious facility. *Courtesy of Al Dotoli.*

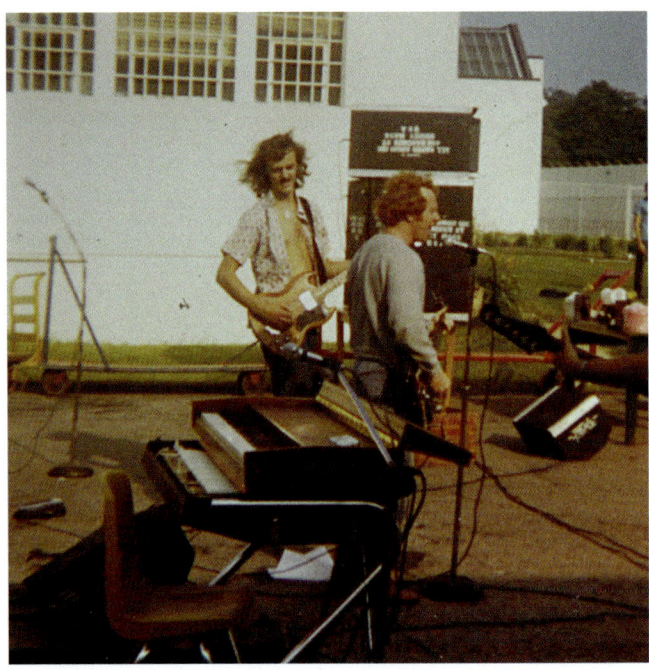

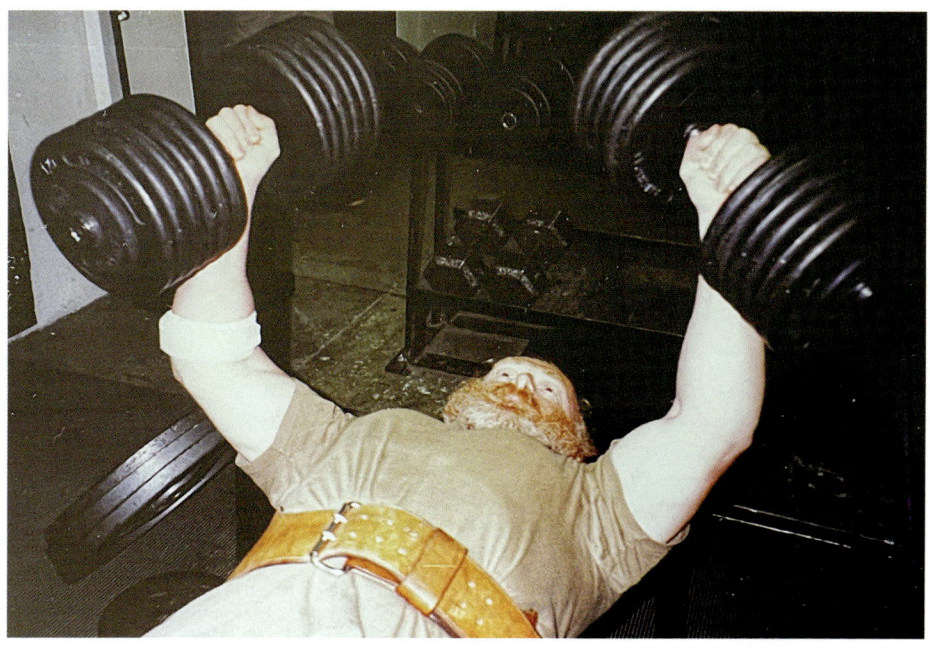

ABOVE: Connor lifting weights in prison. His feats of strength were the stuff of legend. He once bench pressed 445 pounds while weighing just 135 pounds. *Courtesy of Myles Connor.* BELOW: Connor outside the Norfolk County Courthouse after his acquittal in the case of two murdered teenaged girls. *Courtesy of Al Dotoli.*

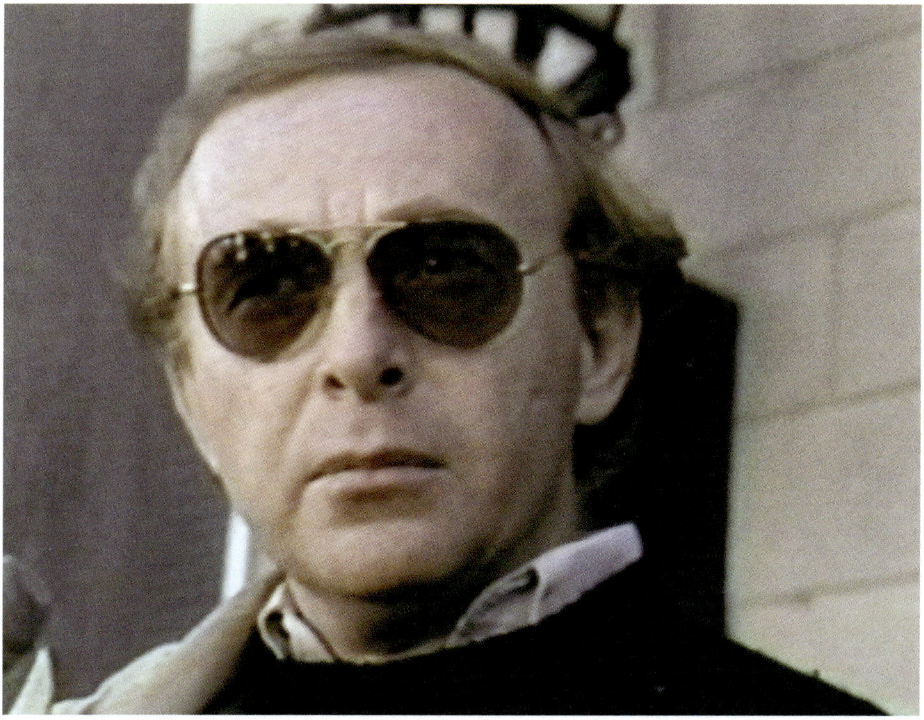

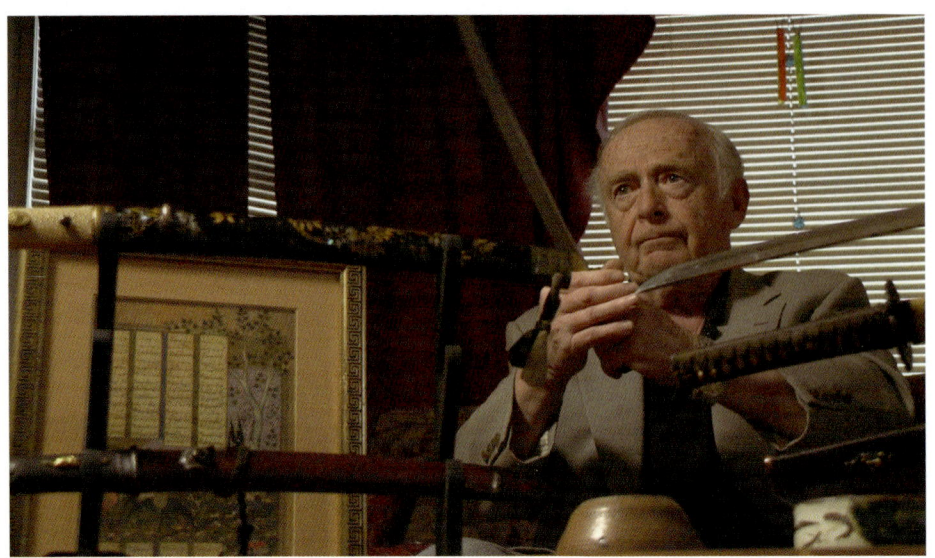

ABOVE: Myles sits for an interview amongst a collection of the artwork that he treasured most—samurai swords. *Courtesy of Al Dotoli*. BELOW: Over lunch with the author, Connor discusses one of his newly acquired swords. *Courtesy of the author*.

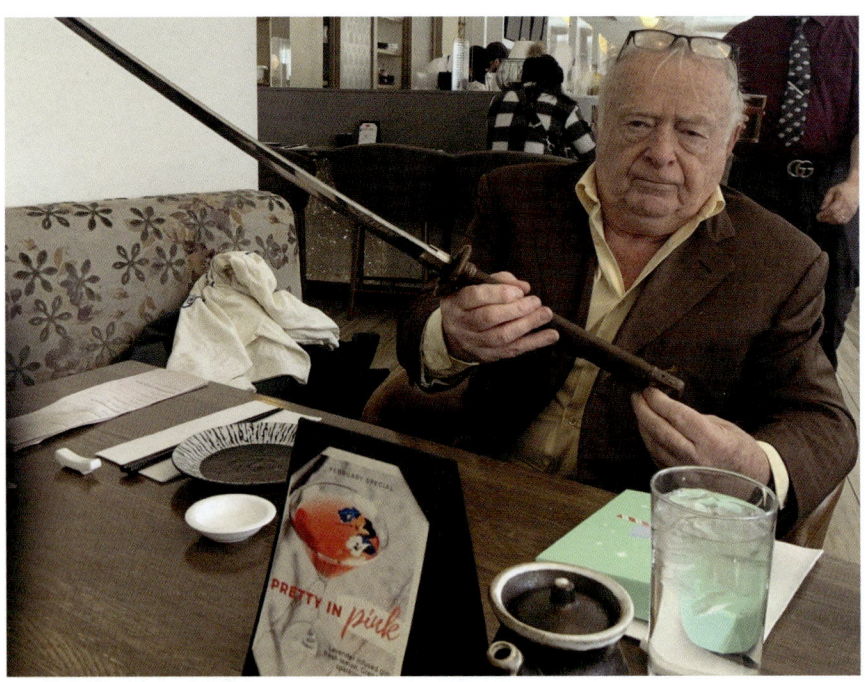

Dotoli was putting the finishing touches on the last of a three-night series of concerts in Mashpee at On the Rocks, a large, popular nightclub on Cape Cod. It featured two large rooms, with one so big the owner hosted clambakes inside it. This bigger room would feature Sha Na Na, a well-known headliner with a large national following, specializing in early rock hits and doo-wop songs and led by Dotoli's friend Lennie Baker. Opening for the Shas, as Al called them, would be the legendary bluesman James Cotton. In the smaller room, what was now simply called the Myles Connor Band would take the stage. Both rooms would sell out, as they did each of the three nights. As far as summer concerts on the Cape went at the time, there was no bigger draw than this. Dotoli had put a lot of work into making this the local musical event of the summer. He even had T-shirts made to mark the occasion. To promote it, he lined up an interview for Myles on Cape Cod's most popular radio station, WCOD. It would be a short spot, but it would air in an age when the radio was the only listening option while behind the wheel. It would garner a lot of attention on what was to be a busy day for Connor.

It's safe to say that Myles's to-do list for July 18, 1974, was unlike anyone else's in the world. He'd start by driving the Ryder van he had rented the previous day out to Northampton, to Martha Ferrante's farm where he stashed the stolen Woolworth art. It was a solid three-hour drive from and back to Cape Cod, so he got an early start. He grabbed all the Wyeth works, including the reproduction, packed them safely in the van, and drove back to Mashpee where his partners, including Charlie Crafts, had set up in an area motel for a few days. That errand completed, Myles and the gang went over the plan for selling the works. After a couple of hours, he drove to WCOD for his radio interview.

Despite his criminal instincts, Myles is blessed with many enviable gifts. In addition to his musicality and intellect, or maybe because of them, he is a captivating storyteller. He was the perfect guest to promote the concerts in a memorable way, especially given the reputation he had throughout Massachusetts as perhaps the most authentic rock and roll outlaw in the business. Once he was on-air, it was the rare person who would turn the dial. Myles answered all of the host's questions with his trademark wit and, given his vocations, unusual elocution. There were the usual questions about some of his more famous criminal pursuits, but it didn't bother Al that they were being addressed. There was no point trying to hide the stories that dominated the front pages of newspapers over the years. Besides, that very evening, he had an important phone call scheduled with Ed Cleven, his predecessor as Dionne Warwick's concert producer. She had a big show coming up in Philadelphia at Constitution Hall and Dotoli wanted to compare notes to make sure it all went well. He was perhaps more concerned than Warwick. Once, she told Al that all press is good press, recounting shows when she knew her performance was off, yet received rave reviews, and others when she was at her best and was panned. "It doesn't matter, Al," she said with her famous thousand-watt smile. "Either way, I was in the news."[6] Dotoli never forgot this lesson, and understood that the same rule applied to Myles, though his front-page notices were admittedly a bit more notorious than anything ever written about Warwick.

The interview was just about over when the host said he had just one more question for Myles. Aware that his audience had to be wondering about Myles's lawless escapades, he asked if he had put his criminal past behind him so that he could finally focus seriously, and solely, on his music career. Myles didn't have to think long to answer. With all the sincerity he could offer, he assured the host that all the criminality was behind him and that his attention was now fixed squarely on performing. Music—not mayhem—was his sole pursuit. It was enough to make Al Dotoli smile from ear to ear, even if he had heard it all before. It's also more than likely that Ralph Petrozziello was listening and gravely concerned that his most valuable partner was really going straight.

Some listeners who heard Myles's claims of turning over a new leaf could only laugh. FBI agents, led by Special Agent Bernie Murphy, were among them. Murphy, a Maryland native and graduate of the University of Baltimore Law School, worked in the Boston field office's Interstate Transportation of Stolen Property squad (ITSP). Agents on the ITSP team enjoyed working truck hijackings, and Murphy did those cases, too. But, he said, "I had a little something in me that went after artwork as well." That's what attracted him to the Woolworth case.[7] He and a cadre of federal agents were parked in their government-issued cars in a Mashpee parking lot listening to the Connor interview while waiting for him to return in the Ryder van. They knew what was afoot. The green van with the Massachusetts license plates connected to the Woolworth heist and the Crafts's camp had been identified immediately, and state police detectives working with the FBI found it parked in Everett soon after. They knew it belonged to Petrozziello, and it didn't take a lot of imagination for investigators to deduce that if his van was used to commit an art heist, then Myles Connor was the likeliest perpetrator.

The FBI tailed Myles Connor, Charlie Crafts, and others to the motel they were using as a makeshift headquarters. Agents interviewed the co-owner and manager of the Merry Meadow Motel, who positively identified Crafts and his blue station wagon. She also remembered another man who came in to use the restroom and described him as a white male, 30–35 years old, around 5'8", and 150 to 160 pounds. And, she added, he had bright red hair. She had described Myles Connor as if he were standing right before her during the interview.*

---

* As in the previous chapter, some details of the Woolworth heist and investigation come from an FBI Freedom of Information Act request.

Police surveillance teams discretely followed the men from Mashpee to a home in Harwich and back for a full day before Myles's appointment with Dickie Donati's connection, which was to be his third important task to accomplish that day. They patiently waited in their unmarked vehicles for Connor to make a move. Finally, Myles and two other men—ostensibly antique dealers from New York—appeared at the van and opened its rear doors. An agent nonchalantly coasted by and could see paintings in the rear. With Myles behind the wheel waiting for Donati's contact to show, police officers swarmed the vehicle and arrested him.

Connor remembers what seemed like an entire cavalry of federal agents rushing him with weapons drawn to take him down. He thought it was far too dramatic, maybe even overkill. But from the perspective of law enforcement, they were arresting a career criminal—a felon known for his martial arts skills and jailbreaks who had once shot a police officer. There was no point in taking chances. A show of overwhelming force was what was in order, even if Connor felt it was much ado about nothing. Murphy, a handsome, light-haired man who looked like an FBI agent straight out of central casting, cuffed Connor and eased him into the back of his cruiser.

Murphy had reeled in a big catch. Donati's contact, unbeknownst to him, was an undercover FBI agent, and he had set up the sting operation. Murphy led the operation, recovered the Wyeths, and arrested one of the state's most notorious targets. The man so adept at staying one step ahead of the police and prosecutors was now secured in the back seat of Murphy's cruiser. No one got away. No one got hurt. It was an operation and outcome about which every FBI agent dreams when they receive their badge and gun, like Murphy did from J. Edgar Hoover. Triumphant, Murphy looked in on Connor in the back seat of his car. There, he didn't find an agitated tough guy spitting vitriol at him or complaining about his handcuffs. Instead, Connor was calm—Zen-like, even—calculating who the turncoat might have been. Murphy, affable yet professional, couldn't help but mildly taunt Connor, just how every cop in the Commonwealth would have liked, saying, "Let's see you get out of this one, Connor."

Myles, too cerebral and experienced to take the bait, remained calm. He looked at Special Agent Murphy and replied, "Really? Wait and see."

Myles was then transported directly from the Mashpee shopping center parking lot to the Barnstable County Jail for processing. Newspapers would report that two additional men were arrested on the scene: James Bishop, forty-six, and Donald Melansky, forty-eight, an antiques dealer, both from New York.*[8]

As all of this was occurring, Al Dotoli was just down the street from the action at On the Rocks. Ever the responsible one, he arrived early to ensure everything was set for that evening's double bill. He confirmed that the equipment was still in its proper place. Every plug and cable had to be double-checked. The sound system had to be tested. The rooms needed to be set up just right. A stickler for detail, Dotoli wasn't one to leave these sorts of things to chance. It didn't matter where the show was or who was performing, if it was his show he strove for perfection.

None of the musicians for the evening's concert had arrived yet, so Al had some time to relax and have a beer or two at the bar with the club's management. Though On the Rocks was a wildly successful spot, it didn't compare with the many of the other venues at which Al was now handling production. So, the venue's managing partner who dealt with all the bands, Fred Scaglione, paid rapt attention as Al answered

---

* Despite this description, no antiques dealer by the name Donald Melansky could be identified.

his questions about touring with the big names in between swigs of Rolling Rock. Suddenly, Al heard a police siren in the distance. Then two. Then three, and yet more. They spun toward the front windows to see what the commotion was just in time to see squad cars zooming by. Based strictly on this, and nothing more, Al looked at Scaglione and told him, "Myles isn't coming."

It was the sort of sixth sense that develops among close friends, the result of experiencing all the vicissitudes of life together. In Al and Myles's case, those ups and downs would involve the typical life events enjoyed or suffered in any friendship: school, work, marriage, childbirth, success, loss, good works, and trouble. But it was the latter that would not just forge ever-stronger ties between the pair but would send them down a treacherous path requiring cunning and guts and ending with one of the most audacious deals in the annals of American crime.

July 1974 turned out to be a good month for fans of the Wyeths. In addition to the recovery of the works that Myles stole, all in good condition, the Olson House, a structure that had been featured in more than three hundred paintings by Andrew Wyeth, including the seminal work *Christina's World*, was given to the State of Maine. Its owner, Joseph E. Levine, a film producer whose work included *The Graduate* and *A Bridge Too Far*, had turned the house into a museum filled with Wyeth's works and had considered dismantling it and moving it to New Jersey, but decided it belonged where Wyeth had painted so much of his oeuvre. As with everything, though, the move had its detractors in the form of locals who were displeased by the influx of Wyeth admirers who came to town to see the collection.[9] Mainers describe such folks as being "from away."

Equally as important to the legacy of the Wyeths was a major exhibition in Japan, the first international exhibition of works by Andrew Wyeth, which took place in Tokyo and Kyoto. The twelve-week run, featuring eighty-eight of the artist's works, was seen by 329,000 visitors—more than triple the estimates. Incredibly, Wyeth was virtually unknown in the country three months before the show, a fact the show's curator, Perry Rathbone, director of the Museum of Fine Arts, Boston, described as "astonishing" given the turnout. Rathbone added that with the exhibition, Wyeth had "conquered the Japanese art world."[10]

The irony of the American artist Andrew Wyeth gaining great fame in Japan while one of America's greatest admirers of Japanese culture was facing prosecution for stealing Wyeth's works was thick. Myles Connor was facing big trouble from federal prosecutors related to the theft, possession, and interstate transport of stolen art. He was also facing a firearms charge based on a gun that the police found in the Ryder van upon his arrest in Mashpee. Moreover, there were also criminal complaints out of two other Massachusetts municipalities. Despite the bevy of charges facing him, Myles was released after just a couple of nights in jail on $50,000 bond.[11] Once again a free man, if only temporarily, even the fearless Myles Connor knew that he had to find a way out of the predicament he had created for himself.

CHAPTER 8
A SEED IS PLANTED

Myles Connor's arrest by the FBI for the Woolworth Estate heist presented him with the biggest problem in his criminal career to date. This was no case in which witnesses could be doubted or discredited on the stand, or where his clever attorney could convince a jury he was nowhere near the stolen goods. This time Connor had been caught by federal agents meeting an undercover agent posing as a potential buyer of stolen goods. He was illegally in possession of a firearm. And he was behind the wheel of the van containing a small fortune in stolen paintings that had been transported from one state to another. A reliable informant had led investigators directly to him, and they were able to begin building a strong case against Connor even before that rendezvous in the Mashpee parking lot. One of Connor's closest pals, Dickie Donati, had inadvertently led the FBI to him via the undercover agent, as did the clumsiness of Charlie Crafts, who, among other blunders, was in possession of the tool used to break into the home. The use of a van owned by well-known Connor confederate Ralph Petrozziello, which was so easily traced back to the thieves, was a major unforced error. The gang rented a Ryder van for the sale of the stolen paintings—why didn't they do the same for the theft?

What had at first appeared to be a perfectly executed heist proved to be anything but. In fact, it was uncharacteristically sloppy, not just for a master thief like Connor but also for a pro like Donati. Perhaps their past successes made them a bit too comfortable. Maybe the score lacked the sort of inspiration that Connor's other thefts featured: personal umbrage, revenge, Japanese treasures. Perhaps the act of simply joining in on someone else's art theft left him without the need to use his stunning capacity for planning a job from start to finish. Whether onstage or in a museum, Connor always took the lead. He had never before, and would never again, simply tag along on someone else's job.

Compounding the problems Myles faced was the despair his actions had once more caused his father. Though Sergeant Joe Connor was by now used to his son making the newspapers for his criminal exploits, this situation was different. This was no local crime. In some ways, it even exceeded the shooting of Corporal Jack O'Donovan because, in that instance, Joe believed his son had acted in self-defense and was too worried about his survival to be concerned about repercussions. The elder Connor also knew that federal sentences were not like those served at the state level, where one could expect to be released long before the issued sentence was over, based on "good behavior" and lenient parole boards where strings could be pulled. Federal sentences traditionally meant a much longer stretch behind bars in a far-off penitentiary. In this instance—and on the federal charges alone—Myles was facing ten years or a $10,000 fine, or both. Given his priors, a mere fine was virtually impossible.

Joe pleaded with his son to cooperate with the police, but it was a losing proposition. Myles would sooner serve a life sentence than roll over on his collaborators. Joe understood this, but as a concerned parent, he felt compelled to put the option out there. His son's instant and definitive dismissal caused him to shift to Plan B.

"Myles, would you at least talk to John Regan to see if he can help?"

Father and son locked eyes for a beat. Myles didn't have it in him to disappoint his father any further. Finally, he nodded. "Okay, Dad," he said, agreeing to something that would have been contrary to his instincts if any other detective had been mentioned. "I'd known John since I was a youngster," Myles recalled. "I had great respect for him. He was one hundred percent ethical and a friend."[1] It would prove to be a prudent decision in a way neither his father, nor Regan, nor even Myles could have ever predicted.

By 1974, Massachusetts State Police major John Regan had already established himself as something of a legend. After serving his country as a corporal in the Marine Corps during the Korean War, Regan was just twenty-three years old when he joined the state police, and his talent for the job was evident right from the jump. In 1958 he was honored by the department for his undercover work that led to the arrest of a trio of drug peddlers who were driving Regan to what they said would be his execution. When the car was pulled over by another officer, all three dealers were apprehended. He was lauded again in 1963 when he helped take down bandits who engaged in a shootout with troopers following a robbery. That same year he received commendation for his successful efforts to take down a narcotics ring on the North Shore. Accolades from the FBI, the Federal Bureau of Narcotics, local police departments, and the Massachusetts Crime Commission filled his employee file. It surprised no one when, in 1967, at the age of thirty-four, Regan became one of the youngest state troopers ever appointed detective.[2]

In 1973 Sergeant Regan was involved in his first major art heist when he investigated the theft of more than six thousand priceless ancient gold coins stolen from Harvard University's Fogg Museum in a daring overnight raid. Thieves used an ingenious ruse to gain entry after closing by leaving a shopping bag behind earlier in the afternoon and phoning the museum, asking that it be held until later when the owner could retrieve it and its important contents—ostensibly, a birthday gift. When the purported owner showed up at around midnight, the night watchman opened the door for him and was met with a revolver in his face and five thieves ready to enter. In all, the coins were valued at the equivalent of $8.5 million in today's dollars. Some were recovered in Canada, others in Rhode Island.[3] After years of dogged investigation, Major Regan was led to an undisclosed location on the South Shore, where he was instructed to dig. He did so and found a military-style duffel bag and a red fishing tackle box encased in a plastic bag containing two thousand of the missing coins. A former state trooper and Harvard Police chief told *Harvard Magazine* that Regan was aided in the effort by Myles Connor.[4] Myles does not recall the incident.

It was this sort of results-oriented work on the most dangerous of cases that earned Major Regan the respect of virtually everyone. Norfolk County district attorney William Delahunt, for whom Regan worked for years, said, "He was successful because he had an unimpeachable integrity . . . he was fair, intelligent and very resourceful. He undertook an investigation without preconceived notions and had a reputation for fairness."[5]

District Attorney Delahunt's description of Major Regan was uncannily similar to the way Sergeant Joe Connor would be described not only by his son, but by those in his own community. It's no wonder that John Regan and Joe Connor were longtime friends. Joe Connor was the man who taught the future Marine how to shoot a gun. And, like Connor, Regan was a self-made man in a time and place where pulling strings was the prescribed method of advancement in civil service work. Regan's ascent was so noteworthy that *The Boston Globe* wrote that he had advanced through the ranks "without the benefit of the political clout which was the usual ladder for advancement in the organization not long ago."[6] He was a man who could be trusted to do the right thing, without regard to personal consequences. It was for this reason that when his son lay in a hospital clinging to life after the shootout in 1966, Joe Connor asked John Regan to watch over him in case any of the other officers assigned to monitoring him had any ideas about doing him further harm in retribution for shooting Corporal O'Donovan. Though O'Donovan was a colleague of Regan's, he accepted the request, for he was unwilling to allow any further extrajudicial punishment against the man he had known as a boy. Eight years later, Joe would again call Regan to ask for his help with his wayward son.

Myles, who had been released on $50,000 bail, met Regan with an idea in mind. While he was unwilling to give up any of his friends in exchange for leniency—and Regan knew this going in—perhaps he might have something else of great value to offer. If he sensed any interest on Regan's part, perhaps he could impose upon him to bring an offer to the federal prosecutor assigned the case, Assistant United States Attorney (AUSA) David Twomey. Twomey, barely thirty years old, had been appointed as an AUSA just a year earlier, but despite his youth had already gained valuable experience prosecuting criminals as an assistant district attorney in Suffolk County. He had quickly proved his mettle in his new job by coordinating the efforts of federal agents in taking down a sex trafficking ring in Boston.[7] In short, it would be foolish to mistake Twomey's youth for naïveté.

Connor met Regan at a coffee shop. Regan, who prided himself on his professional appearance, was in a jacket and tie and cut an impressive figure. It was still the era during which the Massachusetts State

Police adhered to a strict height requirement and a decidedly militaristic ethos. But despite the agency's emphasis on hard-nosed uniformity, Major Regan was a gentleman. He greeted Myles warmly and spoke with him not as a cop to a con but as an old friend. After exchanging pleasantries, they cut right to the core of the meeting. Regan explained that it was his understanding that the feds were eager to do what state authorities often could not: put Myles Connor away for a long time. There was little mood for mercy, especially given Connor's hard-and-fast rule against cooperating with law enforcement against his fellow lawbreakers. So, Myles pulled out his only chit. He told Regan that he might be able to recover various stolen and still missing items in return for leniency. Of course, he was not about to say outright that he was, in fact, the holder of the items he would be locating. While there was no way he'd part with his precious Japanese swords, there were still items he held back from the Forbes House Museum, pieces from the Boston Children's Museum, and a host of other objets d'art taken from a wide array of institutions by the fictitious Dr. Michael Joseph. And, if pushed, he could offer up the two paintings from the Mead Art Museum that he was still holding.

Regan was quite aware of Myles's obsessions and his habit of illicitly obtaining things he coveted. It remained unspoken by both parties, of course, that what was being offered was property that he had stolen and kept for himself. Myles was in enough trouble. There was no need to get into these other crimes. For his part, Myles respected Regan far too much to expect him to ignore admissions of guilt, so he kept his references broad and descriptions vague. But it didn't matter. Despite Myles's best overtures, the detective was pessimistic. These were prosecutors for the US government. They weren't going to be moved by esoteric Asian antiquities or paintings by artists who weren't household names. If they were going to be interested in any sort of negotiation, they would want headlines of the bold, capitalized, front-page variety.

Major Regan looked at Myles Connor sympathetically, shaking his head slightly. "I'm sorry Myles," he said. "Nothing short of a Rembrandt could get you out of this."

To find a person in history whose criminal acumen and boldness was in the league of Myles Connor, one would have to look back to the late nineteenth century at a man named Adam Worth. A remarkably prolific felon, Worth's story bears an uncanny similarity to Connor's. Both were short, fearless men who led gangs of fiercely loyal hoods and could take down men of much larger stature. Both robbed numerous banks of extraordinary sums of money. Both were known for their intellect (Worth was the inspiration for James Moriarty, the ingenious foil of Sherlock Holmes). Both were from Massachusetts. Both were frequent convicts as well as fugitives. Both used aliases to portray themselves as members of the elite. And, most notably, both men not only stole high-value art, but did so with unique motives. If Worth had also had a successful career in music, it would be as if Connor were his reincarnation.

In 1876 Worth was at the top of the criminal world, plying his crooked trade in the United States and abroad, endlessly stealing jewels and robbing banks. His bank heists were legendary. He and his men often tunneled their way into vaults from abutting structures and made off with hauls that would still be considered massive 150 years later. His faithful gang followed him everywhere, eager to partake in his breathtaking robberies. In return, he gave them the same measure of devotion. In just one example, Worth broke one of his confederates out of jail and together they robbed the Boylston Bank in Boston of $1 million before moving to London to lose the investigators hunting for them, including the legendary Pinkerton detectives.[8] But now Worth had a problem. His brother John had been arrested and imprisoned and the master thief wanted to free him. As was his habit, he came up with an audacious plan.

Agnew and Company, a world-renowned dealer of Old Master paintings located amongst the high-end shops on Old Bond Street by Piccadilly had recently purchased from Christie's a true masterpiece: *Georgiana, Duchess of Devonshire* by Thomas Gainsborough. The sale made a huge splash in the media, as Agnew had paid what was then the princely sum of $53,000 for the painting. Moreover, the Duchess, Georgiana Cavendish, the great-great-great-grandaunt of the late Princess Diana, had much in common with her descendant. Beautiful and prone to making headlines, she was the talk of Georgian society, as was her portrait a century later. The financier Junius Spencer Morgan took a fancy to it and sought to buy it for his son, J. P. Morgan. Agnew took advantage of the fuss made over it and displayed the painting in a second-floor window for maximum exposure.[9]

That would prove to be a mistake. One evening, Worth took one of his oversized henchmen to Old Bond Street. So not to draw suspicion in the tony neighborhood, he dressed in his best clothes, including a top hat. Then, when the coast was clear, the diminutive Worth climbed up his much larger goon, accessed the Agnew gallery through the window, cut *Georgiana* from her frame, rolled it up, and made off with it in mere minutes.

With the painting in hand, Worth planned to cut a fragment from it, send it to Agnew for authentication, and use it to free John. Before he even had a chance to do it, his brother was released on a writ of habeas corpus that Adam had engineered through an attorney. Worth no longer needed to part with his beautiful *Georgiana, Duchess of Devonshire*. Instead, he carried it with him often, concealing it in the false bottom of a trunk for twenty-five years, knowing that he had not only a captivating work of art, but an insurance policy should he be arrested. Ultimately, in 1901, working through William Pinkerton, Worth traded the painting back in return for $25,000.[10]

It's not known whether Major John Regan was aware of Adam Worth's mischief. It certainly wasn't common knowledge. But there was a recent case in Massachusetts where a stolen painting was returned to curry favor with the authorities about which he might have known. In this instance, two thieves who were facing a long prison sentence for an armed home invasion in Worcester County got wind of the theft of four valuable works from the Worcester Art Museum. While the Worcester Police Department and the FBI were busy trying to build a proper case against the mastermind of the heist, a local thief named Florian Monday, the men hatched a plan. They would employ measures that the police couldn't. Free on bail as they awaited the judge's sentence, they confronted Monday and demanded the paintings. When he balked, they shoved a gun into his ribs and made it plain that they weren't merely asking him for the artworks. Monday, who was no fool, quickly acquiesced and directed the men to a hay loft at a pig farm in Coventry, Rhode Island, where he had hidden the paintings. The men then arranged their return to the judge in their case. At sentencing, they were shocked to find that he reduced their sentence by what they saw as a negligible amount of time. Their ploy was perhaps flawed by the mistake of turning them over right away. They had made it too easy for the authorities. Monday fled to Montreal before being captured and returned to serve time in prison. So even if Regan was aware of this Rembrandt-for-leniency ploy, his only takeaway could have been that it was minimally effective.

The Worcester case once again demonstrated the folly of stealing a highly recognizable and valuable work of art for profit. It was a lesson Myles Connor learned from the attempted sale of the Wyeths. Interestingly, despite all of his jaw-dropping crimes related to art, he had never been able to sell a true masterwork. He wasn't alone. Before the Worcester heist, Monday believed he could fence his paintings. Immediately after, he realized he could not. The paintings—especially the Rembrandt—were front-page news in the United States and beyond. No one wanted to touch them except the two criminals who forced him to hand them over. And in the case of Worth's Gainsborough, even journalists as far back as 1931 understood that these sorts of works could not be trafficked. "Worth was now in sole possession of the Gainsborough," one story read. "But it was quite a white elephant, for no one in his senses would have dreamed of trying to dispose of it in the open market."[11] The very thing that had made these paintings attractive targets rendered them valuable only for bartering.

Fully aware of the Worcester crooks' failure to see any substantial payoff, Myles thanked Regan for his time and left. He should have been dejected. He knew the detective to be an honest man and understood that his message was pessimistic. From where he sat, Regan conveyed that there really was nothing that Myles could do to escape the trap he had walked right into. He shook the young thief's hand as he saw him out of the office and went back to work. It was hard not to think of his friend Joe Connor. Regan, too, had sons, and he could imagine how hard it must have been for Joe to watch his boy face at least a decade in a federal penitentiary. They had both been in the business long enough to know that the feds don't lose cases. The young man was finally going to get his comeuppance.

Myles should have turned to working with his defense attorney, Martin K. Leppo, to pull off an improbable victory. Perhaps a guilty plea might get him a softer sentencing recommendation from the government. Or maybe Leppo could come up with some unforeseen way to win at trial. Marty Leppo was something of a magician when it came to some of the direst predicaments, though even he would have probably admitted that such maneuvering was much more doable in state court than it was in federal. It was in the state courts where Lenny Bruce's quote that "in the Halls of Justice the only justice is in the halls" was most applicable. But even now Leppo tried to temper Connor's expectations. He'd be wise to mentally prepare himself for a long stretch behind bars.

Myles, however, never thought the same way as everyone else. Major John Regan's remark about how it would take a Rembrandt to get him out of trouble was spontaneous, meant to illustrate the severity of the situation. He was trying to relate to Myles that he understood the nature of the things he had to offer in exchange for leniency and that they weren't big enough. He had resorted to hyperbole, mentioning the painter who was unquestionably one of the world's most famous artists. It was tantamount to a parent telling a teen who wanted a used car that they had a better chance at getting a new Ferrari. Something out of reach. Something impossible. But Regan hadn't thought through what he was saying and to whom he was saying it. Myles didn't think in terms of the impossible. He might not have thought that Regan was speaking literally, or even coyly. But it didn't matter. What Regan had said had inadvertently planted a seed in the mind of one of history's great criminal geniuses. There, it instantly began to germinate. The words were meant to discourage, but they inspired.

THE REMBRANDT HEIST

Stealing a masterpiece to use as a virtual Get out of Jail Free card wasn't something on anyone's radar screen, least of all at the Office of the United States Attorney in Boston. AUSA David Twomey had a full caseload to occupy his time. Though it certainly was the highest-profile prosecution on his desk, the Connor case was just one of many. While the work of Special Agent Murphy and his team at the FBI was fast paced, allowing for improvisation and intrigue, Twomey's work could be plodding, filled with research and procedural filings. It required more intellect than bravery. But it was vitally important that everything be done perfectly. There's no room for error, and the US Department of Justice was not known for flubbing major cases. It has long prided itself on its conviction rate. How to do it was ingrained in each assistant US attorney and encoded in the Federal Rules of Criminal Procedure and the First Circuit Rulebook. After all, this was still the US government, and even courts are bureaucratic. In short, no one in the austere offices of the Department of Justice in Post Office Square was thinking creatively about outlandish ideas like trading art for leniency. Guilty verdicts were the name of the game. Besides, that was the stuff of novels, not *Black's Law Dictionary*.

None of this mattered to Myles. He wasn't going to leave his freedom to chance or even to his defense attorney. If there was something he could do—or even just try—he'd do it. And from the very moment that Rembrandt was mentioned to him, his thoughts were directed to the institution that he had known best: the Museum of Fine Arts, Boston. All the visits throughout his life, beginning back when he was a boy visiting with his Japanese artifact-loving grandfather, Charles Johnson, meant he knew every corner of the cavernous institution, which occupies a large city block sandwiched between Huntington Avenue and the Emerald Necklace in Boston's storied Fenway neighborhood. Myles was Charles's only grandchild from his daughter Lucy, and the boy who inherited his passion for the arts and walked the endless galleries with him for hours. It was only natural that Connor's memories of the galleries housing the MFA's world-class collection of Netherlandish art were rushing to the fore. Should he steal something there, he would have a lot from which to choose.

There were seven Rembrandts in the MFA's collection at the time. And, for that matter, an almost endless supply of other works by just about every artist in the pantheon of those who are household names and are, therefore, thought to be very valuable. Vincent Van Gogh, Pierre-Auguste Renoir, Claude Monet, Paul Gauguin, John Singleton Copley, Pablo Picasso, Donatello—the inventory requires a large database. Every room, every hallway even, presented Myles Connor with options. But Major Regan had said Rembrandt, and Rembrandt it would be. But which to take?

The first Rembrandts in the MFA's collection predate the Huntington Avenue building. Acquired in 1893, while the museum was still occupying a Gothic revival building in Copley Square, were a pair of portraits, *Portrait of a Man Wearing a Black Hat* and *Portrait of a Woman Wearing a Gold Chain*. The paintings capture an unidentified married couple and were gifts to the MFA from the widow of the railroad magnate and cofounder of General Electric Frederick Lothrop Ames.[12] As if to illustrate what Rembrandt represents, Ames was considered the richest man in Massachusetts at his death.[13] Two paintings of another married couple—this time identified—were also in the collection. *Maria Bockenolle (Wife of Johannes Elison)* and *Reverend Johannes Elison* were acquired by the museum in 1956, just nineteen years prior to Myles Connor's dilemma for $360,000. The latter two works are more than twice as large as the former, measuring well over five feet tall.[14] Surely Myles would find these cumbersome. But there is a much smaller yet far more famous Rembrandt work in the collection. *Artist in His Studio*, completed when the Old Master was still quite young, is a perfect little study of the artist contemplating a canvas on an easel. He is standing a distance from it, holding a brush in his right hand, his face expressionless but for his wide-open eyes. Measuring less than 10 x 12 inches, it's an unusual piece, given its size and perspective. In the coming years, Rembrandt's self-portraits—and there would be many—would almost exclusively focus on his face and torso. For the most part, only his drawings and etchings would be so small.

Paintings aside, the MFA was also home to works on paper by Rembrandt, including *Self-Portrait Leaning on a Stone Sill*, *Christ Crucified Between the Two Thieves*, *Christ Preaching*, *Saint Jerome in a Dark Chamber*, and *Saint Francis Praying Beneath a Tree*. These and other works are typically off view due to light sensitivity and in the museum's storage along with nearly a half million other pieces. While one would think that such a location would make the works on paper less likely to be targeted by Connor, one would be forgetting that stealing off-view pieces was the expertise of Dr. Michael Joseph, his academic alter ego. But there were problems with the imposter approach. First, it wasn't guaranteed that he could gain access to the works. The Dr. Joseph ploy required a fair deal of convincing. If he failed, or if the MFA simply wasn't willing or able to accommodate his immediate request to peruse storage, he'd be turned away empty-handed. An institution the size of the MFA would require that a prior appointment be set. Though the ruse had been quite successful in the past, this time Myles was under strict time constraints. His trial for the Wyeth paintings was due to begin on April 23, 1975. He needed a plan that could be pulled off quickly and with little room for error or failure.

Second, Rembrandt's works on paper, while precious and valuable, might not be the sort of big-ticket items to which Major Regan was fancifully alluding. Paintings draw headlines. That was no mystery.

Third, outside of stuffy professorial garb and a false identity, there was no true disguise in the Dr. Joseph hoax. Anyone who dealt with him would have the opportunity to get a clear and sustained look at him and identify him later, especially now that his image would be everywhere during the Wyeth trial. The ruse required close-up interactions and in-depth conversation, and a false wig and/or mustache might be too obvious.

Lastly, Myles had his heart set on a particular painting on view at the MFA, one that he had talked about with his grandfather. It was known as *Portrait of Elsbeth van Rijn*, the artist's sister.* He was aware from conversations with Grandpa Charlie that the painting had a significant provenance. It was not the property of the MFA; rather, it was on a long-term loan to the institution from the descendants of one of Boston's, and America's, leading families, that of Robert Treat Paine, a signer of the Declaration of Independence.

Moreover, even among a lifetime of masterworks, *Portrait of Elsbeth van Rijn* was clearly an extraordinary piece of handiwork. The Rembrandt was on display in the Dutch art gallery, and it was the perfect size to take from the wall and make a mad dash for the exit with it in hand. No cutting from the frame was required, as the work was on a wooden panel. Myles found that not only time-consuming but disgraceful. Damaging fine art was anathema to him. His impressive analytical skills made the decision easy and quick. He would take *Elsbeth*. With the Dr. Joseph approach ruled out, he just needed to figure out how.

---

* In 1975 the painting was also referred to in various publications as *Portrait of Elizabeth van Rijn* and *Portrait of Elisabeth van Rijn*.

CHAPTER 9
SMASH AND GRAB

With his federal trial for the theft of the Wyeth paintings set for April 23, 1975, Myles Connor was under pressure to act. He had decided which painting he would steal and the venue from which he'd take it. Now all that was left was to come up with a plan. For a skilled practitioner of the art of the heist like himself, there were many options.

He had already decided against the Dr. Michael Joseph deception. Most of his other museum jobs were overnight burglaries, breaking into the buildings when they were closed and empty. But those were not institutions on par with the mighty Museum of Fine Arts, Boston. The MFA is a huge, robust facility. Nothing about it is small or temporary. Rather, when closed, it became a giant stone fortress. Breaking a basement window at night wasn't as simple as it had been at the Forbes House Museum, and even if Myles could penetrate the reinforced and possibly alarmed glass, it wasn't likely to provide him with easy and direct access to the second-floor gallery where his target was hung.

Talking his way in by tricking the overnight guard, as in the earlier heist at Harvard University's Fogg Museum, was a coin toss. If the guard did his job correctly and refused him entry, the plan would fail, and the museum would be on high alert. There would be no second chances. He could try to recruit an insider to assist him in gaining entry after closing, but there was hardly enough time to develop someone he could trust.

There was the stay-behind approach, wherein Myles could hide somewhere in the building until after closing, at which point he would emerge. "Overpower the night watchman. Tie him up. And the place is yours," he thought.[1] That was high on his list of possibilities. He and his friend Steve Gorski, a helicopter pilot, even considered resurrecting an old plot to land a chopper on the roof of the MFA.[2] In the end, after much deliberation, Myles settled on a daytime raid.

While Hollywood has convinced most of the world—including many law enforcement officials—that art theft is something perpetrated by slick cat burglars, that's rarely the case. Reality is far more mundane, far less attractive. It's typically perpetrated not by the urbane and sophisticated, but by the brutish and uninformed. It is for these reasons that it continues to happen, even though masterworks are nearly if not completely impossible to fence. The thugs who filch the art don't know this because they don't do research into what became of past heists. They care about only two things: that art is more accessible than other valuables, and that the biggest names are probably worth the most money. Thus, works by Rembrandt and Pablo Picasso are the most frequently stolen. As professional thieves (as opposed to professional art thieves, another Hollywood creation), they understand that the path of least resistance is the best way to execute a heist. Though Myles Connor was cast from a far different mold than the ordinary thief, he understood this last point extraordinarily well. He knew that robbing a museum while it was open allowed him to completely bypass the myriad security measures activated when the building was closed. Why risk trying to break into a fortress at night when you are welcomed in with open arms during the day? Half the challenge disappears. A smash-and-grab job was the surest path to success.

All that remains is taking the painting and sprinting out of the building, which of course is not as easy as it sounds. The MFA had a full complement of guards, many of them retired police officers. They took their jobs seriously and cared about the art, walking the museum's halls like they had for decades walked their beats. Others were retirees, and it was common for them to develop an attachment to the paintings and statues that they guarded like they were family. It's difficult to work every day with some of the greatest works of beauty humankind has ever produced without forming a bond with them. Being a custodian of cultural treasures has a way of doing that. The MFA's guards weren't likely to stand by and watch thieves steal what they were charged with protecting. For this reason, Myles said, "An accomplice may be used to distract . . . guards from chasing you."[3]

There was also the question of members of the public. While the average museumgoer isn't exactly known for their brawn, the public can play a useful role in preventing crime. If the heist is set to take place at an inopportune time—say, during a large tour or very busy day—a quick getaway can be difficult. An outraged visitor might even try to intervene and stop him from lifting the painting off the wall. This was long before everyone was carrying a high-resolution camera in their pocket, so the threat of being photographed in the act wasn't a concern. But if visitors even just raised a commotion loud enough to summon assistance, it could derail the theft. This could all be averted, however, by making the heist an armed robbery and bringing along an accomplice. It would be tough to hold a gun and ward off wannabe heroes while also lifting *Portrait of Elsbeth van Rijn* from the wall, so a second set of hands made sense.

Of course, the aftermath of the heist—should they succeed in getting out of the museum with the painting in hand—required great planning. First, the getaway route. Boston, even then, was notorious for traffic and its labyrinthine city layout inherited from the very beginning of the country. One-way streets appeared out of nowhere. Narrow roads blocked by delivery trucks impeded movement in the Fenway neighborhood and everywhere else. And if there was a Red Sox game down the way from the MFA at Fenway Park, one should expect gridlock. The escape required intricate planning, as did the plan for where to hide the painting.

For a safe house, Myles turned to a trusted friend, Lenny Biondi, an expert auto mechanic on the South Shore. Lenny and Myles discussed a few options. They might hide the painting in the garage where Lenny kept vehicles that he either owned or repaired. There was also an apartment complex nearby being constructed. Perhaps they could hide the painting behind the drywall that was in the process of being installed. Then, when the painting was needed, simply break into the apartment and retrieve it. On second thought, however, that seemed excessive. One of the reasons that thieves don't destroy or dispose of the paintings they steal is because they are so easy to hide. The targeted painting was only two feet tall and a foot and a half wide, plus a frame. Ultimately, they settled on a far simpler solution.

Myles Connor assembled his team from the most trustworthy of his allies, except of course for Al Dotoli. Unsurprisingly, many of them were men he had met and come to trust at Walpole State Prison. Ralph Petrozziello would be on hand, of course, though Myles was concerned about his propensity toward violence. Though there would be no shortage of hard men armed with firearms involved in the heist, it was imperative that no innocents were harmed. This was true for two reasons. First, shooting a civilian, such as a museum employee or visitor, would be strictly contrary to Myles's code. He was wise and experienced enough to know that warning shots—at most—would suffice in warding off anyone who tried to stop the thieves or impede their escape. Second, he knew that the museum guards were unarmed. Also, Myles understood that shooting a person in the commission of the heist would exponentially increase the law enforcement response to it, not just in the moment but in the aftermath. In the Worcester Art Museum heist just a few years before, the thieves shot an elderly security guard when they were confronted upon their departure. Though he survived, the criminals had escalated their offense by nearly murdering the employee. While the theft of four masterpieces would certainly have warranted an in-depth investigation, the involvement of armed and dangerous bandits at large and willing to kill meant that a veritable army of police officers and FBI agents would be assigned to the case. And indeed, they were. Finally, and maybe most importantly, Myles's intent was to use the stolen Rembrandt as a bargaining chip with prosecutors looking to lock him up for a long time. A massive theft to get out of a jam related to a slightly less massive theft. Adding an attempted murder would be an extreme act of self-sabotage, rendering the whole endeavor meaningless and escalating things to an unwanted level.

Petrozziello would be in the getaway vehicle, which would be another stolen van he supplied. This one would have untraceable license plates that he had created and lifted during his time at Walpole State Prison. He would ride shotgun, a term he took almost literally, arming himself with a handgun and a rifle.

The rest of the team Myles Connor assembled were no strangers to violence, but more easily controlled than Petrozziello. Billy Skinner, another Milton native and ex-convict who had served time with him at Walpole, would go into the building with Myles. Skinner, known to his friends as "Billy Irish," could be trusted to control himself under pressure. He had served with the US Army 1st Cavalry Division and wasn't one to lose his cool or his nerve. Myles knew he was the right man to be at his side during the robbery, so he reached out to him first. He asked Skinner, "Can you help me out with this? I need to borrow this painting for a couple of months." Skinner didn't hesitate. "Sure," he said. "We can help you out with that."[4]

Mickey Finn, a boxer, was behind the wheel of the van. Joe Rego accompanied him in back. Two more local criminals drove crash cars, which would cause seemingly innocent accidents on the road should any first responders need to be intercepted. Tommy Maher was assigned to drive a sedan rigged by Biondi to overheat upon demand. Maher would tail the van and crash cars and stop on the street, incapacitate the vehicle, and block traffic, thereby preventing the police from reaching the museum quickly. Myles even arranged for a woman with a baby carriage (complete with a baby doll hidden under a blanket) to be near the entrance as he and Skinner ran out of the building. Should the doors begin to automatically close in response to alarms, she was to use the carriage to block the doors and keep them open for the getaway.

As far as museum heists go, the planning was intricate, surpassing nearly any other of its sort in complexity, complicity, and cunning. It took a special crook to be able to assemble such a large team of people he could trust on short notice. It also took an unusual mind to connive the plan from start to finish, never mind the motive behind it.

Myles decided on April 14 as the day on which the heist would take place. It gave him a full nine days before his trial was set to begin. He chose a Monday afternoon, ensuring the crew would avoid the busy crowds that packed the MFA on weekends. What's more, the Red Sox were on the road, so there would be no game-day traffic with which to contend.

With the date and details set, there was one last item on the to-do list. Myles needed to know how the painting was secured to the wall and whether it was alarmed. This was vital. He couldn't very well go into the robbery unaware of exactly what to expect at the apex of the event, when he would lift the target of the whole affair from whence it hung. He came up with a daring assignment to obtain this information.

Twenty-one-year-old Steve Gorski was a friend of Myles's who, by his own admission, looked up to the notorious figure, and was game for just about anything. Like the others, he had accompanied Myles on a wide variety of adventures, and he was part of the inner circle that was together almost around the clock, even with their girlfriends. When it was time to discuss business, the men simply repaired to another room. Gorski found Connor to be charismatic and funny. "When I was in my twenties, he was already a legend. A genius, a karate expert, master cat burglar, shot in a shoot-out. I looked up to him, the fun guy part of him," Gorski said. The two became close. Gorski, another Milton resident, recalls that Connor would often stay over at his house. His father was successful and owned a large home with plenty of room, unlike Lucy Johnson's home, which Gorski recalled being full of clutter.[5]

Gorski was well-liked by Myles's friends, including Al Dotoli, who hired him to help with road management for Myles's musical act. This soon morphed into criminal activity alongside Myles. In 1974 Gorski helped him rob an antique auction house in the Faneuil Hall area, from which they took mostly Native American artifacts. That same year, Steve, Myles, and Petrozziello's brother Sal attempted to rob a warehouse of fur coats, but the facility had been emptied out the day before. Police officers responded, and they fled. Sal shot at the police, who returned fire. Myles and Steve took refuge under a large evergreen bush as the pursuing officers ran by them, at which point Myles turned to Steve and said, in his best Oliver Hardy voice, "Another fine mess you've gotten me into."[6]

Clearly, Gorski was eager to participate in anything Myles could dream up (including the previously mentioned helicopter proposal). While his next task didn't involve aircraft, Gorski's mission would take just as much courage. Myles told Gorski that he wanted him to go to the MFA on the eve of the heist just before the museum closed, find Rembrandt's *Portrait of Elsbeth van Rijn* and, when no one was looking, momentarily remove it from the wall. Amazingly, Gorski thought it a good idea and agreed.

Gorski went to the MFA on Sunday, April 13, as directed. "It was a very slow day, and it was towards the end of the day. Closing time. So, there weren't a lot of people around to notice," he recalled. When he got to the painting, it wasn't long before he was alone with it. He approached it, looked around one last time, and nervously lifted it from the wall. If a guard happened by, or an alarm sounded, he would say that he had "just jiggled" the artwork. He found it was merely hung on hooks and easily taken. But now he was alone with it, the masterpiece in his hands. He could feel the adrenaline surge inside him. It was heavier than he expected, probably because it was painted on a wooden panel, not a canvas. He stood there, alone, for what he approximated to be about two full minutes, just looking at the woman in the portrait as she stared back him, blank-eyed and emotionless, unlike Gorski, who thought it "was neat" to have the encounter with greatness. Then he placed it back on the wall. There were no security screws. No alarm had sounded, either audibly or silently. No one responded to the area. He could report back to Myles that the painting could be easily removed from the wall without any tools or effort, and that it would alert no one. Everything was in order. There was no better time than now.[7]

Early the next day, Myles and his posse assembled at Ralph Petrozziello's car wash in Brockton, Massachusetts, about an hour due south from the museum. Myles went over the plan again. The men listened, rapt by his directions and leadership. He reiterated again that violence was not to be used, and that the guns were to scare off any wannabe heroes. "Warning shots, but only if necessary," he told them, looking each of them in the eye, especially Petrozziello. "Alright, let's go," he told the team.

Myles and Skinner climbed into the van with Petrozziello and Mickey Finn. The other men got into their crash cars—Bobby Fromm in a black-and-gold Torino, Billy Hogan in a black Monte Carlo. Under a cloudy sky, the gang headed north, nervous about the heist they were about to pull off. This was no simple bank job. The take would be worth ten times what a bank robbery would bring. But beyond that, they knew that this job was vitally important to their leader's freedom—the difference between a long prison term far away and a short term near home. Everyone had a role they had to execute perfectly. No one wanted to be the reason the plan failed.

Finally, they arrived at the Museum of Fine Arts, Boston. Myles's plan called for entry to be made through the Fenway entrance to the museum as opposed to the more popular main entrance on Huntington Avenue. This was a wise strategic decision. The Fenway entrance features a circular driveway in which the van and crash cars could wait for Connor and Skinner to return with the painting in hand. Then they could speed off onto the Fenway, a one-way road that lent itself well not only to the broken-down-car ploy that Maher would enact, but led directly to Storrow Drive and points east or west. From there, one could quickly access Route 93 north or south, or the Massachusetts Turnpike, which runs east and west. In other words, even if the police were just thirty seconds behind the getaway, it would take a lot of luck (and avoidance of the crash cars) to follow the route that the thieves took. While the Huntington Avenue entrance also has a drop-off area, reentering onto the road from it would be tricky. One could expect to be blocked by vehicles stopped at traffic lights located just yards away. And a U-turn wasn't an option because Huntington Avenue is divided by train tracks for the aboveground rail that are impossible for a motor vehicle to cross.

Under a dark gray sky, Myles and Skinner climbed out of the van at around noon. It was go time. But before proceeding, they stopped, took a breath, and looked at the imposing thirty-six-foot-tall Ionic columns standing at the MFA's portico, guarding its glass entrance. The pavilion appeared larger to them now than when they had previously cased it. It was somehow slightly more intimidating. The two men, neither over six feet tall, were facing a majestic megalith. Myles read the inscription on the facade to himself. ROBERT DAWSON EVANS GALLERIES FOR PAINTINGS. He remembered his grandfather telling him that Evans's widow, Maria Antoinette Evans, funded the construction of the wing entirely on her own, spending $1 million (the equivalent of $32 million today). They walked in lockstep up the stairs, pulling open the heavy glass doors and entering the lobby.

Both men were in disguise. Myles wore a brown leather chauffeur's cap over a long blond wig that completely obscured his telltale red hair. Dark glasses obscured his blue eyes, and he wore a coat. By modern standards, the outfit sounds a tad outlandish, but this was 1975, an era of gaudy extremes in men's clothing and hairstyles, so Billy Skinner's wig of shoulder-length dark hair didn't stand out, either.[8]

They purchased tickets, entering the museum as any other visitor would. They then squeezed through the turnstiles that kept track of attendance. Skinner was focused on the job ahead as they headed to yet another tall staircase. He was nervous, hyped for what was to occur in just a matter of minutes. Myles admits that though he wasn't nervous, this heist, with its extremely high personal stakes, had an added sense of urgency. But that wasn't enough to keep him from being cognizant that he was in a temple to the arts, constructed of beautiful Deer Isle granite and, as he made his way toward the second floor up the hemicyclic marble staircase, the splendor and beauty of the building beguiled him, despite his intentions. Whereas Skinner was focused, pupils pinned and watching for any trouble, Connor couldn't help but look around at what architect Guy Lowell's draftsmanship, and Maria Antoinette Evan's money, had wrought.

In less than a minute, they were on the second floor, heading for the Dutch and Flemish art. Hanging to the immediate right of an open foyer among works by Peter Paul Rubens and Anthony van Dyck they found *Portrait of Elsbeth van Rijn* tucked just around a corner. Myles's assumption about the museum being quietest on a Monday afternoon was accurate. An MFA spokesman would later say that "the thieves had chosen the quietest hour of the museum's least active day." He added that many of the people who were in attendance were at that hour having lunch in the museum's restaurant at the opposite end of the building. "The timing was real good," added Gerard Shirar, the museum's director of security.[9] With no one in sight, the pair reached for the painting, each standing on one side of it to lift it from its hooks.

Just then, MFA security guard Vito Magaletta, who was patrolling the area, happened upon them and noticed what they were doing. Astonished by what he was witnessing, Magaletta confronted them in a thick accent from his native Italy.

"What are you trying to do with the painting?" he demanded.

Myles pointed his trusty Walther semiautomatic pistol at him menacingly. "Shut up or I'll kill you," he growled.

Magaletta wisely retreated, ducking behind a wall in the gallery, then blew his guard's whistle—a measure widely employed in museums in the era before handheld radios became the norm. John Monkouski, a guard on the first floor by the Fenway entrance, heard the piercing sound of the whistle echoing down the staircase, bouncing off the granite and marble. The two thieves fled down the stairs, Myles's hands full with the heavy panel. When they reached the first floor, Monkouski rushed toward them from his post by the turnstiles. Though sixty-six years old, he presented a formidable challenge. Big and strong, he had just retired from the Boston Police Department after more than thirty years of service, and he wasn't about to let the thieves get away without a fight. He confronted them, but the younger, stronger Skinner pistol-whipped him in the head, sending Monkouski to the ground.

Magaletta, who had given chase when the thieves ran off with the painting, saw the whole thing. "I saw them hit John. I saw blood," he said, badly shaken by the scene.[10]

Bloodied, dazed, and unarmed, Monkouski would have been wise to stay down. But the ex-cop was from a different age. Born in 1909 in Boston, he joined the Boston Police Department in the 1940s and spent the next three decades patrolling Roxbury Crossing. The job wasn't for the faint-hearted, nor for one who wasn't dedicated to service and selflessly doing what's right. No, Monkouski didn't stay down. Instead, the instincts he developed after so many years patrolling the streets of Boston kicked in. It wasn't in him to cower. He struggled to his feet and ran after the two younger armed criminals, leaving drops of blood on the stairs.

Skinner made it out the exit unimpeded. Myles, however, ran into trouble trying to exit through the turnstile with the painting in hand. His smallish stature and the rigidity of the painting and its frame betrayed him, and he and the artwork were momentarily delayed when they became wedged in the turnstile. Myles squeezed himself through, but not before causing four pieces of the frame to break off and fall to the floor. Once freed, he was relieved to find that the doors had not automatically closed and locked as he had feared they might. The young woman with the baby carriage he had planted there to prevent such an event had not needed to act. He trailed Skinner as he fled down the fifteen stairs outside the entrance toward the waiting van and cars. Just as quickly as they had burst outside, Monkouski sprinted after, belying the fact that he was nearly twice the age of the men he pursued.

In fast-moving, shocking, and dangerous incidents like this, eyewitness reports are notoriously unreliable. Unusual events like these are hard for onlookers to process. People miscount the number of shots they heard, where they came from, and who fired them. Even the perpetrators have jumbled memories of exactly what transpired due to their instinct to focus strictly on their own immediate safety and plight. For instance, Myles recalls Petrozziello firing from the van intending to warn off Monkouski. Witnesses also reported three shots being fired, but that they came from either Skinner or Connor (though it couldn't have been the latter, since his hands were occupied with the cumbersome painting). When Myles heard the gunfire, he could only hope that no one had been hurt. The thunderclap of the gunshots terrified onlookers both inside and outside of the museum. But Monkouski was undeterred, running in the direction from which the bullets were being fired. He wasn't thinking about taking cover; he was thinking about saving the Rembrandt. By now, a phalanx of his fellow guards had joined him in pursuit. Myles remembers that after he handed off the painting to someone in the van, the guard got close enough to grab hold of the wooden panel and would not let go until one of the gang pointed a machine gun at him. Myles yelled out a clear order: "Don't shoot!" The order was followed. Monkouski, still aching from the blow to the head, wisely let go when the barrel of the automatic rifle was in his face. As his boss Shirar said of his guards to *The Boston Globe*, "These men did their job. But what can you do in the face of a gun?"[11]

The van sped off, as did the crash vehicles. The Boston Police Department squad cars navigating the busy city streets toward the MFA didn't make it in time to give pursuit, thanks in equal parts to Myles and Skinner's speed and Tommy Maher's purposely overheated sedan on the Fenway.

What had been a sleepy early afternoon at the Museum of Fine Arts, Boston, turned into a mélange of flashing police and ambulance lights outside the Fenway entrance. Emergency medical technicians tended to John Monkouski's head wound and transported him to a local hospital for treatment. Boston Police Department detectives and FBI agents were soon swarming the scene, taking statements from witnesses. In total, eleven Boston detectives were assigned to the case, along with twelve FBI agents.[12] Those bystanders and employees they spoke with described the getaway car as a 1972 Ford Torino coupe, gold with a black roof, and bearing Massachusetts plates. This was a crash car. Boston Police Department reports do not mention the van, but this is perhaps due to the fact that witnesses saw Skinner jump into the Torino before the vehicles sped off. They therefore described the gold-and-black Ford as having "picked up accomplices and fled toward Hemenway Street."[13] The eyewitnesses provided descriptions of the two thieves that were accurate in terms of attire and hair color, and close to Connor and Skinner's height and weight. However, they were off by at least a decade on the approximate ages, estimating the thieves to be around twenty years old.[14] Based on these descriptions, an all-points bulletin went out for "two unknown white males, one with long blond hair and glasses and leather cap. Both armed with 9mm automatics."[15]

Investigators searched for physical evidence, but there was little. Aside from the vehicle descriptions and license plate numbers, they recovered near the turnstiles the four pieces broken from the ornate gold frame from which they held out hope fingerprints might be lifted. They also found a spent bullet and a discarded rubber glove that they suspected came from the thieves.[16] DNA evidence was not yet existent in 1975. Investigators simply looked for clues left behind, dusted for prints, and watched as the crime scene photographer took an endless series of photos of a latex glove that may have belonged to the thieves, some old wood fragments, a bullet, and two empty hooks.

Myles's gang ignored the getaway route that might have appeared obvious to the rest of the world and stayed local. They went first to Bromley-Heath, housing projects located in neighboring Jamaica Plain, where they transferred the Rembrandt from the van to a Ford LTD that had been brought there by Connor's friend Ozzy DePriest. The local housing project was a clever choice—no one expected that the art thieves would simply go to a nearby neighborhood instead of fleeing on an interstate highway. Bromley-Heath also made for an unintentionally ironic venue, as it was part of a project that had its roots in construction begun in 1889 and financed by Robert Treat Paine II, the very same descendant of the signer of the Declaration of Independence whose family owned, and loaned, *Portrait of Elsbeth van Rijn*.[17] After the transfer of the painting and the vehicles, two of the men drove the Torino to Station Street in Roxbury Crossing, where they ditched it. It wasn't found until four o'clock the next morning. As the responding Boston Police Department officer wrote in his report, "Picture of Rembrandt not found."[18]

Portrait of Elsbeth van Rijn was now in the hands of Myles Connor. He understood perhaps better than any other thief in history exactly what he was holding. He possessed an appreciation for the impact that

Rembrandt van Rijn had not just on the Dutch Golden Age but on the art of painting for the next almost four hundred years. It was not lost on him at all just how unusual a situation he was in, sitting in his car alone with a masterpiece. He held the panel in his two hands and considered the look on the subject's face, her thoughts in that moment a mystery to all who observed her. He wondered if this young woman, said to be the Great Master's sister, bore any resemblance to him. Rembrandt was a lifelong student of character study, and the subtleties of her facial features were not something he'd miss. Throughout his time with the painting, Myles remained fully aware of the rarity of someone of his station of life being the sole possessor of such an object. The painting was the stuff of a multimillionaire's collection, not a rock-and-rolling career criminal. This, however, brought him pleasure, not worry.

That moment when the thief is finally alone with a masterwork they have stolen can be hard to fathom. A painting might hang on the same wall for decades, undisturbed, looking back at an endless stream of visitors staring at it. Then, in a flash—chaos, and even violence. Soon, and for a short period, a one-on-one encounter with a felon. Finally, either a return to the wall from which it had been taken or years of darkness and solitude, hidden, waiting patiently to be rescued. The offender might be in awe of the work because of its immense value, or because of a sudden understanding of its beauty and not simply its acclaim. They might be scared, unsure if they are about to be caught, or because they are overcome with the realization of what they have just done. Rare is the man or woman who simply steals a high-value painting and calmly sits with it as did Myles Connor—taking it in, studying it, understanding it. One is reminded of the famous Dutch thief who, in 2002 burglarized the Van Gogh Museum in Amsterdam, the stylishly named Octave Durham. Oky, as he prefers to be called, took two van Goghs valued in the many millions of dollars. One, his earliest seascape, was painted on the seashore while the artist stood in the sand during a windstorm. Much had been made of the fact that a fair amount of the sand was imbedded in the wet paint where it remained. Durham, who was proudly uninterested in the paintings but for their black market value, picked up *View of the Sea at Scheveningen* and licked it, curious to see if he would taste the sand. He did not. "It tastes like licking a telephone book," he recalled.[19] Unlike Durham, Myles looked at the painting with the eyes of an aesthete. His great passions—music, samurai swords, even karate—were all rooted in his love of artistry above all else.

After he spent a short while enjoying his private encounter with *Portrait of Elsbeth van Rijn*, he snapped to and got back to business. It was time to deliver the painting to Lenny Biondi down on the South Shore. He drove to his Randolph home and the two wrapped the painting in a sleeping bag. Biondi's elderly mother-in-law was living with him at the time, and they decided to slip it under her bed. The old woman went to sleep each night completely unaware that about thirty-six inches beneath her lay a Rembrandt worth millions.

On April 23, 1979, Myles's attorney, Martin K. Leppo, drove to federal court ready to begin his defense in the government's prosecution of his infamous client in connection with the theft of the Wyeths from the Woolworth Estate. There were also state charges and a revocation of his parole to handle, but that would be after the trial in US District Court. Connor was in Quincy, as far as anyone knew, and would meet Leppo there. At 9:00 A.M., Leppo and his opposing counsel, prosecutor David Twomey, were seated at their respective tables, and Judge Andrew Caffery was on the bench in the august federal courtroom.

Everyone was ready to begin. Everyone, that is, except Myles. Once again, he had no intention of facing a trial he didn't think winnable. Instead, he went on the run. With his unconventional bargaining chip safely secured, he needed to come up with a strategy for beating the rap that awaited him.

Leppo had no idea that Myles had taken the Rembrandt. He pleaded with the court to give him more time to get his client into the courtroom, but the judge was having none of it. He revoked the $50,000 bail on which Connor had been freed after his arrest in Mashpee. The FBI obtained a fugitive warrant, and Judge Caffery ordered that the defendant be brought before him immediately upon capture. Police officers throughout the region were warned that Myles should be considered "armed and extremely dangerous." He had, after all, previously shot a police officer after a pursuit and had been armed when the FBI arrested him in Mashpee.[20]

While it's tempting to envision a fugitive on the run hiding in abandoned buildings and stealing whatever morsels of food he can from random bodegas while fleeing to one town after another (or secreting himself in a library, as he had done in Maine), Myles Connor was hardly roughing it. Instead, he was renting an apartment in one of the many stately homes in Cohasset, Massachusetts, an upscale oceanfront locale, in the town's highest-rent district: Jerusalem Road. He wasn't wanting for company, either. His girlfriend, Martha Ferrante, left her farm to stay with him. The two shared walks on the beach and enjoyed themselves as if they hadn't a care in the world. Never mind that the FBI was hunting for him, nor that he was facing a long prison sentence, nor that he had to come up with a plan to redeem a stolen Rembrandt for his freedom—a painting that the entire art world and virtually all the law enforcement officers in Massachusetts were hoping would be found soon.

CHAPTER 10
CRISES

Stunned, saddened, and scared, museum officials met to discuss how best to act in the wake of the Rembrandt heist. Crisis planning and response—especially for an event of that nature—wasn't top of mind for businesses, least of all museums, in 1975 in the same way it would later develop as an essential tool for organizations. How exactly should a museum respond to a major theft conducted at gunpoint and resulting in the injury to an employee and witnessed by visitors? That was the question that vanquished all other business from the desks of the executive team at the Museum of Fine Arts, Boston.

After the gun smoke had cleared, John Monkouski was ambulanced to the hospital, and some semblance of calm had been restored, MFA director Merrill C. Rueppel made the museum's first official response by placing another Dutch masterwork in the place where *Portrait of Elsbeth van Rijn* had hung. The museum chose a self-portrait by Barent Fabritius, who is thought likely to have studied with Rembrandt. The painting, outfitted in an ornate gilded frame, would serve as a replacement, or at least a placeholder, to cover the now-barren space. This wasn't the storied Isabella Stewart Gardner Museum across the street, where nothing can ever be changed or replaced, according to the founder's will. The thieves had taken the frame, so it couldn't be hung empty and in situ as the Gardner would famously do fifteen years later (and some other stricken institutions would later do as well).

Director Rueppel had been on the job less than two years when the theft took place. He was just forty-nine years old—relatively young by the standards of the day. Rueppel joined the MFA from the Dallas Museum of Fine Arts,* where he built a reputation for advancing that institution on a tight budget.[1] Despite this, his ascension to the job in Boston was met with a great amount of skepticism from some who wondered how the director of a thirty-seven-year-old museum with a "fledgling" collection and small budget could end up leading one of oldest and largest museums in the country. While MFA board president John Coolidge stated tersely, "You pick the best man available," many were left pondering how that equated to Rueppel. It wasn't so much his intellect (he was described as "brilliant" by members of the Dallas community) as it was his pedigree. An exposé on his hiring explained, "Rueppel had not studied at the Fogg, the West Point of American museums, where a majority of U.S. museum directors are trained: he had a doctorate in art history from Wisconsin." In addition, because of his expertise in pre-Columbian art, with its concomitant concerns about the smuggling of artifacts, Rueppel's acquisitions raised some questions. This was a particular concern around 1970, the year of the UNESCO Convention on the Means of Prohibiting and Preventing the Illicit Import, Export or Transfer of Ownership of Cultural Property. A Mexican journal alleged that one piece in particular, a Mayan stela that he acquired for the Dallas Museum of Fine Arts in 1966 had been looted. Though Rueppel denied the allegation, the specter of illicit trafficking made him a surprising candidate for

---

*   Now the Dallas Museum of Art.

the prestigious directorship he won in Boston given the controversy that led to the job vacancy.[2]

It all began across the Atlantic. Rueppel's predecessor, Perry Rathbone, purchased a painting of a young woman attributed to the Italian Renaissance master Raphael for $600,000 from a Genoese art dealer. The painting was to be the centerpiece around which the MFA would celebrate its centennial jubilee in 1970. Soon, however, two emerging scandals simultaneously besieged the purchase. First, an Italian investigator specializing in looted and smuggled art began looking into the purchase for possible violations of that nation's cultural heritage laws that prevented the export of important artistic property. And second, art historians in the United States and Europe began questioning the attribution of the work to Raphael. Both developments spelled big trouble for the MFA. In January 1971, US Customs officials surprised museum officials with a search warrant and seized the painting. Soon, both MFA director Rathbone and curator Hanns Swarzenski, who carried the painting to the United States in a suitcase and failed to declare it upon entry, were subpoenaed to appear before a federal grand jury. Though no indictment was returned against them, the MFA's trustees voted—in Rathbone's absence—to return the painting to Italy. To make matters worse, the institution was unable to recover the $350,000 it had advanced the Italian art dealer because he had died in prison awaiting trial for illegally exporting the alleged Raphael.[3] In the end, both Rathbone and Swarzenski had to leave their positions. So, while one art crime had paved the way for Rueppel's high-profile new job, he was soon thrust into the spotlight by another.

It was understandably a difficult time to be an employee at the Museum of Fine Arts, Boston. A violent crime anywhere lingers in the minds of eyewitnesses, especially staff members, who would have to walk and work in the same spaces where traumatic events took place. There were police officers and FBI agents crawling around and questioning employees, subtly looking into any prospect of an insider. Some staff members feared a repeat crime. They worried about John Monkouski and his injury (and who, despite his heroism, was incorrectly listed as "George" in some *Boston Globe* coverage). Might the thieves target him for retribution? Might eyewitnesses who provided their names be at risk? Would the MFA have trouble recruiting guards? Would additional security be brought in, if only for at least the short term? Stories about what happened swirled throughout the building, changing ever so slightly with each retelling, as they always do. Everyone, from curators to custodians, waited to hear what Rueppel would have to say.

Speaking to the media, Rueppel addressed the first question that the press always asks when a piece of art is stolen: what is it worth? He fumbled it somewhat, at first saying that the value was "inestimable," then adding "a half million dollars would not be surprising." He would go on to explain that the dollar value of the painting would be determined in part by the amount for which the owners of the work had insured it, adding that he didn't know that figure.[4] The press ran with the half-million-dollar figure as if it were written in stone. Some went a step further. *The Boston Globe*'s Ellen Zack posited that *Portrait of Elsbeth van Rijn* "could be the most valuable single work of art ever stolen in the United States."[5] Her colleague at the *Globe*, Richard Connolly, described it as "virtually priceless."[6] Neither explained their reasoning. United Press International upped the figure, inexplicably, to $1.5 million.[7] When the whole affair would come to a close, estimates escalated to between $1 million and $5 million without any real examination into these approximations.

To be fair, museums don't provide valuations of their artwork to the public. There are several reasons for this. The most obvious is security.

Making known the dollar value of pieces in a museum collection (or any collection outside of an auction house, really) can be tantamount to providing thieves with a shopping list, enabling them to prioritize certain pieces over others by leveraging the known value against things like portability, security hardware, distance from points of egress, and so on. Another reason is that museums, and the art historians working within them, are focused on the intrinsic value of an artwork. They do not acquire pieces based on their price tags. A painting or object is acquired based on matters such as curatorial interest, educational value, and artistic significance, not merely to flaunt an acquisition. There are exceptions to this, of course. One could argue that the 2017 purchase by the Abu Dhabi Department of Culture and Tourism of *Salvador Mundi*, attributed in whole or part to Leonardo da Vinci, for a jaw-dropping $450.3 million was based on a desire to draw attention to a new museum project rather than any educational purpose. The fact that this professedly important work hasn't been seen since the sale seems to bolster this point.

Museums do, however, have pieces appraised when necessary for insurance purposes. But insurance values can often be misleading and are not exact indicators of what a particular piece might bring at auction. None of this arcana would likely interest reporters, however; what they seek are big numbers for big headlines.

Rueppel spoke openly about his opinion of the thieves, expressing astonishment that they would take such a highly recognizable work. "I can't believe that a professional art thief would choose this picture. It's too easily identifiable." He went on, "I think they're crazy . . . It would be virtually impossible to find an art dealer to handle this. It's like stealing a statue of Paul Revere," he said, perhaps referring to the famous equestrian statue of the patriot sculpted by Cyrus Dallin that stands across from the Old North Church in Boston's historic North

End district.[8] He was correct, of course, about the painting being too hot to sell. Elsbeth's image was plastered on the pages of newspapers around the world. No one would touch it, at least not for any dollar amount that would justify the risk involved in stealing and selling it. But what Rueppel couldn't know, of course, was that in this case profit wasn't the motive.

Rueppel also spoke with contempt and shock of the brutality that the thieves employed in the heist, flashing semiautomatic weapons and injuring a guard. "The thing that is appalling is that as far as I know it is the first theft by violence in an American museum."[9] That misbelief was a surprise. Just three years earlier, and only forty-five minutes away, the Worcester Art Museum armed robbery had occurred and made big headlines at home and across the world. A Rembrandt had also been stolen in that theft, his 1633 rendering of *St. Bartholomew*. Sadly, the violence in that episode exceeded that of the MFA attack. The two thieves making their escape from the Worcester Art Museum with stolen paintings didn't pistol-whip the elderly employee stationed at the doors. Instead, they shot him. It was a serious wound, too, striking guard Phil Evans in his lower abdomen. Miraculously, Evans's life was saved thanks to the visitor he had been speaking to just seconds before being shot. The woman, it turns out, was a nurse who knew just what to do to keep him alive until paramedics could transport him to the hospital. The fact that works by big-name artists were stolen (in addition to Rembrandt, there were two Gauguins and a Picasso), combined with the grotesque drama of a shooting, garnered the whole affair a lot of attention. Similarly, the theft at Harvard University's Fogg Museum, in which thieves pointed a gun at an overnight guard and forced their way into the building en route to stealing millions in ancient gold coins, dominated a news cycle in Massachusetts and across the nation.

None of this notoriety had gone unnoticed during Rueppel's short tenure at the Museum of Fine Arts, Boston. Thirteen months before *Portrait of Elsbeth van Rijn* was stolen, Rueppel hired a retired US Army Intelligence and Security Command veteran as his new head of security. When Colonel Gerard Shirar was brought on board it was reported that enlisting a man of his experience was necessitated by "the rash of major art thefts" that had recently occurred. "It's unfortunate but necessary for museums to now beef up their security," Shirar said, adding that he planned to implement a number of changes, including restricting the size of packages allowed in the galleries, adding Plexiglas to protect certain items, and more intensive training for guards.[10] It was wise to bring in a serious-minded professional, but not even the retired army colonel could foresee what Myles Connor had in store. And even if he had, it is extremely difficult for a museum to prevent an armed daytime raid. Museum guards are rarely, if ever, armed—and for good reason. A standoff—or, worse, a shootout—in a museum is not an option. The average gallery guard might spend an entire career without dealing with anything more daunting than a cranky visitor or unattended children wreaking havoc on the furniture. Taking on hardened criminals just wasn't what they were hired to do, and they certainly weren't paid a salary commensurate with such a hazard, either.

While recent thefts at other areas' institutions might have been the impetus to hire Shirar, the MFA had been victimized by thieves at least four times in the previous twenty years—a large number for any institution. But strangely, Rueppel told the media that the MFA had never suffered a theft.[11] In 1954 an engraving by Albrecht Dürer was stolen; less than a year later, in January 1964, a John-François Millet painting titled *The Fruit* was taken; a month later, seven sets of sixteenth- and seventeenth-century dueling pistols, seascape paintings, and other items were stolen by a former museum employee; and in November 1970, five pieces of Victorian jewelry were pilfered. In addition, in April 1969, paintings by luminaries such as Pablo Picasso, Claude Monet, Paul Cézanne, Henri Matisse, and Paul Gauguin were taken from the museum's walls in an attempted theft that was foiled by a gallery guard.[12]

That wasn't the only close call for a painting in Boston that month. A thief stole a Picasso destined for Milwaukee from a freight office at Logan International Airport. The painting was dropped off at the MFA by a taxi driver who fled before he could be questioned. The painting was still in its shipping crate but was accompanied by a handwritten note that read, "Please accept this to replace in part some of the paintings removed from museums thruout [sic] the country." It was signed "Robbin Hood." The MFA shipped it to its original destination, the Irving Gallery in Milwaukee.[13]

With the recent flurry of activity related to art crime totaling nearly $35 million worldwide during the year of the MFA Rembrandt heist, the police had their work cut out for them. The culprits could have been from anywhere, especially given the misperception of the time that there were professional art thieves at work around the globe who specialized in high-value fine art.

Nevertheless, investigators were inclined to consider as potential suspects anyone who in the past had stolen art in Massachusetts or internationally. Images of the painting were distributed nationally, and to border officials who might intercept it if it was destined for a foreign land.[14] Of course, one didn't have to look far to find a long list of criminals operating in the Boston area at the time to find men capable of pulling off the daring noontime armed raid at the MFA. The city was filled with gangs of criminals looking everywhere and anywhere for a score. Nothing was safe: Oriental rugs, home stereos, televisions, fur coats, leather jackets, jewelry, armored cars, and myriad other valuables were targeted. The city was uniquely under the auspices of two powerful organized crime factions: the so-called Irish Mob in the form of the Winter Hill Gang and the Italian Mafia, with an underboss operating out of the city's North End but with its headquarters an hour away in Providence, Rhode Island. Operating with their permission, as long as tribute was paid, gangs of criminals—call them disorganized crime—were running rampant in Greater Boston. Where to begin?

There didn't appear to be any immediate leads that signaled to the MFA that a recovery was imminent. FBI agents and Boston Police Department detectives were still conducting interviews with witnesses and employees while also rifling through tips as they came into their respective offices and to the museum. In a case as big as this one, with huge local headlines and reports circulating throughout the Western world, there would be no shortage of calls. While on the surface this may sound like a good thing, the fact is that there exists a large chasm between *a lot of tips* and *a lot of good leads*. What investigators were hoping for were a few actionable pieces of information, but what they received were masses of people offering theories, psychics offering locations, and con men hoping to profit from others' misery. In any case, it becomes essential that the investigating agencies act quickly to identify the logical leads and prioritize those that hold the most promise. In the MFA case, investigators also were charged with determining whether there was any inside element.

It was evident from the start that no employees were complicit in the crime. Vito Magaletta's background was spotless, and he had done nothing to facilitate the theft. Logic dictates that, had he been involved, he would simply have avoided the area and concentrated his observations to other zones to which he was assigned. Likewise, Monkouski put life and limb at great risk to save the Rembrandt. On a larger scale, a daytime raid meant no one was needed to let the bad guys into the building. Investigators were correct in their assumption. Myles hadn't lined up anyone in the museum's employ to assist. He simply didn't need to do so.

One by one, investigators considered local thieves who had stolen art. The two men who had pulled off the Worcester heist had already been arrested. One cooperated and was given probation, while the one who pulled the trigger was sentenced to eight to twenty-five years in prison. Florian "Al" Monday, the mastermind, had been captured by the Royal Canadian Mounted Police hiding out in Montreal under a false identity a year before the MFA job.[15] They could rule that gang out. Similarly, the Fogg Museum thieves were also captured in 1974, and the mastermind in that heist, Anthony Vaglica, was already being held on separate charges when arrested.[16]

Investigators were, of course, aware that the area's most notorious thief, Myles Connor, had been arrested by the FBI for the Wyeth paintings but was not in custody. By 1975 he had long been a newsmaker, and there were very few police officers who were unaware of Connor and his status. However, while it might seem unfathomable that he would have robbed the museum, especially ten days before he was due to stand trial in federal court for art theft, Connor was well established as no ordinary criminal. He never fit into any available offender profiles. So, while it might not have made sense that he would be involved, investigators remained suspicious.

FBI Special Agent Bernie Murphy, who had arrested Myles in Mashpee, was certain he had done it. The moment he heard about the MFA robbery, the bright young agent recalled Myles's confident retort when he had challenged him to get out of the fix he was in: "Wait and see."[17] Though neither of the descriptions of the thieves were a match for Myles, it would have been foolhardy to eliminate him as a suspect altogether. Given his history, it was hard to make an argument for not placing him near or at the top of the list of suspects.

Investigators kept their ears close to the ground for word from informants about who had taken *Portrait of Elsbeth van Rijn*. They also worked with colleagues who were close to breaking two other area art thefts that garnered less attention in the months following the MFA robbery. In May, four paintings were taken from the Childs Gallery on Newbury Street in the Back Bay worth an estimated $90,000: *The White Clipper* by Montague Dawson, *Bald Eagles in Winter* by Frank W. Benson, and two works by Erastus Salisbury Field. In that robbery, two men—one armed—stole the works at gunpoint. The paintings were recovered a day later when a ransom was paid. Then there was the theft in July of a Winslow Homer painting, *The Whittling Boy*, from the Converse Art & Archives at Malden Public Library, financed by Mr. and Mrs. Elisha Slade Converse, the rubber-soled shoe manufacturer. A Boston native and one of the country's best-loved marine artists, Homer's painting was insured for $100,000 and was the most valuable piece in the collection. It was recovered by the office of the Suffolk County District Attorney three months later. A ransom was reportedly paid for that work as well.[18] In both cases, the authorities were tight-lipped about the status of the paintings, still uncertain if either had a connection to the MFA.

The investigation into the Converse and Childs thefts illustrates law enforcement's grudging respect for Connor's cunning. Though he had been arrested in May 1974 on charges for the Wyeth heist, he was out on bail when the two heists were committed. Myles Connor on the streets, regardless of his circumstances, was a threat to any building holding art or cash. That was a truism that couldn't be denied. This meant that despite his daunting predicament after the Mashpee arrest, he was still being eyed for the two lesser thefts. But, as usual, the police couldn't pin them on him, and for good reason: he hadn't had anything to do with either crime.

As was necessary, the police sounded a confident note to the public. They referenced the four pieces of the frame that were broken off and touched by the thieves that might have fingerprints on them. One of the thieves had left behind a rubber glove, so a bare hand might have touched at least one of them. They were able to determine from whence the getaway car had been stolen—Norwood, Massachusetts, about forty-five minutes south of the MFA. Though no evidence was left in the car, there was a chance fingerprints might be discovered within. And they made note of the detailed descriptions of the culprits that witnesses had provided.

As early as the day of the robbery, Boston Police Deputy Superintendent Leroy Chase told the press that, based on a tip, a break was expected at any moment. He boasted that he was "waiting to hear from my detectives who are in close pursuit of the person or persons responsible for this robbery."[19] His confidence in a quick resolution was palpable. "It's just a waiting game right now," he said. "I would say before the day is over I would anticipate something concrete. I can't say when."[20] Chase's counterpart in the Intelligence Unit, Deputy Superintendent John Doyle, spoke dismissively about the culprits, perhaps to irk them into some sort of response. He openly described them as "rank amateurs," adding that it would take mere "routine police procedure" to bring them to justice.[21] Someone even leaked to United Press International that the police knew "the identity of two of the three bandits."[22] Myles was no fan of Doyle's, who he described as "a devious old devil who I thoroughly despised."[23] Despite the confident tone of the messaging from the two deputy superintendents, the day came to a close with investigators no nearer to arrests of the robbers or recovery of the painting. Connor was aware of the boasts coming from the Boston Police Department implying imminent closure. They were "constantly on the tube stating how close they were to recovering the Rembrandt," he said.[24] The obviously incorrect messaging from the Boston Police Department brought him no small measure of amusement.

Meanwhile, the head of the Boston office of the FBI, James Newpher, who was just weeks away from retirement, was more reserved. Considered to be one of the most accessible special agents in charge to have run the Boston office, he was uncharacteristically unforthcoming, saying only that the descriptions of the thieves were "fairly good" and that composite drawings were still in progress.[25]

In addition to the nearly two dozen or so police and FBI investigators out knocking on doors and squeezing sources for information on the missing Rembrandt, private detectives were on the case, too, hoping to get a piece of whatever the painting's insurer might be offering for the safe return of the masterpiece. The impetus was a reward notice posted in *The Boston Globe* on April 28, exactly two weeks after the heist. Despite the early confidence expressed by the police, there seemed to be no progress in the effort to capture the thieves and recover the painting. That prompted the owners, who opted not to be identified by name, to appeal to the public for information leading to the recovery of the painting. The promise of a reward, they must have reasoned, would do more to shake free useful tips than anything the police had been able to accomplish to date. After all, the conjecture from the very start was that the painting was taken for a ransom, so dangling the promise of a payment made sense. Interestingly, no specific reward amount was provided, which might have been because the owners knew more about the actual value of the painting than anyone was letting on. It also might have been a strategic move, intended to lead possible informants to let their imaginations run wild with gigantic payoffs for information. Maintaining an element of mystery behind the prize meant that no one would disregard it as not worth their time.

The organization representing the owners was First Security Services Corporation of Boston, founded by Dick Barry, a retired Massachusetts State Police officer. Barry had been an investigator working for the state's Crime Commission and the district attorney's office when, in 1967, he decided to take a leave of absence from the State Police for a dramatic change: he accepted an offer from Andrew Tuney, a former fellow Massachusetts State Police detective, to join his private investigative firm and lead his new Beverly Hills office. It was the sort of thing that made headlines. Tuney had played a leading role in the investigation into the infamous Boston Strangler, a serial killer and rapist who terrorized the area in the early 1960s, murdering thirteen women. The murderer was finally caught and identified as Albert DeSalvo and was defended in court by the legendary attorney F. Lee Bailey. Though Tuney was on the side of the prosecution, he soon bought from Bailey the Boston-based firm Investigative Associates, Inc. He then went on to work with Bailey on another legendary murder case, that of Dr. Samuel Sheppard, who was convicted and later acquitted of murdering his wife.[26] It was hard to imagine more high-profile work, and the lure of bringing his family to Beverly Hills and overseeing the new office was too much to resist for Barry. By 1972, though, with his family missing their East Coast roots, he started First Security Services Corporation in Boston and quickly grew the firm into one of the leading investigative and security firms in the area.[27]

The weeks that followed the reward announcement featured great drama surrounding the heist and the Museum of Fine Arts, Boston. In May, *The Boston Herald Advertiser* was reporting that First Security was secretly negotiating in person with the thieves, who were demanding $250,000 for the return of the Rembrandt. Boston Police Deputy Superintendent John Doyle assisted in the effort but took a back seat to Dick Barry's negotiators. The media reports alleged that contact was made with the bandits the day after the heist. Barry's spokesman was unwilling to share details. "All that we can say at this time is that we are negotiating with some people concerning the return of the painting."[28]

As certain as the negotiators—and the press—sounded, the negotiations with the purported "bandits" dragged on but were fruitless. The disappointment of the failed effort was not the end of the troubles for the MFA. In the first week of June, news had spread that the museum's trustees had already decided that Rueppel's contract as director would not be renewed at the end of his tenure in two years.

Then, on June 4, another reward advertisement appeared in the papers, but this time it was not from the owners of the painting through First Security. Instead, a notice under the heading LET'S MAKE A DEAL appeared, offering a "substantial reward" for the return of the Rembrandt. Oddly, it also stated that a heretofore unknown individual, Richard Carter, was the "only person authorized to negotiate for the return of the missing item." The ad, placed by a California attorney named Donald Calabria, made no mention of who exactly either he or Carter represented.

The notice led Dick Barry from First Security to hold a press conference. He reiterated that his company, working on behalf of two unnamed insurance firms, was still the only authorized negotiator for the Rembrandt, adding that others—that is, Calabria and Carter—"appear[ed] to be acting on a frolic of their own." Barry also addressed the so-called ransom stories that speculated as to the potential size of the reward. "No one actually interested has ever thought about the amount of any possible reward for information leading to the recovery of the painting, but it was certain the amounts mentioned in the article were ridiculous and would not even be considered," he said.[29]

While Barry was correct in saying that only he and his company were authorized representatives of the owners of the painting, it defies belief that when the decision was made to post a reward notice in the region's biggest newspaper, no one considered what they would be willing to pay. Certainly, when First Security was negotiating with that first group of pretenders in the days immediately following the heist, they had to have had some idea of how much of an offer they were authorized to make. In any event, the announcement by Carter and Calabria introduced confusion that the MFA and investigators could ill afford.

On the very day the press conference was being held, it was reported that the MFA's security guards, who were attempting to form a local labor union, wrote to Merrill Rueppel to advise him that it did not support his efforts to fight the trustees' executive committee as they sought his ouster. The guards wrote that Rueppel's "insensitivity" led to the "destruction of security morale." The guards noted that while the rest of the museum's staff were receiving pay increases, they would be realizing a decrease in take-home pay due to reduced work schedules.[30] The guards based nothing about their decision on the theft, but in light of what had happened less than two months prior, the MFA could ill afford a security team beset by poor morale.

Rueppel did not need tea leaves to tell him that both the board and the staff had lost confidence in him. The curatorial team was waging a revolt over his new policy that dictated they could not teach outside of the museum. He reasoned that five days a week their focus should be making the galleries look "interesting," but the eight curators would have none of it. On June 9, 1975, the board of trustees terminated Rueppel's contract. He was out as director, replaced by Asiatic art curator Jan Fontein who would serve as interim director. The move put the MFA's troubles in the spotlight, with multiple long stories about the changes in leadership due to the foibles of Rueppel and his predecessor, Perry Rathbone, filling newspapers. Much focus was placed on the difficulties facing the institution, which now included the responsibility of paying the salaries of two summarily ousted directors through the end of their respective contracts.[31] This sort of publicity could have a serious chilling effect on donors.

The decision to make Fontein the acting director would have overjoyed Myles Connor if he hadn't other things on his mind besides researching the curator's background. Fontein was the senior curator for Asiatic art, and earned honors during his doctoral studies in Japanese, Chinese, and the art and archeology of Southeast Asia. In time, he would oversee the renovation of twenty-six galleries dedicated to Asian art at the MFA.[32] One could easily imagine Connor eagerly attending his lectures and exhibitions, reading all his published works, and discussing the art of the Japanese tea ceremony—a subject Fontein had spent a full year studying in Japan.[33] The new acting director was even made commander in the Japanese Order of the Sacred Treasure, an honor that certainly would have thrilled Myles.[34] Years later, Fontein would host a special exhibition to mark the reopening of the Asiatic Wing at the MFA, *Living National Treasures of Japan*, which featured a workshop set up in the courtyard to demonstrate master sword making. It was as if Fontein was the very man Connor himself would choose as director of the institution.

Jan Fontein was a breath of fresh air. While both Rathbone and Rueppel had faced serious accusations of unethical transactions involving art and antiquities, Fontein made news in 1973 when he returned an eleventh-century Indian bronze to a museum in Calcutta (now Kolkata) after he discovered that it had been stolen a few years prior to the Museum of Fine Arts, Boston, acquiring it. Also, in contrast to Rueppel, who was thought to be aloof, Fontein was described by *The New York Times* as "affable" with an "unpretentious style" and "down-to-earth personality."[35] But while it might appear that Fontein had a very low bar to overcome in order to make an improvement in what was quickly becoming a beleaguered institution, he had enormous challenges to face. He inherited not only poor morale and financial trouble, but a leadership vacuum created when the museum's board president, John Coolidge, and its assistant director, A. S. Cavallo, had also left the MFA.[36]

On top of all this, this lifelong academic with expertise in far-off lands was expected to oversee the museum's role in a criminal investigation. It is difficult to imagine a field so far from his own. That's not to say he wasn't interested, though. Fontein was Dutch, born about fifteen miles from Amsterdam. He earned an undergraduate degree in Chinese and Japanese literature in 1945 at Leiden University—Rembrandt's hometown.[37] He undoubtedly understood the importance of this magnificent painting as well as anyone. Even though his curatorial interests were Asiatic, his heartstrings were pulled by the theft of the best-known Dutch Master from his own institution. If only he knew that it was at least securely stowed away from the slightest risk of harm, safe from damaging direct light, where no one could touch it, and, most importantly, under the control of a man who not only appreciated its importance but who fully intended to give it back.

CHAPTER II
THE YOUNG WOMAN

B ecause of Myles Connor's exploits, *Portrait of Elsbeth van Rijn* was being mentioned in newspapers and on broadcasts around the world throughout the rest of 1975. It was not the sort of attention that one would wish for a great painting. Even its imaginative creator could never have envisioned the maelstrom that now surrounded the work. Yet the painting's history prior to its time with Myles was far from dull.

Portrait of Elsbeth van Rijn changed hands at least eleven times dating back to 1726 until it was acquired by the sovereign of Liechtenstein around 1891. During his long reign, Johann II, Prince of Liechtenstein, was well-known as a patron and connoisseur of the arts and was regarded as one of the greatest collectors of the second half of the nineteenth century.[1] He obsessively amassed a huge collection of art and worked to restore landmarks to their original state. But at the close of World War I, he had much more pressing business at hand than acquiring art and cultural property.

As monarchies in Central Europe dissolved, replaced for a time by radical socialist governments, the Princely House of Liechtenstein was in jeopardy of joining the Habsburgs in Austria and others in Saxony,

Bavaria, and elsewhere in a fall from power. Unlike those, however, Johann II made a wise strategic move. He turned to the Bishop of Chur, who was responsible for the Roman Catholic diocese that included Liechtenstein, for assistance. The bishop was willing to help and composed a pastoral letter that was published throughout the nation reminding his flock of their obligation to remain loyal to their ruler.

The letter worked, and Johann II remained as the wealthy nation's leader. A red revolution was thwarted in Liechtenstein. So grateful was Johann II for the bishop's intercession that he offered him any work in his grand collection. The bishop chose Rembrandt's *Portrait of Elsbeth van Rijn*, and the prince happily fulfilled his promise.

Years passed, and as the bishop became increasingly concerned over diocesan finances, he decided that though having such beauty in his residence was pleasing to the eyes, perhaps the sale of such an astounding work might be in order. He believed that the painting might fetch as much as $250,000 in the United States, particularly in Los Angeles, where Hollywood fortunes were forming. He shipped the painting off to a monastery there after summoning the assistance of a wealthy Angeleno woman who would talk up the painting to those she thought might be interested.

In 1929 the woman contacted a friend, Boston art dealer Robert Vose, who was in Los Angeles for annual visit.[2] She implored him to visit the monastery to see the artistic treasures within, hoping that Vose might find a few paintings he would be interested in selling. Vose had little interest in such a visit but acquiesced when the woman—who had graciously acquainted him with the area—said, "I had thought that you were a friend of mine." The art dealer summoned a taxi and went directly to the monastery, none too pleased with the mission.

Once there, he was escorted by a tonsured monk, who led him to works Vose's son, Morton, described as "copies, or minor works 'promoted' by name plates into works by major artists." The poor selection annoyed Vose, who was ready to leave the monastery not long after arriving. But his escort told him, "There are two or three more in the next room." Once there, he was transfixed by what he saw: the bishop's Rembrandt. He knew immediately that it was a special work. Morton described an "astonishment which overcame" his father when he saw it. Vose telephoned the woman who referred him to the monastery and said, "If I ever again disregard one of your suggestions, it will be because I am deaf, blind, or dead! How am I to proceed?" She informed him of the identity of the owner—the Bishop of Chur—and said that negotiations would have to be conducted directly with him.

The bishop, excited at the possibility of selling the painting, immediately booked a voyage to the United States to negotiate directly with Vose. After collecting the painting in California, the bishop arrived in Boston and sold it to Robert Treat Paine II, a descendant of the Founding Father, for $125,000. Though half the amount of what the bishop dreamt, the timing was fortunate, for it occurred just one month before the stock market crash of 1929. By the early weeks of 1930, *Portrait of Elsbeth van Rijn* was on display at the Museum of Fine Arts, Boston, on loan from the Paine family, where it remained for the next fifty-six years, minus the eight months it spent in Myles Connor's possession.

Rembrandt van Rijn's work is so often the target of thieves because he is universally known to be one of the greatest artists in the history of Western civilization. His body of work is large enough that many major museums have at least one of his pieces in their collection, which means they are accessible to art lovers—and art thieves—most everywhere. Even the least cultured thief knows that Rembrandt paintings command a high price. So, while they might not know what makes them special (at least not until seeing one in person), they do see dollar signs when the wicked idea of stealing art germinates in their minds.

The three-year period beginning in May 1972 and ending with the theft from the Museum of Fine Arts, Boston, in 1975, was a dangerous time for Rembrandt paintings in North America, with five of his works being stolen. In addition to the MFA and Worcester Art Museum heists, three Rembrandts were stolen: *Portrait of an Elderly Woman* and *Man Leaning on a Sill* were lifted in a predawn robbery from the Taft Museum of Art in Cincinnati in 1973 and *Landscape with Cottage* was taken from the Montreal Museum of Fine Arts one year earlier.

Myles Connor's criminal connoisseurship was a defining characteristic of the MFA heist. He had chosen the worthiest of targets. *Portrait of Elsbeth van Rijn* is a fine example of Rembrandt van Rijn's breathtaking hand skills and technique. Painted on a mahogany panel, it is a front-facing character study of a young woman with soft, full features and blond wispy curls bearing a strand of pearls and matching eardrops. She wears a lustrous gold-trimmed cloak over an elegantly pleated high-neck white blouse, and her earrings match the adornment in her hair. The sitter is gently lit. The grace of the painting stands in stark contrast to the violence and garishness of the circumstances surrounding its theft. One can imagine the woman's expressionless gaze remaining unfazed while the panel was frantically transported from the museum's wall to the getaway vehicle and all the ruckus in between.

The quality of the painting cannot be overstated. Peter Sutton, a later curator of European paintings at the MFA, said that the painting was "the foundation of his reputation as a portraitist." Fiona Ford of Sotheby's said, "It's a delightful, intimate portrait. It has all the freshness of youth about it."[3] Acclaimed Dutch and Flemish art scholar Arthur Wheelock Jr. said of it, "There is a wonderful sense of life that exists in this painting and the more you look at it she is less static, she's sort of turned and Rembrandt has adjusted the background so that she has earrings and one is against this dark background and one is against a light background. So, he plays off light and dark and subtle shifts in her position that gives a sense of inner life to this figure that is quite amazing."[4]

While the quality of the work is beyond dispute, the identity of the young woman has puzzled art experts. Though originally thought to be a portrait of Rembrandt's sister, that belief was already waning when the painting was stolen. In *Rembrandt: The Complete Paintings* (1969), "the painting is titled "Rembrandt's sister" between question marks of doubt," said the preeminent Rembrandt expert Gary Schwartz, who consulted on the book.[5] Schwartz has referred to the painting as *A Young Woman in an Embroidered Robe*, and not as Liesbeth van Rijn.[*] As to the true identity of the sitter, Schwartz writes, "There is little one can say against the theory of H. F. Wijnman that the model was Hendrick Uylenburgh's wife Maria van Eyck, who was about 30 in 1632. In its favor is at least the knowledge that Maria did pose for Rembrandt." Schwartz adds an intriguing twist, "However, Wijnman saw the same face in several other works of this period . . . the problem with this is that when one begins to compare the faces of the young women in Rembrandt's paintings feature by feature, one discovers that that nearly all of them are different models whom he made look the same."[6] So, at the time of the heist, while the media repeatedly referred to the work as *Elsbeth van Rijn* (using a variety of spellings), that determination had years before been, at best, cast into doubt.

---

[*] Another of the spellings of Rembrandt's sister's name. As with most things related to Rembrandt, Schwartz's is the most reliable.

The Rembrandt Research Project, a collaboration by a group of Dutch art scholars who formed to take on the weighty challenge of authenticating paintings attributed to the master and removing from his oeuvre lesser works wrongly assigned to him, examined the work in a 1970 study. They agree with Schwartz's assessment. "Where the meaning of the picture is concerned, one must assume that the painting is not a commissioned portrait, but a *tronie* (an artistic study of facial expressions and character) that was not painted with the primary intention of being a likeness of a living person," instead serving "as a prototype for a number of [his] studio works."[7]

Unlike so many others, the authenticity of *Portrait of Elsbeth van Rijn* as a true work by Rembrandt is a settled matter. Rembrandt scholar John C. Van Dyke, writing in 1923, claimed that fewer than fifty of the one thousand paintings attributed to Rembrandt in collections at that time were from his own hand, with the great majority painted by his students and studio assistants. But Van Dyke repeatedly pointed to this portrait as an "indubitable example" of Rembrandt's artistry.[8] More recently, the Rembrandt Research Project confidently asserted that it is "a well preserved, authentic work, reliably signed and dated 1632." The only doubt was whether the mahogany panel had originally been rectangular as opposed to its current oval state.[9]

Portrait of Elsbeth van Rijn was completed in an important year in Rembrandt's life. The artist, who was about twenty-six years old at the time, had recently moved from his hometown of Leiden to the bustling port city of Amsterdam. It wasn't his first visit—he had studied under the great Pieter Lastman there years before—but now it would become his home until the end of his life. Though Rembrandt stubbornly didn't visit Italy to develop his skills, he was influenced by the strong light and deep shadow used for dramatic effect by the Italian artist Caravaggio and cultivated it into one of the hallmarks of his portraiture.[10] Upon arriving in Amsterdam, Rembrandt initially moved into the house of the art dealer Hendrick Uylenburgh, and there met his future wife, Saskia van Uylenburgh. Over the course of his career, Rembrandt enjoyed professional success and acclaim but suffered tremendous personal loss. Saskia died at just thirty years old, leaving Rembrandt widowered with a one-year-old child. He later fell in love with a servant, Hendrickje Stoffels, but lacked the finances to marry her. She became his common-law wife, and they shared a child. Rembrandt portrayed Hendrickje in several of his works. She died in 1663, and his son, Titus, also preceded him in death in 1668. Rembrandt died virtually penniless in 1669, but today his body of work is among the most valuable, best-known, and most highly esteemed in the history of art.[11]

CHAPTER 12
ON THE RUN AGAIN

While officials at the Museum of Fine Arts, Boston, scrambled to overcome negative press, staff departures, budget issues, and the loss of its most important Rembrandt, Myles Connor was enjoying the summer in Cohasset, walking beautiful Sandy Beach with his girlfriend Martha Ferrante. Sure, he was a highly sought-after fugitive facing federal prison, and yes, he was a suspect in the biggest museum heist in memory, but Connor was never prone to anxiety. Billy Skinner was making regular trips to Cohasset to bring him up to speed as to what was going on in the city and to deliver to him whatever he might need. Skinner let Myles know that Al Dotoli was feeling some heat and even believed that the police had put a camera outside of his house in case Myles or the painting—or both—paid a visit. This surprised neither Dotoli nor Connor. It was an obvious move. How could anyone looking for Myles not monitor Al? Hadn't he been the person who had been brought to Maine a decade earlier to try to coax his best friend into turning himself in?

As lovely as summer had been, when fall came it meant Martha had to return to her home to continue her studies at UMass Amherst. When it was time for her to leave, parting was sweet sorrow. She knew full well that her lover was on the run yet again, and that eventually a day of reckoning would come. Would she see him again before then? He had pulled off miracles before, but Martha was a smart young woman. She knew that no one could get away with it—no matter what "it" might be—forever. But while she knew Myles was a wanted man, she did not know that he had an incredible chit hidden under a bed in Randolph, Massachusetts, and that he was simply awaiting the right moment to cash it in.

Ferrante had barely begun the fall semester of 1975 when Myles decided to drive out to see her. It hadn't yet been two weeks that they were apart, but while he had adapted well to being a fugitive, he hadn't adjusted to her absence yet. So, Myles hopped in his Camaro, sped west on the Massachusetts Turnpike, and picked Martha up on campus. Then they drove to South Hadley, the location where, just months earlier, he had pulled off a major bank heist. This time, though, he visited the rustic town not to steal money but to spend it, taking his girlfriend to dinner at the Bonanza Family Restaurant (which billed itself as a "The Family Restaurant Even a Father Could Love!" because of its reasonable prices). They never made it to the host stand. Investigators had been monitoring Martha's address, and when Myles suddenly appeared, they scrambled to assemble a unit of FBI agents armed with shotguns to apprehend him in the restaurant's parking lot. The Bureau had to mobilize so quickly that they didn't have time to let the town's police chief know that they were about to arrest the famous felon. "They had to act fast as Connor was considered dangerous," South Hadley chief Henry Decker reasoned. His officers were only alerted when a townie noticed what turned out to be a federal agent with a shotgun in the parking lot. Myles was bundled and pushed into a government car yet again and driven directly to Boston, where he was swiftly deposited in the Charles Street Jail.[1]

As big a capture it was for the FBI's Boston office, it was only the second-most newsworthy apprehension of the week for the Bureau. On September 18, their counterparts at the San Francisco office arrested Patty Hearst, the twenty-one-year-old kidnapping victim-cum-bank robbing radical who had been the subject of the most intensive national manhunt in the nation's history. Hearst, heir to the legendary publishing family, was also arrested at gunpoint, along with three of her comrades. The two arrests in one week marked a fine time to be an FBI agent. It's hard to imagine two bigger successes: they had captured fugitives sought not just by the justice system but by the Hearst and Woolworth families, fulfilling the hopes of two more important American families.

Meanwhile, Al Dotoli was getting overtures from those who correctly assumed that his guitar-playing pal had been the man behind the MFA robbery. Members of his criminal crew remained nervous that as speculation about Connor's complicity in the huge heist grew, they might be facing danger from other gangs. Steve Gorski, the man who lifted the painting from the wall the day before the heist, said, "After the Rembrandt was taken we were very careful for a while. Getting out of my car at night I usually had a gun in my hand. We were thinking [James "Whitey"] Bulger might like to have it without the work."[2] It was a reasonable concern. The notorious Bulger and his cohorts, including Stephen "The Rifleman" Flemmi, were among the most dangerous criminals in the Boston area, committing widespread mayhem and murder. Their chief assassin, John Martorano, was from Milton and was not an enemy of Connor's. In fact, Martorano's brother Jimmy was a good friend of Myles's. But this was a brutal group with little regard for friendship, alliances, or any sort of code. They even murdered young women they felt inconvenient to them, something anathema to traditional organized crime gangs, especially of that era.

In time, it would be found that Bulger and Flemmi were also betraying their confederates by acting as informants to a sympathetic FBI agent, John Connolly, who, in turn, provided them with intelligence about informants and the Italian Mafia. It was beyond a devil's bargain—it was an alliance of the most powerful of criminals and federal agents. Connolly was eager to know what had happened to the Rembrandt so that he could score important points for himself in the agency and continue to elevate himself, seeking to satisfy his ego and assist the Bulger gang. His failure in this regard would lead Connolly to seek vengeance against Myles Connor for years to come.

Special Agent Bernie Murphy, who all along had suspected that Myles had stolen the Rembrandt, and that Al might be the key to recovering it, visited Al's new home to conduct a consent search. Al, unaware at the time of what exactly Murphy might be looking for, asked him for a hint. "Is it something that can fit in a desk drawer?" Al asked, wondering if they were searching for money. "No, bigger," Murphy replied. Al consented, leading Murphy and his partner around the house, taking him to every room, and even getting them a step ladder so they could stick their heads up into the knee space with their flashlights. Of course, they found nothing. Finally, the agents noted three trucks parked in Al's drive, each with locked rear doors. They asked if they could take a look inside. Again, Al agreed, and ran inside to get the keys to the padlocks. He opened the first two, and it was plain to the investigators that there was no painting in them. When he got to the third, which contained a sound system used for years by the rock band Poco, he couldn't locate the key. So, he offered to ask his friends at the Quincy Fire Department to cut the lock.

"Don't worry about it, Al, we believe you," Murphy said.

"Are you sure? I don't mind having them come over with bolt cutters," Dotoli offered.

"No, it's fine. But listen Al, there is talk that some bad actors out there who are thinking about coming here and tying you to a chair or something and beating the painting's whereabouts out of you."

Al thanked Murphy for passing along the intelligence, and the agents went on their way. The next morning, he found the lock to the third truck—and only the third truck—cut and on the ground, leaving the truck unsecured. Nothing was missing from the inside. Dotoli never learned who had done it. On another occasion, one of Al's other vans was stolen. When it was recovered, the cargo compartment, which had plywood walls along the inside, had been disassembled in an obvious search for a painting of an innocent young Dutch woman circa 1632.[3]

Agent John Connolly, who always had his ear to the ground, knew that Myles had emerged as a prime suspect. He, too, paid Dotoli a visit. Dotoli saw Connolly and his partner walking up his long driveway and told his friends, who had stayed over after an all-night party, to grab him three beers. When he answered the door, he was drinking one and still somewhat inebriated from the long night. Knowing that the feds couldn't question him in his home while clearly under the influence, he offered the agents a drink and exaggerated his level of intoxication. Connolly and his partner did an about-face and left.[4]

Private detectives also were calling Al, and not all were clear about their identity or on whose behalf they were acting. While they had hit upon the right person by contacting the lifelong best friend of Myles Connor, they underestimated his shrewdness. Dotoli's reputation as a law-abiding yin to Connor's yang was accurate, but it was a mistake to interpret this as anything akin to timidity or weakness. Al had been negotiating deals with men much older and more experienced than he since before could legally drive. His discernment and executive functioning were at the root of the fast successes he achieved in his business ventures. The difference was that Dotoli's moral compass always pointed true north, while Connor's often found its magnetic pull coming from other directions.

Al could not be bullied or intimidated by government agents, private investigators, insurance companies, or local toughs who suffered from the misbelief that he would fold if the right pressure was applied. But Rudy Guarino represented something entirely different—the Mafia. Al had grown up in an Italian family around Boston's North End, where his father had a restaurant. He had also produced innumerable concerts in clubs throughout the area frequented by made men and their top associates. While he wasn't easily rattled and was on a first-name basis with many of them, he knew that anyone speaking on behalf of "The Office," the headquarters of Raymond L. S. Patriarca in Providence, Rhode Island, represented something more worrisome than any tin star or corporate ID.

Considering the sheer power of the Patriarca crime family, their approach to Al was remarkable. Theirs was a friendly offer of a briefcase filled with $60,000 cash for a painting the papers were saying was valued between $1 million and $1.5 million. They promised that there was more to come. Though there were no threats and no show of force, Al was wise enough to know he wanted no part of the money. He understood that the overture meant, in his words, that "this shit is serious," even if it came without a threat. "Would you ask your friend to consider giving this painting to us?" is what Al recalls Guarino saying to him.[5] There was no "or else" involved. Nothing Guarino said to Dotoli implied any danger might befall him or his loved ones. Of course, the mere mention of Patriarca's name—even a tacit reference to Federal Hill—was portentous enough to any normal person, but La Cosa Nostra in Providence was not known for its subtlety. They hadn't reason to be esoteric.

The fact is that there was deference for Myles Connor on the part of the Mafia. For more than fifteen years he had stolen from a wide variety of organizations throughout New England, all of which was Patriarca's territory. Yet he never paid a penny's worth of tribute to any organized crime outfit, and, tellingly, none demanded it. He was the one major active criminal who ignored the whole concept of seeking permission to operate in any area or paying any portion of his haul up the chain. Organized crime was fully aware of his exploits, but they also understood that there was no point in trying to enforce their rules on him. He'd never follow them. Myles Connor was to be handled gently. Respectfully. Threats wouldn't work with him anyway. This wasn't the Worcester heist where stronger, tougher men merely pointed a gun at Al Monday and demanded he take them to the paintings. Getting the Rembrandt from Myles required diplomacy. Guarino knew this. They all did. The Mafia in Providence was successful in their ventures because their tact was combined with implicit ruthlessness.

Though Al hadn't the vaguest idea where the painting was, too many now believed he did. That was potentially a more dangerous situation for him—the criminal underworld wanting something from him that he truly did not have. Al wisely decided to meet with Myles at the Charles Street Jail in Boston.

Prior to seeing Al, Myles had already had three very important meetings in the dank and filthy place in which he had been held since he was caught in Martha's company. In 1975 the Charles Street Jail was a truly awful place, rivaling Walpole State Prison for its inhumane conditions.* Two years earlier, the US District Court ruled that the jail violated the constitutional rights of its inmates and labeled it unfit for human habitation based on overcrowding, rat and insect infestation, primitive plumbing, and the lack of recreational area.[6] The facility was

---

* The jail has since been converted to a trendy hotel with a hip bar aptly called CLINK.

built before the Civil War, and was among the oldest in the nation. It had housed Nicola Sacco and Bartolomeo Vanzetti, suffragists, and German prisoners of war. In short, it was to the Museum of Fine Arts, Boston, what a highway underpass is to the Omni Parker House. It was in this incongruous setting that work would begin to see that the *Portrait of Elsbeth van Rijn* was returned to its rightful owners.

The first of Connor's meetings was with his attorney, Martin K. Leppo. Marty, as he liked to be called, was in the midst of a high-profile multiyear death penalty case involving the so-called De Mau Mau organization, a group of Black Vietnam War–era veterans who united against the racism and oppression they felt both in the military and after their service had concluded. The group had resorted to violence in some instances, including in Boston, where, in 1973 five members went to the home of Black activist and author Hakim Jamal carrying handguns, carbines, and a rifle. The men held the occupants of the home at gunpoint while another shot Jamal dead. Three of the men were arrested and tried for murder. Leppo's client, William Johnson, and the others were found guilty of murder in the commission of a felony, which, at the time, meant they could be put to death. Johnson was a difficult client to control. When the judge sentenced him to death, Johnson picked up a heavy chair and threw it at the judge, narrowly missing Leppo.[7] So, Leppo had his hands full before he even met with Myles to discuss his latest venture.

Like Connor, Leppo was small in stature but ruggedly built. Moreover, he had been a boxer while serving in the Marine Corps and beyond. He didn't scare easily, not even in the wake of a violent outburst by a cold-blooded killer. He would go on to appeal Johnson's sentence and get him a new trial, sparing him from the death penalty. Now, just months later, he was sitting again in the Charles Street Jail, where Johnson had been held, with another newsworthy client. Leppo met Connor under unusual circumstances—two words that, when placed together, pretty much define much of Myles Connor's life. Leppo was dining at a café in Boston with some friends when he saw something most unexpected outside. "A guy walked by the restaurant in Mattapan Square on Blue Hill Avenue, and he's got a mountain lion on a leash," he said.[8]

Being an adventurous sort, Leppo went outside and introduced himself. He and Myles became lifelong friends. As for the mountain lion—a cougar, actually—it went on to star with Farrah Fawcett in a commercial for the Mercury Cougar automobile.

Leppo was still representing Connor on the Wyeth case and had come to see his now-captured client. He should have been upset that Connor had absconded and left him alone to suffer the wrath of an irate federal judge. But Leppo took it in stride. He was a seasoned defense attorney and resisted the urge to let his temper get the best of him. He was, however, gifted with a sharp mind and an acid tongue, and could take a man down with his wit as well as his fists. Myles enjoyed their banter and the way they could communicate purely through wry humor and sarcasm.

Before Leppo addressed the Wyeth matter, he had a question for Connor. "You wouldn't happen to know who took that Rembrandt painting from the MFA, would you?"

"Why, absolutely not!" Myles replied, with mock astonishment. "How dare you even ask!"

Leppo knew his client and friend well enough to understand that response. He filed it away, suspecting that the matter would surely arise again in the future. Saying no more at this time, though, they moved on to the more pressing matter involving the state and federal charges Myles was still facing.

The next person to visit Myles was his father, Joe. When asked if his father was aware upon his visit that his son had stolen the Rembrandt,

Myles admits that though he hadn't told him, "Of course he did. He knew me."[9] His father wasn't upset. In fact, he never got upset with his son. He accepted him as he was. Similarly, Joe's fellow police officers didn't hold his son's sins against him. Police officers know better than most that families are complex and that children raised in the same household by the same parents often turn out drastically different. Anyone who knew the sort of man Sergeant Joe Connor was knew that his influence wasn't to blame for Myles's misdeeds.

Joe's message for his son was a repeat of the one he delivered immediately following Myles's arrest by the FBI in Mashpee: you should talk with John Regan. Unlike the last time, however, there was an agenda. Without mentioning the missing Rembrandt, his father told him, "Myles, if you were involved, John would like to be involved."[10]

This was exactly what Myles was hoping to hear. "I thought I was going to have to go through the FBI," he remembers. According to Connor, the Bureau had already made an offer. "They offered me an 'out' if I'd become their snitch," he recalled.[11] This, of course, ran contrary to his code and was thus a complete nonstarter. Moreover, unbeknownst to him at the time, the FBI's case agent assigned to the Connor investigation, Special Agent Bernie Murphy, was vehemently against any sort of deal with Myles.

Regan's interest was clearly the key development and a major breakthrough. It met two important criteria Myles felt necessary for a smooth return of the painting. First, he trusted Regan implicitly. "I can't say enough good things about him. He was above board. A good guy. A friend to my dad," Myles remembered. Second, Myles knew that neither the FBI nor the Boston Police Department wanted to see him maneuver his way out of this jam. Not again. Not when they had him right in their grasp. The prospect of frustrating them yet once more appealed to Myles. And coming through on his promise to Special

Agent Bernie Murphy to "get out of this one" would be like a walk-off home run in the World Series. Gloating would be nearly impossible to resist. "Okay dad," Myles said. "Tell John to come visit me." [12]

Regan wasted no time going to the Charles Street Jail to see Connor. For him, too, it was also an ideal situation. Recovering the Rembrandt painting would be both a major career coup for him and a massive win for the Massachusetts State Police. Interagency rivalries are very common, but few are more contentious than that which exists between elements of the FBI and the Massachusetts State Police. Members of the latter often view those of the former as receiving—if not blatantly claiming—all the credit for work that they've shared. To be fair, much of that is due to the public affairs apparatus that the FBI has had in place since the days of J. Edgar Hoover. The legendary director was known to put outlaws on his famous MOST WANTED list only after obtaining reliable information as to their whereabouts, thus guaranteeing a strong record of success. To be sure, there's a vast difference between the FBI's Washington careerists and line agents who spend decades working the streets in local offices across the nation. Nevertheless, headlines crediting the state cops with solving the FBI's case were the stuff from which law enforcement dreams—and careers—were made.

There was another incentive for John Regan that was less about his work than his heart. Regan genuinely cared about Joe Connor and his family. He had grown up in the Irish enclave of South Boston just like Joe, and both had climbed out of the lower class and earned, through hard work and integrity, the American Dream of middle-class homeownership in beautiful Milton. There is something to be said about this sort of bond between men, especially those from their generation, who never lost sight of from whence they came.

During their meeting, Regan was aware via Joe that Myles had taken the Rembrandt (though he truly had no idea that the idea had started with him). Nevertheless, Myles told him that he hadn't stolen it. There was no point in admitting to a crime or putting Regan in a position to have to lie for him. Besides, Regan wasn't there to determine who stole it, only to get it back. "I believe I know who has it and I can have someone I trust get their hands on it," Myles told the detective. "But that will come with a price." Regan expected this, of course—Myles wasn't in it for humanity's sake. "I don't want to spend the next ten years in a federal prison. Twomey is going to have to make a deal."

"Okay. He's probably going to want some proof of life that the painting is out there before any deals are cut," Regan advised.

"I know," Myles told him. "Let me see what I can do."[13]

Regan left the meeting confident that they were on their way to a recovery. That is, if Assistant United States Attorney David Twomey was willing and able to cut a deal with Myles Connor's attorney. What Myles had going for him is that the US Attorney's Office craved the good press associated with recovering the Rembrandt. What's more, the US attorneys throughout the country are political appointees, nominated by the president of the United States and confirmed by the Senate. The man occupying the office for the District of Massachusetts was James Gabriel, himself a political creature. He had been active in Republican politics in his hometown of Cambridge, Massachusetts, before serving under Republican state attorneys general, eventually becoming an assistant US attorney. In that role, he had been involved in the surrender of Daniel Ellsberg, the former Pentagon researcher who had provided *The New York Times* with the Pentagon Papers. In 1971 President Richard Nixon made Gabriel his US attorney for Massachusetts.

The politically astute Gabriel understood the importance of currying favor with the influential Board of Trustees at the Museum of Fine Arts, Boston, a group eager to see the Rembrandt affair righted. Surely, they'd be grateful if his office could pull it off. Conversely, it wouldn't serve

Gabriel well if the Rembrandt was not recovered because Twomey ruined a deal squabbling over the number of years by which some miscreant's sentence would be reduced. He had little to worry about in that regard. His young prosecutor was very much on the side of making a deal.

For the federal prosecutors, it would be a win-win situation, just like it was for the Massachusetts State Police. The painting gets returned and Myles Connor still goes to prison. The office's sky-high conviction rate stays intact. So what if Myles served a very short sentence? The public would be fine with it all. And the FBI would be left out of the equation—something that even their compatriots in the US Department of Justice didn't mind at all.

Agent Murphy argued vehemently against a deal. "I had no interest in having another Rembrandt. I mean, God love him and it's nice for people who like that, but to me, trading Myles for a Rembrandt didn't make any sense. I was unalterably opposed to it. I was overridden ultimately because it was a Rembrandt, because it was the Boston Museum of Fine Arts, because the state police wanted to do it, the US Attorney's Office wanted to do it. I was opposed to it, and I fought it about as hard as I could. I had no interest in making that bargain," he later said.[14]

Over the course of about eight weeks, Leppo and Twomey, with Gabriel's participation, worked together to drum out a deal that worked for both sides. Things shifted into sixth gear when Connor arranged with Lenny Biondi, in whose house the painting was hidden, for a photo of the back of the Rembrandt to be delivered to Leppo. He showed it to Twomey as proof that his client could truly make the masterpiece materialize. The image showing the back of a painting with a newspaper was a most convincing identifier. This was the age of the instant photograph—there were no high-definition cameras available to the common person. A blurry Polaroid picture of the front of a painting that might have been taken in the past or doctored based on some publicly available copy might lead nervous experts to say it couldn't be ruled out. But the back, or verso, of a painting holds information that only the possessor of the work could describe or photograph, and it is almost impossible to fake. A thief would have to know exactly what the back of a painting looked like, including what labels and markings might—or might not—be there. Not even a curator could perfectly describe this without the painting right before them. There could be no doubt: Myles Connor could produce the painting. A deal was to be made.

Myles met with Leppo, who explained the agreement that he and Twomey had finally crafted. Leppo could get the feds to reduce the ten-year sentence to four years. On top of that, he was able to get the federal sentence to run concurrently with the state parole violation sentence. It was a deal too good to pass up, and Myles jumped at it. He understood that between the Wyeths and the parole violation, he was looking at too much prison time to walk away from the whole affair a completely free man. As a bonus, the feds were willing to agree to allow him to serve his time in a Massachusetts state prison instead of some far-off federal facility, with parole on the first possible date and release to a pre-release center, or "halfway house," before that.[15] Myles told Leppo that he accepted the deal. Now all he had to do was see to it that the painting made it safely out from under the bed where it was hidden and into the waiting arms of Major Regan and AUSA Twomey.

This was no small feat, and Myles understood this. Fortunately for him, there was one man above all others in whom he could place his trust to make sure nothing—not greed, not disloyalty—would spoil the deal. And that man was, at that very moment, planning to visit him at the Charles Street Jail.

CHAPTER 13

HIGH FIDELITY

Knowing he could no longer simply brush aside the nuisance calls, visits from the feds, and, most ominous of all, the Mafia, Al Dotoli decided to see Myles Connor at the Charles Street Jail before the sound of Rudy Guarino's engine was even out of earshot. It was far better to be in the cops' spotlight than Raymond L. S. Patriarca's. The infamous Mob boss had been paroled earlier in 1975 and wasted no time looking for ways to earn. In August, he even commissioned the massive Bonded Vault heist in Rhode Island in which seven men stole an estimated $30 million from safe deposit boxes there, including many belonging to members of his own criminal organization. Simply for giving the nod, Patriarca received two shares of $64,000 from the score.

The FBI office in Providence, Rhode Island, was receiving word that his associates throughout the area were using his name to earn. Patriarca told the feds, "I cannot prevent these people from using my name, but I am not breaking any laws."[1] The Bureau knew better. No one who valued staying above ground dared drop Patriarca's name without permission, including Rudy Guarino.

Fully aware of how the Mafia operated, Al wasn't leaving anything to chance. "It got dangerous," he said.[2] Just as he had been when Myles was on the run in Maine, and like he was when the antiques from the Forbes House Museum had to be moved, Al would have to be part of the solution to a problem Myles had caused. Fortunately, unbeknownst to Al, the cagey Connor was also working on a plan to bring the matter to a close by arranging for the return of the painting as negotiated by his attorney Marty Leppo and the federal prosecutor David Twomey. His attorney arranged a meeting between Connor and Dotoli at the jail.

In typical Myles Connor fashion, he had somehow finagled a private office for the pair to strategize. Dotoli explained the visits that he had received over the previous weeks. He relayed that FBI Special Agent Bernie Murphy mentioned the stolen painting, and Al, who had developed an amicable relationship with Murphy, posited that perhaps he could work through him and the FBI to return the painting. That idea was met with a quick and definitive "no" from Myles. Then Al pivoted to the Rudy Guarino overture. Myles was amused by the $60,000 offer. When asked if he was worried when he learned the Patriarca crime family was interested in his stolen painting, Myles just laughed loudly and joked, "Why would I be? That was Al's problem!"[3] In fact, while Myles didn't fear the Mafia, he didn't want his best friend troubled. Al made it clear to him that the painting had to be returned. "Once that thing is gone," he reasoned, "I'm off the hook."[4]

Myles was in complete agreement. The only reason he had taken it in the first place was to negotiate a softer sentence for himself. Putting his best friend in peril was never part of the equation. Though they were in a private room alone, Dotoli leaned into Connor and asked in a hushed voice, "What do we have to do to give this thing back?"[5]

Myles, ever relaxed, started by assuring him something was already in the works. "It's being addressed right now. Somebody is going to be in touch [with you] soon." For Al, that was good news. But it also told him that he would be part of the plan before he had even volunteered. "There was no question I was going to be involved," Al said, aware that for a matter this important, this big, Myles would turn to him. "I chose you as the one who should return the Rembrandt," he said, "primarily because you were the one person . . . whom I could trust, without question, and implicitly, to handle such an operation."[6] But just what did that involvement entail? "Did he want someone to hide it in the speakers so someone could sneak it out at a concert? Did he want to put it on my truck?" With Myles Connor, anything and everything was on the table. Myles explained his plan. Al would take the lead in the return. The Massachusetts State Police, in the person of Major John Regan, and the US Department of Justice, represented by Assistant United States Attorney David Twomey, would be on the receiving end of the transaction. There would be no FBI, no Boston Police Department. Connor didn't know Twomey, but he was the only option to avoid the involvement of men from agencies who historically had a bloodlust for him.

The difference in the strategies they had dreamt up showed the disparity in the mentality of the two men. Dotoli's idea for the return of the Rembrandt would be more John le Carré than Ian Fleming—thoughtful, strategic, methodical. Myles's plan, of course, was more sensational. He told Al to seek out the loudest fireworks he could find so that when he handed off the painting, they could be thrown from his car to give the impression of machine gun fire. Al, who is far more pragmatic than Myles, stopped him right there. He looked at him for two beats from across a small table. Then he deadpanned, "Are you out of your fucking mind?" He told his friend, "I'll tell you one thing. I'll get this thing back, but we're doing this my way."

"Okay Alfred," Connor said with a chuckle. "Next time I call you, I'm going to ask you to go see my pal," directing Al to go to the Sands Café in Dorchester where he would receive a letter with advice for the return of the painting from a man with the curious moniker "White Cliff." Giving Al the document in the jail was too risky, thus the need for such a stealthy delivery.

Despite Myles Connor's theatrics, Al Dotoli was pleased. The twenty-eight-year-old thought the whole operation was "pretty fucking cool." He could right a wrong and help his friend out doing it. "To me it was all good. Myles would get out of jail, the MFA would have their painting, and the police would get their notoriety. And all these goddamned fools who were chasing me around, showing me money . . . wouldn't do that anymore because there was nothing to look for."[7]

Eager to get down to it, Al sat in his office and put his mind to work crafting a return plan. Where Myles was adventurous and daring, Al was tactical and precise. Throughout his career, his ability to handle a dizzying array of logistics to make a stadium concert happen exemplified his capacity for the executive functioning that he would employ in this endeavor. Perhaps that's why he excelled in business while Connor's forte was crime. Though he didn't yet know who had the painting, that information was forthcoming, and he knew Myles was handling it. The fact that whoever was holding onto the Rembrandt hadn't cashed it in was proof the mystery man could be trusted.

Drawing on his experience maximizing press attention for a big show, Al decided that it would be of the utmost importance that the recovery happen on a Saturday to ensure it would be a front-page headline in *The Boston Sunday Globe*, thus garnering maximum attention. In other words, everyone would know it was pointless to bother Al Dotoli about the painting once the world knew that the feds and the MFA had it back.

In late December 1975, while most of his hard-partying friends were getting ready to rock in the New Year, Al Dotoli was busily making plans of a different sort to ring in the bicentennial. To that end, as his closest friend recommended, he visited a bar called the Sands Café. So, he made the drive from his newly purchased home on Myrtle Street in Quincy along the Southeast Expressway to the tough yet historic Dorchester section of Boston. It was located not far from where George Washington had fortified the city and ended the British siege. Dotoli was familiar with the Sands Café; a friend owned the Lucky Strike Bowling Alley next door and he had visited the place often for a beer or two with friends.

Al took a seat at the bar. It was the early afternoon, but the Sands Café was the sort of place that was perpetually dark, and he disappeared into the scenery as he took the last barstool on the right. He ordered a beer and, as Myles had suggested, he asked the bartender a scripted question: "Hey, by the way, is White Cliff here?"

"Oh, yeah, he'll be around," the bartender nonchalantly assured him as he walked away, leaving his only customer alone to drink his beer. When Al finished his lager, the bartender returned. He didn't ask if there would be another round. "That'll be a buck," he said, casually.

Al placed a five-dollar bill on the bar. With his change the bartender slid a blank white sealed envelope across the bar. Al left the change and grabbed the envelope. He waited until he got into his car to examine its contents and found carefully composed instructions written in neat, organized cursive. As expected, it had nothing to do with celebrating New Year's Eve. Instead, Myles's missive explicitly spelled out key reminders when conducting the elaborate return. Not only would Al have one of the most valuable Dutch Master paintings in the world in his hands, so too would be holding Myles's future.

Though the operation was fraught with the risk of arrest and danger, the letter read like a memorandum prepared by a manager to an employee. It was addressed to "Kevin," which would be Al's code name for the operation, and consisted of five enumerated directives. The first addressed confidentiality. Myles knew Al intended to enlist the help of his close friends, Bobby Gioiosa and his brothers, and he reminded him to direct them not to speak of this operation even after it was completed.

Second, Connor assured Dotoli that the person holding the painting, from whom he would take delivery of the Rembrandt, was a man he completely trusted. He described this person, code-named "Charlie" and not yet identified to Dotoli, as "very bright and capable and I hope that he will go along with the plan and be included in the delivery; take effort to explain why it has to be done this way and explain that he has a guarantee of immunity should anything unforeseen develop."

Third, Connor reminded Dotoli to be sure that his "backup" (in this case, Bobby Gioiosa—code name "B"), would not act in any way that might raise the antenna of local police. Moreover, he urged Dotoli not to leave the Rembrandt unattended in a vehicle, lest it be stolen by car thieves. Of course, Dotoli knew this and would never make such an error, but one can sense from the memo, and this point in particular, a bit of worry. However, it was clearly rooted in the complexity and criticality of a process in which Myles could not take part. His future was at stake, and being confined in a jail while others acted was a difficult position, even if it was his oldest and most trusted friend at the helm of the operation.

The penultimate point warned Al that Agent Murphy could very well be lurking about, hoping to steal credit for the recovery. Myles was dead set against any sort of involvement on the part of the FBI. Similarly, Al should be on the lookout for a bothersome private investigator. "There is one very obstinate insurance investigator who has been trying to get involved and he has made several mob contacts," he warned. "Be very careful about being followed and also make sure your backup man is armed and with you at any time you're near your home and business."

The fifth point was portentous: "If anyone tries to interfere (or does interfere) or foils this in any way, I don't want the backup to hesitate, he is to shoot." Al knew beyond a doubt that this directive was as sincere as it was absolute, and he also understood the intent. He understood that there existed a possibility that he was being followed by dangerous people looking to take the painting from him. If so, they wouldn't simply politely ask for it.

Connor ended the document with a postscript. "Thank you. I appreciate your part and B's (a reference to Bobby Gioiosa) part to the extreme in gratitude and ultimately will repay the kindness." Then, another. "Don't remove the painting from the frame."[8]

Both afterthoughts were superfluous. For one, not for a second did Al expect any sort of remuneration or favor for his help. He wanted only to get his best friend out of a serious predicament and to get back to his business without the Mafia pulling into his driveway ever again. As to the frame, Al didn't even want to look at the painting. He didn't care what it looked like, was indifferent to Rembrandt, and didn't want to handle the artwork one second longer than required to get it back to the authorities without getting robbed or arrested. Removing the frame was not something he considered.

Still, one can understand Connor's consternation regarding all of these matters. He was relying on his most law-abiding friend to play the lead role in a play that was as dangerous as it was audacious. Despite his good character, Al never considered saying no. This was Myles who needed him. No further discussion was necessary. But the stakes couldn't be higher, for art history or Myles Connor's life.

On New Year's Eve, Al told his new girlfriend, a flaxen-haired beauty from North Quincy named Rena Worth, that he wouldn't be available to attend any of the evening's parties that his rock-and-roll friends would be throwing. She understood. Perceptive beyond her years, she could tell something unspoken was in the works and knew how close he was to Myles. In fact, she met Al while attending one of Myles's shows at the Beachcomber. Soon enough, they were a couple. Dotoli pulled out the big guns to win over her parents, taking them to see and meet Dionne Warwick in concert. His thriving career, combined with his friendly countenance, made him an easy sell to the Worth family.

In his own charming, gentle way, Al promised Rena he'd make it up to her. Instead of holding her in his arms as the countdown to the bicentennial year began, he was making plans to hold another blond woman—one 340 years old and clad in a gold-trimmed cloak. Utilizing a stopwatch, he repeatedly drove his shiny new Chrysler Cordoba from his home in Quincy through Randolph, tracing the route he would use during the operation.

Al's plan was complex, consisting of multiple carefully considered steps, each essential to the safe return of the art while also assuring his own safety. This was nothing new to him. Putting on a major concert is intensely complicated work, filled with endless logistics, difficult personalities, and the need to plan for the unexpected. He had long since become a master of managing many moving parts on a tight and immoveable deadline. He was also comfortable being the man behind the scenes rather than the star of the show. In many ways, he was the perfect man for this job.

Despite their wild reputation, the Gioiosa brothers were essential to the plan. They could be trusted to provide protection if the plan went awry or if there was a double-cross. They eagerly accepted their role. The brothers were the sorts who wouldn't need fireworks to imitate the sound of automatic weapons—they'd bring the real thing. These were the men who Myles insisted in his letter should start shooting should anyone try to intervene. They wouldn't have to be told twice.

Next came identifying a suitable location. Al chose the Holiday Inn in Randolph, a suburb south of Boston that he knew well. He didn't know at the time that "Charlie" lived in the town, nor that the painting was stored there. It was a serendipitous benefit. Al did know that the hotel's two ground-level access points would ensure that he could enter and exit covertly through either rear or side doors. He directed Bobby Gioiosa to rent him two adjoining rooms with a connecting door using a false name. They did so in cash—an acceptable form of payment at the time. One of the rooms would serve as his base of operations, the other as an escape route should there be a raid by either the good guys—or the bad.

Another advantage that the Holiday Inn afforded Dotoli was easy access to two means of communication that could not be traced back to him. In addition to the phones in the rooms, there was a working pay phone—the preferred mode of covert communication in the pre-burner cellphone days—next to the hotel parking lot.

Finally, Al needed to arrange a place to contact Regan and his partner, but not on their own turf where he could be set up. His first thought was Peter's Place, a popular nightclub in Randolph. He visited it and sat alone at the bar while loud partying was taking place upstairs at a discotheque. He jotted down the number to the house phone and noticed that Peter's Place had multiple lines that ensured callers never found the line busy. He wouldn't have trouble getting through. It was the perfect spot for him to send the police to await his further instructions.

On Friday, January 2, 1975, confident in the plan he had crafted, Al decided all systems were go. He called John Regan at his home and said, "It's Kevin. It's on." Regan, who had been provided with the code name in advance, understood and agreed to Al's direction to wait by his phone. Later, just before dusk, Al called him again and asked, "Who owns that '69 black Buick in your driveway?"

"My wife," the trooper answered.

"Well, you need to come in that car and bring two sets of keys."

Regan resisted. "Oh no, I can't do that," he said. "That's my wife's car."

"Then it's off," came Dotoli's reply.

"Oh," Regan said. "Well, then I *can* do that."

Al was adamant that the plan be followed to the letter. Because he intended to briefly get in the back seat of the cop's car, he wasn't willing to risk trapping himself in a police vehicle from which he couldn't escape. For all he knew, it could be rigged with some sort of device to identify him. By forcing Regan to use a personal car—especially one belonging to the detective's wife—so late in the game, he left no time for police to booby-trap it, giving Al the surety he needed. Al directed Regan to go to Copeland Farms, the bottling plant where Myles worked as a teen, and wait by the pay phone.

Compulsively committed to self-preservation, Al's next step was a ruse to determine if he was being followed. He sent his backup to a nearby parking lot, where they sat in a van armed for battle. He took a framed mirror roughly the size of an average painting from a wall in his home and wrapped it in a sleeping bag. It was a perfect decoy. He slowly walked outside with the bundle, making no effort to conceal it so that anyone who might be doing reconnaissance couldn't miss him. He walked across a marsh to the parking lot to meet Bobby Gioiosa.

As he approached the appointed parking lot, he could see Gioiosa's van and a car they had rented at his request waiting alongside it. Al put the mirror into the rented Plymouth Fury.

Al directed Bobby to follow him. He stopped at a convenience store pay phone and called Regan and told him to come to that very pay phone. Al drove off quickly, leaving the spot before Regan could arrive.

Then, with Gioiosa still trailing him, Al drove to a ballpark just behind the Holiday Inn. The drive, though short, was fraught with anxiety. He kept a constant eye on the rearview mirror to see if he was being followed. When they arrived at the ballpark, it was completely empty save for their two vehicles. Al hid the swaddled mirror between two trash barrels to see if anyone went to grab it. If he did have a tail, they'd surely think the cheap mirror was the Rembrandt, and Al would soon either be ambushed by thieves or, if there was a sting, arrested by the police.

Bobby waited ten minutes—no one took the mirror, so he retrieved it and departed. Just as he had hoped, nothing happened. There were no sirens, no flashing lights. No thugs pulled up on them. No guns were drawn. Al was comfortable that the whole operation just might work.

Now it was time for Al to contact the person holding the painting, the man Myles had code-named "Charlie." Al called him from the hotel room using a phone number Myles had provided. He told "Charlie" exactly where to meet him—the decidedly unglamorous parking lot at Mister Donut in Randolph.

Lenny Biondi, aka "Charlie," was another longtime friend of Myles's, and though Al knew Lenny, he didn't know it was he who was holding the Rembrandt. All he knew—all he wanted to know—was that someone code-named Charlie would deliver the painting to him when directed. Al phoned Charlie his location and informed him that upon arrival, he would flash his headlights three times so that Charlie would know it was him. Biondi didn't reveal his identity to Al during the call, and his terse responses didn't lend themselves to voice recognition. Biondi arrived on cue, acknowledged the flashing headlights, and pulled behind Al's car, tailing him tightly through the streets of Randolph.

Meanwhile, John Regan, who was accompanied by David Twomey, was waiting at the bar at Peter's Place as directed earlier by Al Dotoli. Al phoned the bar, and the call was quickly answered. The bartender gave the handset to Regan, and Al and told him they were now to get into the detective's wife's car, which they dutifully did. Al approached their Buick clad in deep blue denim pants and matching jacket, concealing his identity with a dark green ski mask. The dramatic irony of the cloak-and-dagger operation still excites him. While Myles had used a disguise to remove the painting, Al was disguised to give it back. "I wasn't stealing anything, I was returning something!" he would recall with an incredulous smile, surprising himself at times with what he had done.[9]

Major Regan rolled down the window and, using scripted words to confirm that the handoff was still a go, said from the front seat of the car, "It's a beautiful night out." Al replied, "Yes, there's a lot of stars." These were the magic words. Dotoli climbed into the back seat, demanded identification (which both Regan and Twomey readily flashed), asked if they were armed (both lied and said no). He told them to get out of the car and go back into the bar and leave one set of keys with him. They quickly did exactly as they were told. Al climbed into the driver's seat and sped off in their car with Biondi still following him to the Holiday Inn, which was only about three hundred feet away. Once there, Biondi got out, took the Rembrandt out of his trunk, and gingerly placed it into Regan's car, which Al was driving.

Coincidentally, like the decoy mirror, the actual painting was also wrapped in a sleeping bag.

Al was pleased and relieved to see that "Charlie" was Lenny Biondi. He knew him to be a serious and trustworthy individual. He needn't worry that his identity as the return agent in this affair would be revealed. Like Al, Lenny was a legitimate businessman—he owned and operated a successful gas station and garage in Quincy. He was well-liked and respected and, also like Al, would be happy to see the whole matter with the painting come to a beneficial conclusion for all involved.

Dotoli carefully pulled back the sleeping bag. It was facedown. He confirmed that he had the actual painting by comparing it to a Polaroid image of the back of the wooden panel. Incredibly, he never bothered to turn it over to cast his eyes upon the face of the painting, missing out on a moment of artistic intimacy few could ever know. But Al wasn't there for aesthetics. "I didn't want to see this thing for a second more than I had to," he said.[10] Curiosity aside, there was no need to flip the painting over. It was a match. He threw the second set of keys into the trunk of the detective's wife's car and slammed it shut. Then he went back up to his hotel room. He called the bar and again summoned Regan and Twomey. Over the phone, Dotoli could hear them falling over each other to respond to the bartender's beckoning. He instructed them to run—not walk—to their car and to look in the trunk. "If what you want is there," he said to them, "turn and face the Holiday Inn, open your coats, and put your hands on your waist. If it's not what you want, close the trunk and go back to the bar." When they opened their trench coats, Al saw that they were indeed carrying weapons.

Al watched from a window and saw them confirm that the true Rembrandt was indeed in the trunk. They got into the car and left with the painting. The operation was complete. Al's plan worked without as much as a single pentimento.

Al Dotoli immediately left Boston on a business trip, traveling by air to the Waldorf in New York City. Relieved that the whole episode was in his rearview mirror, he went to Christos, the famous haunt of East Coast celebrities of the day. Because of its proximity to his New York office, Al was a regular there. The maître d' greeted him warmly.

"Hi, Mr. Dotoli, how are you tonight?"

Al smiled and crooned, "I'm just fuckin' *marvelous*."

The next morning, after a few meetings, he checked the New York papers and saw that the recovery of the Rembrandt was on the second page of the city's tabloids. This boded well for *The Boston Sunday Globe*. He called Rena to check in. After a bit of small talk, she coyly said to Al, "My dad was reading the paper this morning. He put it down and looked at me for a second and said, 'Your boyfriend was very active last night.'"

"Was I active on the front page?" he asked with a guilty laugh. Rena confirmed that he was. Apparently, however, neither Rena nor her father disapproved. She and Al went on to marry and spend the rest of their lives together.

Now all the area wise guys, investigators, and fortune seekers—from Boston to Providence—would know that the painting was no longer available. The calls would stop, and so would pressure from the Mafia. Just as he planned, *The Boston Globe* had splashed the headline PRICELESS REMBRANDT RECOVERED in bold and above the fold, complete with a large photo of the MFA's acting director, Jan Fontein, with the painting. Al Dotoli's plan had gone as smoothly as any Frank Sinatra show. Myles Connor described Al's performance as "a work of art."[11] He had come through for Myles once again.

CHAPTER 14

PRESERVATION

After the painting was placed in the trunk of his wife's car, Major John Regan pulled out of the nightclub's parking lot ever so gingerly. Regan and Assistant United States Attorney David Twomey nervously drove back to Boston, visited by an irrational fear that the worst of luck would strike and they'd be rear-ended on the highway, the painting reduced to mahogany splinters. Precious artwork is usually packed in a bespoke cushioned crate and transported in a box truck, strapped snugly into the cargo compartment to prevent it from being tossed around or even shaken. But on this night, as the sky fell dark, Rembrandt's *Portrait of Elsbeth van Rijn* was wrapped in a sleeping bag in the trunk of a six-year-old Buick sedan.

Rather than delivering the painting to the Museum of Fine Arts, Boston, they drove directly to US Attorney James Gabriel's office, located in the Federal Building in Post Office Square. They arrived at 6:30 P.M., elated by what they had accomplished. Still, the Rembrandt was evidence—a highly valuable piece of property taken in the commission of a crime—and had to be handled as such until officially turned over the MFA. The authorities also wanted to be sure that they controlled the messaging, and there was no better place from which to do that than Gabriel's office. As the top law enforcement official in the state, it was important for the public to know that the recovery had been orchestrated by his office and the Massachusetts State Police.

The day before, when Regan and Twomey informed their superiors that the transfer was to take place, plans to authenticate the painting were formed. Upon the painting's arrival at Gabriel's office, Lucretia Hoover Giese, a young assistant curator in the MFA's Department of Paintings, examined the panel and confirmed its authenticity.[1] It wasn't a difficult task. Pigment analysis wasn't necessary. Everyone involved in the recovery knew that it came from the correct party. The nineteenth-century frame, a work of art itself, was damaged exactly in the manner the remnants left when Myles Connor became momentarily snagged at the turnstile indicated. Giese compared known information about the back of the painting with the work before her. It was a perfect match in every respect, including its dimensions. Later, the delay in announcing the recovery until the morning was attributed to time spent authenticating the painting. But in truth, the assessment took very little time or effort, like a parent confirming the identity of a child who had gone missing. A person of Giese's experience would recognize the quality of the painting upon first glance. The rest was just details.

On Saturday morning, January 3, 1975, US Attorney James Gabriel, flanked by acting MFA director Jan Fontein and law enforcement authorities, held a press conference in his office and announced that the stolen Rembrandt painting had been recovered the prior evening in a transfer made in a restaurant parking lot in Boston. It had spent the night in a vault at Gabriel's office and protected by an armed deputy US marshal. Of course, the actual handoff took place at Peter's Place in Randolph, about fifteen miles south of the city, but there was no point in exposing the nightclub to any suspicion or inference of criminal involvement. Fabricating the location also prevented any speculation about who might have been involved. Though no one outside of Al Dotoli and Myles Connor knew that Lenny Biondi had participated, many knew that he and Myles were good friends. Had it been announced that the recovery took place in Randolph—Biondi's hometown—speculation about him would have begun immediately. Without even knowing it, the authorities had protected his identity. Until the publication of this book, it has never been revealed.[*]

Gabriel told the media that details of the recovery could not be disclosed because "there are some people involved here who are fearing for their safety in the return of this picture."[2] There was a measure of truth to that, of course, though neither he nor the pair who were given the painting knew that it was Al Dotoli who placed it in their trunk. The US attorney told a carefully crafted version of the circumstances surrounding the return of the painting.

"A public-spirited citizen who desired to see the portrait returned came forward with some information, which eventually led to the final negotiations and recovery," Gabriel said, using an interestingly flattering term to describe the unnamed Connor. This led to "several months of delicate negotiations." He reiterated that "certain individuals who had knowledge of [the painting's] whereabouts became concerned for their safety and the safety of their families."[3] This tortured version of the fact would be the theme—the painting was returned out of fear, not stolen and returned to be used as a bargaining chip.

Then Gabriel went into full spin mode. With Major John Regan and his boss, Public Safety Director John Kehoe, to one side and Twomey and Fontein to the other, Gabriel said, "No deals of any kind have been made with any federal prisoner."[4]

---

[*] Valenti "Lenny" Biondi passed away in December 2024.

The only way in which this could be stated was that, throughout the negotiations and at that moment, Myles Connor was being held at the Charles Street Jail, a state institution belonging to Suffolk County, Massachusetts. With the painting returned as promised, Myles would not be serving his time as a federal prisoner. The deal that Marty Leppo had cut with Twomey allowed Connor to serve his sentence in a state penitentiary. Gabriel employed the most lawyerly parsing of this fact, allowing him to make the statement and stick to it. Of course, this would aggravate the situation with the FBI yet further. Myles had been captured thanks to their work, led by Special Agent Bernie Murphy, and now they were not only cut out of the glory of recovering one of the world's great masterpieces, but their prisoner was also being tacitly considered a guest of the Commonwealth. In addition, Gabriel, Kehoe, and Regan all made it plain to the media that no money had changed hands. This much was true. But, when pressed, they added that "no consideration of any kind was paid for its recovery."[5] *The Boston Sunday Herald Advertiser* reported that it had "learned that Myles J. Connor, Jr., of Milton, currently in Charles Street Jail on federal charges in connection with another art theft, may have been instrumental in the safe return of the Rembrandt."[6]

This was not the message that the authorities wanted conveyed. Instead, they attributed the success to a secret three-month investigation conducted by Regan with Twomey and Boston Police Department detective Richard Hudson.[7] It's unclear why Detective Hudson received credit. Perhaps it was a hat tip to the Boston Police Department, the responding agency for the heist. The FBI snub aside, law enforcement agencies are loath to offend another department, especially one with which they will likely work again. Connor, of course, had no interest in seeing the Boston Police Department receive any credit in the recovery, but this was a minor matter, and he wasn't about to quibble over it.

What was key was that the work had been returned, the deal sealed, and a long federal sentence averted. Clearly, though, consideration was paid for the recovery of the painting. To say otherwise was plainly false, and the claim couldn't be attributed to legalese or semantics of any kind.

Gabriel and the Massachusetts State Police had good reasons to hide Connor's involvement. First, and most important, any indication from the government that a masterpiece was not just ransomed but used to drastically reduce a major prison sentence would set a precedent that no one wanted to see established. Ransoms are an anathema in the art world, as they encourage further theft. With masterpieces difficult to fence, the Connor deal would create a new market for stolen art in the form of prosecutors. Any active criminal would be tempted to steal and hold onto valuable cultural objects as chits should they be nabbed down the road. Gabriel had little choice but to extinguish talk of a so-called Get out of Jail Free card.

There was also the question of Al Dotoli and Myles Connor's safety. From the government's perspective, the identities of those who help the police essentially undo a crime must be kept sacrosanct. It's a hard-and-fast rule of law enforcement. Though neither Myles nor Al had any concern about their safety, both the feds and the state police had to maintain this stance. Any betrayal of their identities could have a chilling effect on future cooperators. Information from the criminal element is key, and it would be unwise to appear careless with such sources. This kept Gabriel tight-lipped about details. "People's lives have been threatened and there are certain questions we cannot answer," he repeated. "We will have to be deliberately evasive on certain questions that may be asked." Gabriel did explain that "underworld elements" had wanted to get their hands on the painting when rumors of a $300,000 reward were spread.[8] Those rumors had begun with the private investigator and attorney from California who crossed the country and swooped into town with questionable claims to be the sole representatives of the painting's owners. Fortunately, their reckless fortune hunting did not interfere with the return.

Gabriel and Regan gave the press a general sense of the recovery operation. They intertwined truths (the painting was wrapped in a sleeping bag and placed in their trunk) with inconsequential falsehoods (the return took place in a parking lot on the Southeast Expressway). But they said nothing to implicate Connor. They couldn't implicate Dotoli or Biondi even if they had wished to do so, as their identities were unknown to them. Regan described the ski-masked man accurately. He was "intelligent, real cool and a professional type," the seasoned detective said, demonstrating his keenly developed ability to assess his fellow man, especially under trying circumstances. He couldn't have described Al Dotoli better had he sat with him for an hour over beers.

The speculation about Myles's involvement from *The Boston Sunday Herald Advertiser* aside, it appears that all confidences were maintained. The misperception that the painting was returned simply out of fear of Mafia interest missed the bigger picture as to why the painting was stolen and what it elicited for its thief. One of the private investigators who involved themselves in the hunt for *Portrait of Elsbeth van Rijn* correctly told *The Boston Globe* that the potential reward lured in the interest of underworld figures. But this was common knowledge. He incorrectly stated that the person behind it all "just wanted to dump it."[9] In fact, nothing could be further from the truth. The painting was strategically managed currency created by Myles Connor and accepted by the US government.

More good news for the art world followed. With the Rembrandt returned, and certain there was no connection to the MFA robbery,

Gabriel was free to announce that the Winslow Homer painting stolen from the Converse Art & Archives at Malden Public Library and the works taken from the Childs Gallery in 1975 had been recovered. The information had been held back to ensure there was no connection to the Rembrandt heist. Curiously, they did mention that ransoms had been paid to get those works back. They declined to state the amounts, likely for fear of inspiring more theft.[10]

MFA acting director Jan Fontein was understandably ecstatic. "We're very grateful and happy that such an important work of art has been returned in fairly good condition," he said. The qualified statement was due not only to the damaged frame but also a result of three "rubs" found on the surface of the varnish that protected the work. The rubs were described as appearing on the girl's left cheek, near the right side of her jaw, and on the left of her chest. But these were purely superficial. "At first glance there appears to be no serious damage to the painting," Fontein said. "Elizabeth Jones of our research department will give it a thorough examination tomorrow."[11]

Despite the minor marring of the surface, Fontein was expansive in his feelings about seeing the painting returned. "The whole art world will be pleased that such a beautiful painting by an important artist has been recovered." Smiling, he added, "Being a Dutchman myself, I am little partial to Mr. Rembrandt."[12]

At the conclusion of the press conference, with smiles all around, *Portrait of Elsbeth van Rijn* was loaded into a vehicle and transported back to the Museum of Fine Arts, Boston, accompanied by a detail of state troopers. It was the sort of escort typically reserved for important dignitaries. And that was perfectly appropriate.

Once back in the Museum of Fine Arts, Boston, the Rembrandt would receive more special treatment. Though Fontein had described the three superficial abrasions on the painting, a complete examination to determine any other changes in the panel's condition over the eight months it spent outside of the institution was required. For this, *Portrait of Elsbeth van Rijn* was placed in the care of Elizabeth "Betty" Jones, the MFA's paintings conservator.

Considered to be one of the top painting restorers in the world, Jones arrived at the MFA just a year earlier after spending twenty-two years as the chief conservator at Harvard University's Fogg Museum. A graduate of Vassar College, she worked as a draftsperson for Pratt & Whitney during World War II. After the war, she studied restoration techniques at the Fogg before she took a job directing a restoration project at Independence Hall in Philadelphia for the National Park Service. She conserved paintings of the Founding Fathers there before returning to the Fogg in 1952.[13]

Jones went immediately to work on the Rembrandt panel, studying the paint surface and the layers beneath it. She used a binocular microscope, X-ray technology, and even infrared light to identify any damage to the painting. "We went over the portrait centimeter by centimeter," Jones said.[14] She was relieved to find it relatively unscathed despite its recent plight. The work was painstaking and took many hours to complete. But Jones was no stranger to patient, methodical approaches to conservation. In 1966 she was asked by the Committee to Rescue Italian Art to travel to Venice after a tidal wave wreaked havoc on the historic city. She analyzed two sides of the famous St. Mark's Basilica, taking photographs of the Byzantine church stone by stone with a telescopic lens. To her, it was a matter of duty. "Somebody had to do it," she reasoned. "They needed help." While at the Fogg, Jones restored a Renoir drawing suffering from the paper's own acidity. "We had to shear off the second layer [of paper] with scalpels, and remount the drawing on silk. It took three months, and we held our breath while we were doing it."[15]

Jones's next several weeks would be spent in the conservation lab performing a careful restoration of *Portrait of Elsbeth van Rijn*. She found that "there are two dents in the picture, but you can see them only through the microscope. There are also two smears in the varnish, but the paint was not harmed. We'll be able to revarnish it and smooth it out." The two dents were likely caused by the culprit holding the face side of the painting against his body and the buttons on his coat leaving impressions, according to Jan Fontein.[16] He and Jones agreed that the good condition of the painting was "a miracle."[17]

It's reasonable that Jones found the condition of the newly recovered painting to be miraculous. When precious art is stolen, those who work in museums—especially those whose job it is to care for art on a very granular level—tend to catastrophize, or at least prepare for the worst. Imaginations run wild about things like climate control, light exposure, water damage, and even just clumsy handling. They also fear that the work will be destroyed by its captors, as is believed was the case with a Rembrandt portrait of his wife, Saskia, stolen from Chilham Castle in England in 1938.[18] Fortunately, in the expert hands of conservators like Betty Jones, stolen paintings are almost always brought back to a condition suitable for display. It is in art conservation labs where the actual miracles often occur. Besides, Jones did not know—and could not know—that the painting had spent the previous eight months safely tucked under a bed, in ideal room temperature, and away from any light whatsoever. Nor that it was stored there by a true art lover.

The recovered and restored Rembrandt remained at the Museum of Fine Arts, Boston, for ten more years. Then, on December 10, 1986, twenty years after the Paine family loaned what had been called *Portrait of Elsbeth van Rijn* to the MFA, the painting was returned to the family, who decided to sell it at auction through Sotheby's London. The December sale was expected to be a big hit for collectors of Old Master paintings. Along with what was now titled *Portrait of a Girl Wearing a Gold-Trimmed Cloak* were two paintings by Frans Hals of an unidentified man and his wife. The latter two paintings were expected to bring in an estimated $2.8 million apiece, and the Rembrandt a bit less at an estimated $2.5 million. But, to the shock of the art world, neither of the Hals paintings met their reserve prices and were withdrawn from the auction. And when the gavel fell on the Rembrandt, the surprise at the final price was palpable: £7.26 million ($10.3 million)—more than four times Sotheby's estimate.

The esteemed auction house was elated. "It's an outstanding price," said their spokesperson. "We knew it was going to go high, but not that high."[19] Despite her happy tone, the spokesperson understated the news. The sale marked a new record for a Rembrandt painting, far outpacing the $2.3 million paid in 1961 by the Metropolitan Museum of Art in New York City for his *Aristotle with a Bust of Homer*. Four years later, his *Portrait of Titus* sold for only $2.2 million to Norton Simon, he of the later eponymous museum, at Christie's London.[20] The latest sale, however, removed any doubt about Rembrandt's popularity and any question as to whether the value of his works had peaked. Not only was this a record price for one of his paintings, but it was, according to Sotheby's, the third-highest price ever paid at auction for a painting up to this point. Only Andrea Mantegna's *Adoration of the Magi* ($11.7 million) and Édouard Manet's *La Rue Mosnier aux paveurs* ($11.1 million), both sold within the year before the Rembrandt, brought higher prices.[21]

The big art sale numbers—which also included millions of dollars paid in recent months for works by Piet Mondrian, Georges Braque, Pierre-Auguste Renoir, and others—led art market experts to speculate about the startling price boom. As usual, nearly every expert posited a different motive. One major art gallery owner attributed it to an increase in discretionary income. An editor at *Art Business News* reasoned that there was a greater awareness of art on the part of the public. One interesting factor might have been tax considerations. An increase in capital gains taxes scheduled for January 1987 pushed the Rembrandt sale up to December 1986.[22]

Clearly, Myles Connor had chosen well. Of the Rembrandts on display at the MFA in 1975, he stole what one expert described as among the most popular pieces at the museum. The record price matched the quality, it was reasoned.[23] But one part of the equation for the high price paid for the Rembrandt that went unmentioned was the new and noteworthy addition to its provenance. *Portrait of a Girl Wearing a Gold-Trimmed Cloak* would forever be the Rembrandt that was stolen from the Museum of Fine Arts, Boston, in 1975, and returned in a remarkably clandestine manner.

Consider the difference between a beautiful antique Ford Mustang and the 1968 Highland Green Ford Mustang GT 390 Fastback driven by Steve McQueen in the classic film *Bullitt*. The bragging rights equal dollar signs. One can almost hear a future owner of the Rembrandt boasting, "Yes, that's the one taken at gunpoint in Boston and used by a genius thief to lessen his prison sentence."

The unnamed buyer of the Rembrandt painting held it out of sight for nine years. No one knew who had it, and no one aside from that very private wealthy art lover, and perhaps their closest family and friends, was able to see it. Scott Schaefer, then the J. Paul Getty Museum's senior curator, who had long coveted the work for the Getty's collection, said, "No one, and I mean no one, knew who had acquired the picture."[24]

Then, in 2007, George Wachter at Sotheby's New York learned that Thomas S. Kaplan was buying Dutch masterworks for his collection. "I kind of realized this is a moment to try and get [the Rembrandt] back, and so we went to where it was, and we talked the owners into giving us an opportunity to sell it." The owners were interested but set very strict conditions for selling the painting. They wished to move very quickly, and they refused to allow their identity to be revealed. Further, if Wachter's buyer was interested, he would be allowed to have just one person view the work and give him advice. Kaplan agreed and asked fine art dealer Otto Naumann to have a look. "I'm glad he did," Naumann said.[25] When Naumann saw the painting, he was floored. Kaplan recalled receiving his call immediately after he viewed it. "Holy shit! That's incredible! That is one of the greatest Rembrandt pieces!"[26]

Still, Kaplan mulled it over. When his wife asked if he would buy it, he replied that the price tag was very high.

"Sweetheart, it's a masterpiece. Do it," she said.

A wise art collector, Kaplan took his wife's advice and purchased *Young Girl in a Gold-Trimmed Cloak* for an undisclosed price.[27]

When news of the sale reached Scott Schaefer at the Getty, he phoned Wachter at Sotheby's and asked why he didn't give the museum the first shot at the painting. Wachter told him that the institution would have taken longer to decide than the buyer was willing to wait. Whereas the Getty had internal bureaucracy with which to contend, Kaplan merely had to hear the opinions of his expert—and his wife—to make a major purchase.

In the end, however, the Getty made out quite well, thanks to Kaplan's magnanimity. The collector called Schaefer and asked, "How would you like to have it on a loan?" Schaefer was understandably thrilled. "You have to understand that this is the painting that I always wanted at the Getty." And so the painting resides in Los Angeles, California.[28]

Years later, Steve Gorski, who at twenty-one years old was sent by Myles Connor the evening before the heist to lift the Rembrandt off the wall to check for alarms, visited the Getty Museum, unaware that the painting was there on loan. He perused the masterpieces on the walls of the East Pavilion when he happened upon the face of the young woman he held in his hands nearly forty years earlier. He was shocked to see it, and, for the second time, stood transfixed by the beauty of the work. This time, he kept his hands to himself. Like Giacomo Medici, who would visit museums and pose with the antiquities he'd smuggled, Gorski posed for a photo standing with his kids by the Rembrandt.[29]

CHAPTER 15
TRIALS AND TRIBULATIONS

State and federal prosecutors kept their bargain and ensured that Myles Connor's demands were met. Instead of a fifteen-year stint in prison, he served only four. FBI Special Agent Bernie Murphy was none too pleased with the outcome and had vehemently opposed the idea only to be overruled. Murphy had good reason: not only was Connor a remarkably active criminal, but the bargain also inadvertently set an ugly precedent. Despite their efforts to keep these details from the public, so that exactly this situation would not happen, in the years since the heist there have been untold numbers of stolen paintings taken or held by criminals with the hope that they might later be used as Get out of Jail Free cards.

Al Dotoli doesn't recall Myles ever thanking him for the clandestine risks he took returning the Rembrandt in 1976. But he didn't mind. Myles didn't have to thank him. Helping a friend is as much a part of Al's makeup as is his love of the music business. Besides, Myles had already written, "Thank you. I appreciate your part to the extreme in gratitude" on the letter he had surreptitiously delivered to Al at the Sands Café. When it came to their unique and enigmatic friendship,

Myles knew he could thank Al in advance, because his pal always came through.

After serving his abbreviated prison term, Myles Connor was back onstage by 1978. An advertisement in *The Boston Globe* announced, HE'S TRULY BACK! and heralded three consecutive nights of shows at the popular Beachcomber nightclub in Quincy. Billed as "The Real President of Rock-n-Roll," Myles was now playing with guitar virtuoso Scott "The Cat" Anderson as his special guest.[1] Connor was again the club's biggest draw. Crowds packed into the Beachcomber for the high-energy shows featuring the famous ex-convict, standing shoulder to sweaty shoulder and loving every second of it.

Al Dotoli, ever indefatigable in his quest to launch his best friend into superstardom, again worked feverishly to resurrect Myles's music career. But, as Al would say, crime got in the way. The shootout with the police had long-ranging repercussions for Myles, as had his Harry Houdini–like ability to get out of big trouble and long sentences. During his bank robbery days, Myles estimates, "I probably robbed seventeen banks and the smallest [take] was $117,000. They prosecuted me for five different bank robberies. I did every single one and they acquitted me on every single one."[2] Much of this was the result of the legal acumen of his attorneys, especially veteran litigator and law professor Earle Cooley.

These victories, however, would have the undesired side effect of making Myles Connor one of the biggest criminal targets in the state. Some members of law enforcement would work to frame Connor for crimes he didn't commit—an odd fact considering the sheer volume of lawbreaking he did, in fact, pull off. According to Connor, he was implicated in "crimes I was accused of as payback, or vendettas, by immoral law enforcement individuals for wrongs they felt I'd done to them . . . by making them look foolish. The extremes they went to were extensive."[3]

Examining the most serious prosecutions Myles Connor faced and ultimately overcame, it's clear that there were indeed desperate acts to imprison him for major offenses that were far outside the bounds of anything he would have ever done. The first took place in 1967. Police and prosecutors in the area were understandably angered that he had shot a Massachusetts State Police officer. Before he was even released from the hospital for the injuries he had suffered in that skirmish, Connor was indicted on morals charges related to assaults on teenage girls who "positively identified" him during a hearing.[4] When he recovered and was shipped off to serve his sentence in a state penitentiary, an inmate at Bridgewater State Prison, Francis Hathaway Jr., admitted to a cellmate that he had been the one who raped the young girls. Hathaway, who was the same age and size as Connor and shared the same blazing red hair, signed affidavits admitting to the crimes and later confessed to a judge that he had committed the offenses.[5] Myles was exonerated for the crimes.

In 1974 Boston Police Department officer Donald Brown was shot and killed by thieves while escorting a Purity Supreme supermarket manager making a deposit. The trio that committed the crime was Ralph Petrozziello, Tommy Sperrazza, and Paul Cook. Because Petrozziello and Sperrazza were frequent collaborators with Connor in bank robberies, prosecutors seized the opportunity to implicate him in the murder by gaining the cooperation of the actual triggerman. Sperrazza, who was by any measure a bloodthirsty criminal, admitted he shot Officer Brown from the back seat of a vehicle driven by Petrozziello and sought favor with prosecutors by accusing Connor of being the mastermind of the theft. A jury saw through the charade.[6] "I was outright acquitted of the cop killing—via what I always describe as one of the miracles in my life—in 17 minutes," reminisced Connor.[7]

At around the same time, Myles was again implicated in murder by Tommy Sperrazza, the actual perpetrator. As if the cowardly killing of a sixty-one-year-old police officer was not a sufficient sin against society, Sperrazza and his frequent partner, John Stokes, stabbed two innocent eighteen-year-old girls to death in a Quincy apartment in February 1975. The victims, Karen Spinney and Susan Webster, had been witnesses to yet another homicide perpetrated by Sperrazza and his friend, so Sperrazza decided to kill them.

Again, Sperrazza testified that Myles Connor was the mastermind of the homicides, and in return was placed in the United States Federal Witness Protection Program with his family—a far better situation than the double life sentences he would have been serving in a state prison. It was handsome payment for a man that the prosecutor, Paul Buckley, described in court as "a cold-blooded murderer," "a rat," and a "fink," which he spelled out, letter by letter, for emphasis. In Myles's defense, Earle Cooley told the jury that his client "should not be whipsawed into a vicious, knock-down, dragged-out battle between law enforcement agencies—used by one and prosecuted by the other."[8] Despite the unreliable witnesses against Myles, he was convicted of being an accessory to the murders.

The conviction and double life sentences that were levied on Connor were soon set aside based on an immediate appeal by Cooley. A second trial was held, and once again Al Dotoli came to his friend's rescue. When Sperrazza confidently identified the date and time that he alleged Myles had dug a grave for the victims in Northampton, Massachusetts, Al showed Cooley that his meticulous recordkeeping proved his friend was actually performing at a jam session with James Cotton and Sha Na Na at that precise time.[9] Al rallied the musicians to court, where they all testified under oath that Myles was with them, not digging a grave in faraway Northampton as described by the Commonwealth. The jury returned a not guilty verdict, and Myles was acquitted in absentia, and Al Dotoli had once again saved the day for his impish pal. Connor playfully wrote to Dotoli, "Who was it who amassed my defense witnesses? Do you recall?" and then gratefully added, "You were almost single-handedly responsible for getting me acquitted."[10]

This time, the frustrated police turned their ire on Al Dotoli. After the jury's decision, he was issued a vindictive summons on the courthouse steps to appear before a judge on an old minor traffic matter. The judge, greatly annoyed at the police action, immediately dismissed the charge.[11]

As usual, Myles Connor was not totally out of the woods: hours before the verdict was read, he jumped bail, forfeiting the $25,000 that he had posted. That led to yet another warrant for his arrest. When he finally was brought before a judge, he stated his reasons for opting to go on the run. He explained that during closing arguments, the prosecutor had lied and put his case at risk. "I felt rules had been broken... I think it seriously impacted the jury," he told the judge. Jumping bail wasn't something he wanted to do, but he had also heard of a plot to shoot him if he had been acquitted and claimed that a cotter pin had been removed from his car, causing him injury. Sadly, Myles's mother, Lucy Conant Johnson, passed away while he was on the run. The judge was unsympathetic to this and his arguments and sentenced Myles to one year in jail.[12]

In retrospect, the rapes and murders were clearly not the sort of crimes in which Myles Connor involved himself. First, while he was frequently the mastermind of illegal designs, they were for jobs in which he was an active participant. He was never a quasi–Mafia Don, ordering underlings to do his dirty work—least of all Tommy Sperrazza, whom he long considered a loose cannon without a moral code like the one by which he governed himself. Fortunately for Connor, judges and juries saw through this. But efforts by law enforcement to implicate Connor continued. Despite these misguided prosecutions, Connor never displayed a propensity for gratuitous violence, nor had a history of attacks of any nature against women.

In 1979, John Connolly, a federal agent with the FBI's organized crime squad, and, it was later revealed, a member of James "Whitey" Bulger's organized crime organization, tried to implicate Myles in a shocking crime that took place in Boston's notorious Combat Zone a year earlier. During the trial of the shooters who killed five men in a cocaine-related robbery in the infamous Blackfriars Pub murders, a report authored by Connolly quoted one of the shooters saying that Myles had suggested the robbery and wanted half of the proceeds in return for the tip. When Connor was informed of Connolly's report, he was "rocked" and offered to take a polygraph exam to prove his innocence. "I can honestly say that I have not only never been in the Blackfriars but I don't know where it is," he said. Referring to the man who had allegedly implicated him to Connolly, Connor said, "Billy Ierardi and I have never been formally introduced. The last time I recall laying eyes on him was several years ago in Walpole... and somebody pointed him out to me and said, 'That's Billy Ierardi.' Never had a conversation with him."[13]

Connor long suspected that Connolly had it out for him for two reasons. First, the FBI agent was furious that Myles had excluded the Bureau from having a hand in the return of the Rembrandt; and second, and more importantly, Connolly was eager to eliminate any competition faced by Bulger and his partner, Stephen Flemmi, especially from someone whom they could not control.

Myles's suspicion that Connolly discussed him with Bulger and his crew was confirmed in a 1999 judicial memorandum written by federal judge Mark Wolfe during the US government's prosecution of Boston Mob boss Frank Salemme. Wolfe wrote that at a meeting held with Connolly and fellow agent Nick Gianturco at the latter's home, Bulger and Flemmi "provided information on the criminal activities of . . . Myles Connor."[14] It's no surprise, then, that the actual chief suspects in the ordering of the Blackfriars murders were Bulger, Flemmi, and their associates. Connor was never charged with any offense related to the homicides. Ironically, one of the investigators who played an early key role in exposing the dirty dealings between Bulger, Flemmi, and the Boston FBI, was Lieutenant Colonel Jack O'Donovan of the Massachusetts State Police—the very same detective who was shot by Myles Connor in 1966.[15]

When Myles Connor was asked by the media about John Connolly's allegation, he said, "I'm not an angel. My past is my past but right now I'm struggling to get over that. You'd like to escape from all that where you've got a possibility to really go ahead and make vast achievements." He added, "I'm doing very well, myself and the band . . . we're right on the verge of a big record contract."[16] There was truth to this. The band was thriving, Connor had returned to fine form onstage, and the audiences still loved him. As ever, Al Dotoli was working on that big record deal. But just as in past interviews, he had not put crime behind him.

In the waning days of 1988, Myles was in Bloomington, Illinois, meeting a potential buyer for the Simon Willard clock he stole from the Woolworth Estate fifteen years earlier. A month later, he met the same buyer with more items he had for sale: the Dutch paintings he stole from the Mead Art Museum in 1975. For the paintings, Connor was asking $60,000—less than half of what he claimed the paintings' value to be and actually only about a quarter of their true worth. That wasn't all he was looking to sell. Myles told the man that he was prepared to move two kilos of cocaine through him to sell to students at the University of Illinois every week. He also had a small amount of LSD to sell. The buyer was interested in doing business, so Myles used the paintings lifted from the Mead Art Museum—Pieter Lastman's *St. John the Baptist* and Hendrick van Vliet's *Interior of the Nieuwe Kerk, Delft*, as collateral for a loan from the buyer, who also gave him $24,000 to buy cocaine in Florida.

When Myles returned to Illinois with the cocaine in March 1989, he met with the buyer who, much to his surprise, was an undercover FBI agent. Myles had been set up throughout the dealings by a Bureau informant. He was arrested and, because of his history of fleeing prosecution, was held pending a trial. Just a month before, he had told a Boston reporter, "I have tried diligently to go straight over the last number of years, and it has been anything but easy."[17] Once again, he was facing a major federal sentence, but this time he couldn't flee. And worse, he was far from the sort of help he could seek in the past back home in Massachusetts. His only hope was a jailbreak, but a fellow inmate betrayed him and told the authorities that Connor planned to break out of the county lockup. When authorities searched his cell, they found four hacksaw blades smuggled via a hollowed-out hardbound book. There were signs that the operation had already begun.[18]

For the first time, Myles Connor finally ran into something that he hadn't experienced in any of his previous trials: a truly indignant judge. During sentencing, US District Court judge Richard Mills wrote a lengthy examination of Connor's criminal career, laying out all his misdeeds in detail. Judge Mills was blunt, calling Connor "rotten to the core." The federal prosecutor, who referred to Connor as "a menace to society," asked for a strict nine-and-a-half-year prison term based on new federal sentencing guidelines, but Judge Mills wasn't having it. Instead, he doubled the recommendation, ordering that Myles, now forty-seven years old, serve twenty years without parole. "We don't need you," Judge Mills said to Connor. "And we are society."[19]

Myles appealed the sentence and was successful, but still, the earliest Myles Connor would be eligible for release would be after ten years, at age fifty-seven. This time there would be no new trials, no paintings to trade, no jailhouse admissions from the true culprit. The music career that Al Dotoli had worked so hard to develop into a national act was over. Things looked bleak, because they were.

When Myles Connor was ultimately freed from prison in 2000, there was little awaiting him. He had no work history. His name was synonymous with crime in his home state. He would be arrested again a few times for petty crimes. He moved in with his girlfriend, Suzy King, on a farm in Blackstone, Massachusetts, tending to livestock and enjoying the valuable swords and antiques he still legitimately owned.

His final musical performance took place in May 2009 when he packed the Beachcomber. The club's owner said, "The whole place was packed, and everyone was seated and ready before the show even started. We didn't do any special promotion, nothing beyond our usual ad." Myles played a short set, highlighted by his covers of Johnny Cash's "Ring of Fire" and "Don't Take Your Guns to Town." His voice was weaker, but he still nailed Cash's low register. It was his first time back onstage in twenty years, and it would be his last.[20]

Through it all, there was one constant in Myles Connor's life—his friend, Al Dotoli, who remained at his side when he was in the recording studio as a teenager, near death in a hospital bed in Boston, needing to return a priceless treasure to the MFA, falsely accused of murder, and into their golden years. On the cusp of eighty years old, Myles wrote a long letter to Al, acknowledging all he had done for him throughout his life. It was a startling frank and intensely reflective letter, the sort that can only come from deep within and with the introspection that comes late in life. "Because of the widely published accusations and the horrible nature of them, I know you, and your loved ones had to endure the embarrassment of being my supporter and friend. You endured all this, and you did it out of years of friendship and loyalty."[21]

"There is no end to my gratitude and love for you as a friend," he wrote. "I never want our friendship to ever end."[22]

EPILOGUE

Over the years that I have known Myles Connor and Al Dotoli, I have spent endless hours either doubled over in laughter or sitting mouth agape in amazement at stories the two of them have shared with me—some in strict confidence and some widely reported. One of the unique things about our relationship is that I have been able to confirm the veracity of them. One of the most difficult things about writing their story is describing the seemingly outlandish but verifiably true exploits contained within. Men in their ninth decade who have lived incredibly active lives sometimes offer up tales that one hasn't heard before, and in the case of these two, the stories are typically worth repeating. It might be Al arranging for Andy Williams to surprise New England Patriots owner Robert Kraft with a rendition of "Moon River." Or it could be Myles recalling how he ingeniously broke into his own storage locker to retrieve his possessions and save them from the auction block. Every visit with them would result with yet another story that left a lasting impression.

One afternoon, I explained this to Myles, and it was something he hadn't considered, mainly because he hadn't read about these events, he lived them. It hadn't really dawned on him that what he had done in his life was far outside of the ordinary. Neither he nor Al ever spent time reading about other art thefts, at least not until I gave them copies of my first book, *Stealing Rembrandts* (which I at least hope they read). I said to Myles, "Let's play a thought experiment. Imagine you never robbed the MFA of the Rembrandt to get out of trouble. Now imagine I told you that story, but it was about someone else. Would you believe it?" He thought for a second, smiled, and said, "No, I don't suppose that I would."

That's how his entire life has been. In 2024 I took my childhood friend Steve Almagno to see a special showing of the documentary film Al had produced about Myles's life and music career, *Rock and Roll Outlaw: The Ballad of Myles Connor*, at a local theater in Massachusetts. He sat in amazement watching the film. Afterward, we went backstage to a makeshift green room with Al, his wife Rena and his daughter Courtney, and Myles for a beer. There, Myles shared a few more stories, and my friend soon understood my fascination. When we drove home, he asked me, "How do you know all of these stories are true?" I explained that I confirmed them through FBI files, contemporaneous newspaper accounts, and interviews with participants, investigators, and criminals.

In researching this book, I've had access to materials that neither Myles nor Al could possibly see, and they always confirmed exactly what they told me. I interviewed retired FBI Special Agent Bernie Murphy, who hadn't seen Myles in fifty years, and his version of the arrest in Mashpee before his concert was an exact, word-for-word confirmation of what Connor told me. Sometimes, people simply live remarkable lives.

The same is true for Dotoli. Who would have wagered that he would turn a one-night rental of his sound system at a local club into a major career putting on concerts for the biggest names in the music industry?

EPILOGUE

If as a teenager he had told his father that he'd be working with Frank Sinatra, the elder Dotoli would likely have told him to get back to washing dishes in the family's North End restaurant. Yet soon enough, there he was, and with the Rolling Stones, Sammy Davis Jr., Dionne Warwick, and countless others, too. As for pulling off the return of a stolen $10 million painting, well, knowing his friendship with that redheaded fellow, everyone might have seen that coming.

There's cosmic irony in the fact that nearly all of the art and antiques that Myles Connor accumulated throughout his lifetime were ultimately stolen from him by scoundrels willing to risk his wrath. He estimates that a girlfriend's brother stole somewhere between $4 million to $5 million in Japanese swords and sword guards while Myles was imprisoned in the 1970s. Then, while he was in federal prison in the 1980s, he entrusted a tractor trailer filled with what he estimates to be $5 million in antique firearms, Incan gold, Japanese suits of armor, bronze statuary, and, of course, more swords, to a man he believed to be a loyal friend. But he was no Al Dotoli. Unfortunately for Connor, that person turned out to be neither loyal nor a friend. Rather than safeguard the goods, he betrayed Myles and sold everything for what is rumored to be mere pennies on the dollar, allegedly to support a drug habit.

To see Myles talk about these losses decades after the fact is to watch him experience sadness, outrage, and a desire for revenge, all before quickly returning to his good-humored self. On one occasion, as he spoke of some of the items that were lost, Al interrupted him with a question.

"By the way, that Christmas gift you gave us, Rena was asking where it came from."

"You mean the jade?" Myles asked.

"No, that was the anniversary gift," Al replied. He stumbled for a description of the Christmas gift, but with his hands mimicked its shape.

"Oh, the vase!" Myles remembered.

"Yes, where's it from?" Al asked.

"Let's see," Connor said, placing his chin in his hand. "Fogg Museum, 1972." Then he broke out in his unmistakable roaring laugh. Al and I joined in, guffawing so loud that the other diners turned to see what was so funny.

"No, I'm just kidding," Myles said. We left it at that.

In 2018 Myles made one last try to get his hands on what remained of his beloved weaponry. This time, he tried to do it the legal way, enlisting the help of an attorney and petitioning the Norfolk County Superior Court to return to him items seized during a 1986 drug raid of a Dorchester apartment. At trial, he testified to the provenance of the items that the police confiscated, arguing that they had come from the estates of his maternal grandfather and mother.[1]

The list of items in question read like exactly the sorts of things Myles collected. Numerous antique American rifles, three Japanese matchlock rifles, an umbrella sword, and a walking cane .410-gauge shotgun, to name but a few.[2] A woman who had helped Myles move his collection out of his mother's home and into the Dorchester apartment testified in his support, as did Marty Leppo. But the jury was not convinced. The district attorney said that "we felt strongly that [Connor] could not establish a path of ownership to these items, which were comingled with many things that have already been returned to their rightful owners." In essence, Myles's well-known reputation as a thief was the burden he had to overcome, and he could not. It was an unfortunate turn of events. The items truly were his, but his reputation had cost him.

Nevertheless, Myles's passion for collecting never waned. He continued to scrape together funds—typically from Al—to buy more swords. On his eightieth birthday, I offered to take him to lunch at an upscale Japanese restaurant. I arrived before he did and waited by the large windows facing the street. Soon, I saw him walking toward the eatery carrying what looked oddly like a pair of blue jeans on a horizontal pole. He entered the packed establishment with this strange item, and when we sat down, he took the pants off of what turned out to be a beautiful Samurai sword. "It's a twelfth-century sword," he said. The sword was longer than the table, and he described every element of it to me, right down to the rub marks from the polishing stones, while most of the other patrons looked at him with curious stares. Soon, the restaurant manager, a Japanese gentleman, approached the table. Certain he was going to ask Myles to leave, I closed my menu and reached for my keys. But instead, the two struck up a conversation, and Myles gave him a brief tutorial on the ancient curiosity he had brought to lunch. It was pure Myles Connor: his unexpected charm lured the manager in, and the restaurateur walked away with a smile that rivaled the sword in width and gleam.

Many crimes are, by their very nature, transactional. Art heists are no different. When thieves steal art, they envision a transaction. They dream of an insurance company paying a large ransom, or a museum offering a big reward. If these payoffs don't come to fruition, they sometimes use it as collateral, especially in the drug trade. They might even hold onto it for use as a Get out of Jail Free card now that Myles Connor and Al Dotoli set that precedent more than fifty years ago.

Not all of Myles's thefts were transactional. Some of his motives were personal, not pecuniary. Vengeance and obsession were at the heart of some of his major heists, with money being a mere ancillary benefit. This makes him a rarity in the annals of art crime, with less than a handful of others in his company. Indeed, even my overture to meet him was answered with a business proposition from Al—appear in our documentary and we can talk. I quickly agreed. I, too, had something I wanted in return, and that was the insights of a legendary art thief.

Almost instantly, the three of us became friends. Right from the onset, we were in touch at least weekly. I wasn't exactly surprised. I've always been at ease with ex-convicts and members of the criminal underworld. Perhaps that is because both of my brothers served time in prison, one at the federal level and the other in a state penitentiary. And many of the people with whom I grew up—and, indeed, met through my investigation into the Gardner heist—have been criminals. I've learned much from my time with them. First and foremost, I found that very few of them are irredeemable reprobates. They have children whom they love and who love them. Like mine, their parents often suffered, both emotionally and financially, when they got into trouble. They have friends that care about them to whom they are loyal. I quite like meeting with them; their life experiences are interesting. Sometimes they can be tragic. Others, thrilling.

Spending time with Myles Connor and Al Dotoli is like experiencing all this in the extreme. But for them, friendship is never transactional. Al never asked for anything from Myles when he came to his rescue or developed musical opportunities. It wasn't even something he considered, and he still doesn't. Anything the pair asked of each other was rooted in fraternity and genuine affection for each other. It began that day Al rang the Connor family's doorbell when they were teens, and Myles took him in as a much taller little brother. It extends to this very day, nearly seventy years later.

One afternoon, I tried to explain this to Lucia Bay, a paintings conservator at the Isabella Stewart Gardner Museum. Lucia is fascinated by the world of art crime and was eager to hear about Myles. I sometimes have difficulty speaking about him because, as I do, I am myself taken aback by what I am recounting. But she got it, despite my stumbling. "People are complicated," she said, recounting a truism that was never more apt than when describing my friends Myles Connor and Al Dotoli. "Exactly," I responded. "You can't just sum them up in a sentence."

What could be more complicated than an honest man like Al Dotoli volunteering for a mission to return a valuable painting to law enforcement at great risk to himself? Or spending innumerable hours trying to turn Myles Connor into a superstar as he repeatedly squandered the opportunities Al created for him?

Is there anything more complex than a man with a genius-level IQ whose love for Japanese swords would consume him to the point where there was no risk too great to keep him from pursuing them? Someone gifted enough to impress art curators with doctorates about their shared passions only to entrust millions of dollars' worth of his beloved objects to obvious scoundrels who would betray him? In my line of work, I cannot think of anything more complicated.

But despite this tangle of unusual dichotomies, Myles and Al are bound by a sacred code that can be summed up in one word: loyalty. I've found myself wrapped in this enigma. I often tell people that though he is one of the most accomplished thieves in history, if I left $10,000 in cash on a table, he wouldn't dream of taking it. As for Dotoli, I'd probably return to find $11,000, such is his generous nature. Both know I wouldn't dream of ripping them off, either. So, despite this story of astonishing criminality, I find myself comfortable and at peace in their company. There's little we wouldn't do for each other, and none of it would be a transaction, except perhaps for an even exchange of loyalty.

In the summer of 2021, Myles's longtime girlfriend, Suzy King, died after a bout with a terrible infection. Myles spent considerable time helping Suzy with her beloved old horse, Candy Girl, and other animals in Carrollton, Georgia, over the last couple of years of her life. He handled the day-to-day chores on her property while she was away on long road trips. Her loss was a blow to Myles, who, despite his long periods of lawlessness, has a deeply sentimental side to him.

One afternoon he called to tell me that he had seen a medium whom he had asked to communicate with Suzy. He hadn't provided Suzy's name, but he told me the medium knew it and knew Candy Girl's name as well. The medium told him that Suzy was "in a great place" and that she was with Myles at all times. He was as happy as I'd heard him since Suzy had first become ill, and he told me that he had never believed in the afterlife and spiritual matters, but that the medium had made him a believer. It was as if a great weight was lifted from his shoulders.

Suzy's funeral mass was said by Myles's half-brother, Father Sean Connor. It was a lovely ceremony, well attended by many of Myles's friends, most of whom knew that her passing was a difficult loss for him. I sat with Al Dotoli and was heartened to see that so many people had shown up to pay their respects. After the service, I walked outside

EPILOGUE

the church and waited for Myles, who had stayed behind to say goodbye one last time.

Finally, the church doors opened, and he came down the steps smiling. Father Sean stood in the doorway and called to his brother.

"Myles, don't forget what Dad said."

Smiling, Myles turned and asked, "What's that?"

"Stay out of trouble," the priest said.

I turned to Al, who looked back at me with a smile that said, "Good luck with that."

TIMELINE

February 1, 1943: Myles J. Connor Jr. is born to Myles (Joe) Connor and Lucy Conant Johnson Connor in Milton, Massachusetts.

March 19, 1947: Alfred Dotoli is born to Mary and Joseph Dotoli in Milton, Massachusetts.

Early 1960s: Myles Connor begins playing music professionally.

March 16, 1965: Myles Connor breaks into the Forbes House Museum overnight and steals a large number of antiques.

Spring 1965: Myles Connor breaks into the Boston Children's Museum and steals Asian artifacts from its storage space.

July 21, 1965: Myles Connor is intercepted by a police officer in Sullivan, Maine, attempting to steal antiques from a home. He escapes but is later apprehended by state police and jailed in the Hancock County Jail.

July 26, 1965: Myles Connor escapes from the Hancock County Jail using a bar of soap he fashioned to look like a gun.

July 30, 1965: Myles Connor is captured by the police after a massive manhunt. He is released two weeks later pending an appearance in the Superior Court.

February 16, 1966: Myles Connor is indicted on charges related to the Forbes House burglary and flees police officers attempting to serve him an arrest warrant.

April 27, 1966: Myles Connor engages in a shootout with the police as they close in on him. He shoots and injures Massachusetts State Police corporal John O'Donovan and is struck himself. He suffers grave injuries and begins a long hospital stay. He is then sent to Walpole State Prison.

February 15, 1967: While incarcerated, Myles Connor is indicted for a series of crimes, including sexual assault. He is later exonerated when the real culprit confesses to the crimes.

1972: Myles Connor is released from Walpole State Prison.

May 17, 1972: Worcester Museum is robbed at gunpoint in broad daylight of a Rembrandt, a Picasso, and two Gauguins in a heist planned by Florian Monday.

December 2, 1973: The Fogg Museum is robbed of millions in gold coins at gunpoint in an overnight theft. Detective John Regan of the Massachusetts State Police later recovers a large portion of the stolen coins.

Weekend of May 25, 1974: Myles Connor and associates steal antiques, grandfather clocks, and Wyeth paintings from the Woolworth Estate in Maine.

July 18, 1974: Myles Connor is arrested by the FBI in possession of stolen paintings from the Woolworth Estate.

January 29, 1975: Myles Connor and associates rob the Norfolk County Trust Bank in Milton.

February 8, 1975: Myles Connor steals Dutch paintings in an overnight theft from the Mead Art Museum in Amherst, Massachusetts.

April 14, 1975: Myles Connor robs the Museum of Fine Arts, Boston.

January 4, 1976: Al Dotoli returns the stolen Rembrandt to the Museum of Fine Arts, Boston.

January 6, 1976: Recovery of the Rembrandt is announced in *The Boston Sunday Globe*.

1979: Myles Connor is released from prison.

March 20, 1981: Myles Connor is convicted of directing the murder of two teenaged girls.

December 8, 1981: Myles Connor is tried and acquitted of directing the murder of a police officer.

August 25, 1984: Myles Connor's murder conviction is overturned.

March 3, 1985: Myles Connor is acquitted of the murder of the two teenaged girls.

March 6, 1989: Myles Connor is arrested by the FBI in Springfield, Illinois, on charges involving drug trafficking and the attempted sale of stolen art. He is ultimately sentenced to twenty years in federal prison, but the sentence is reduced on appeal.

June 9, 2000: Myles Connor is released from federal prison.

ACKNOWLEDGMENTS

I am forever grateful to my literary agent, my doting sensei Sharlene Martin of Martin Literary Management, for her faith in me and this book. Similarly, I am indebted to Jessica Case and Claiborne Hancock, my gracious and patient editor and publisher at Pegasus Books. Thank you both for working with me again.

Many people have urged me to write about my friendship with Myles and Al, but two people in particular have encouraged me for many years: good friend and gifted writer Kelly Horan and Geoff Kelly, my friend and partner in the Gardner Museum investigation for almost twenty years. I hope that this book is what you envisioned.

Stephen Almagno provided me with encouragement, advice, lunches, humor, and brotherhood. Maxine Hanelt gave me loving sticky notes, cookies, candy, chocolate milk, and, best of all, her contagious joy. Peter and Patricia Crowley provided a sounding board and unlimited Diet Cokes. I received great support and encouragement from my much-adored sister, Lori Giorgi; my mother, Judith Amore (who bought me the laptop on which I am typing this); my nephew Louis Giorgi; and, of course, Stephanie Langfield Charette, who was essential to me completing this work. Lorraine Donati Hanley provided great help and friendship. Ulrich Boser graciously gave me a stack of newspaper clippings that proved invaluable. Patrick Radden Keefe inspired me with his belief in this project. Dr. Victoria Reed provided art provenance guidance and proofreading. Natalie Wolcott Williams provided her usual critical prowess, and Anne Hawley, as ever, inspired. Steve Gorski told me about his involvement with the Rembrandt painting and several funny tales. Bernie Murphy was kind with his time and told me about his career and involvement with Myles with candor and good humor. Jeff Jacoby talked with me about writing, as did my friend Christian Di Spigna. Karen Frascona and Nicki Luongo at the Museum of Fine Arts, Boston, were a great help. My students at Harvard University's Extension Program kept me in a constant state of research. Jessica Gasbarre and friends at the Memorial Art Gallery in Rochester kept me in stitches. The team at Caffe Nero in Winchester provided me with unfailingly excellent service during the innumerable hours I spent there writing. Thanks also go to Tina Bellomy and Jason Hanelt for their kindness at a key moment in the project.

Deborah A. Lang, a liaison agent in the Public Service Unit at Boston Police Headquarters is due a special measure of thanks. Debbie somehow found the fifty-year-old handwritten police report from the April 14, 1975, heist among the tens of thousands of reports on file with the BPD from the pre-automation era. I don't know how she did it, other than to say she is a great researcher and a credit to her job. Sergeant Detective John Boyle of the Boston Police Department's Office of Media Relations was also a great help.

The Reverend Valanarasu Newton-Williamraj and the Reverend Paul Clifford of St. Mary's Catholic Church provided me with spiritual guidance throughout this project and beyond.

I'd also like to thank the countless unnamed people over the past twenty years who have approached me, called me, and written me with stories about Myles Connor, nearly all of which are true (except the woman who told me she was married to him—that was weird).

Courtney, Kacy, and Rena Dotoli provided me with background details and photographs. Charly and Drew Kalell vicariously kept me conscious of every word I wrote in this book. Someday, when you both read this, I hope you are proud of your grandfather. You should be.

And, of course, my heartfelt thanks to Alfred Dotoli and Myles Connor. I'm honored that you trusted me with your story and that you expanded your duo into a trio. Pals forever.

NOTES

Chapter 1: The Office
1. Al Dotoli, interview by author, May 28, 2021, Canton, Mass.
2. Ibid.
3. Al Dotoli, telephone interview with author, September 17, 2024.
4. Al Dotoli, interview by author, May 28, 2021.
5. Howard Zinn, "State Ignores Law for Prison Reform and Release of Inmates into Community," *Boston Globe*, March 28, 1975, 21.
6. United Press International, "Complexes Don't Count," *Boston Globe*, March 1, 1967, 2.
7. Hugh Bigelow, Ken Hartnett, Bob Sales, and F. B. Taylor Jr., "Walpole's Donnelly Was Willing to Resign," *Boston Globe*, April 2, 1972, 46.
8. Myles Connor, telephone interview with author, September 27, 2024.
9. Ibid.
10. Myles Connor, telephone interview with author, March 4, 2023.
11. Ken Hartnett, "Gun Law Leads to a Conviction, Tests a Trooper, Unnerves a Visitor," *Boston Globe*, April 13, 1972, 1.
12. United Press International, "2 Men in Boston Steal a Rembrandt," *Fort Worth Star-Telegram*, April 15, 1975, 5A.
13. Robert Anglin, "Gunmen Flee Museum with Stolen Rembrandt," *Boston Globe*, April 15, 1975, 1.
14. Ibid.
15. Seymour Linscott, "Hub Police Have Art Theft Clues, Descriptions," *Boston Globe*, April 15, 1975, 5.
16. United Press International. "Agents Hunt Stolen Rembrandt," *Republican* (Springfield, Mass.), April 15, 1975, 1.
17. Robert Anglin, "Reward Offered to Retrieve Rembrandt," *Boston Globe*, April 29, 1975, 3.
18. Anglin, "Reward Offered to Retrieve Rembrandt."
19. Al Dotoli, interview by author, May 28, 2021.
20. Ibid.
21. Ibid.
22. Ibid.
23. Allan May, "The Providence Mob," Crime Library, https://www.crimelibrary.org/gangsters_outlaws/family_epics/providence_mob/3.html.
24. Ibid.
25. "Murder Plot Conviction of Patriarca Upheld," *Boston Globe*, October 15, 1968, 58.
26. Al Dotoli, interview by author, September 17, 2024.

Chapter 2: 1975: A Very Busy Year

1. Steve Gorski, interview by author, November 4, 2024, Boston.
2. Traute M. Marshall, *Art Museums Plus: Cultural Excursions in New England* (University Press of New England, 2009), 95.
3. "Benjamin West's Paintings Will Be Seen at Amherst," *Springfield Sunday Republican* (Springfield, Mass.), May 7, 1950, 21.
4. "Stearns Steeple (1873)," Historic Buildings of Massachusetts, December 4, 2011, https://mass.historicbuildingsct.com/?p=3835.
5. "Professor Frank Trapp," Amherst College, https://www.amherst.edu/news/magazine/issue-archive/2005_summer/college_row/trapp.
6. Myles Connor, telephone interview with author, October 8, 2024.
7. Myles Connor, interview with author, October 3, 2024, Boston.
8. Greg Keraghosian, "San Francisco's Most Infamous Art Heist: A Million Dollar Rembrandt That's Since Been Discovered," *SFGATE*, August 26, 2021, https://www.sfgate.com/sfhistory/article/san-francisco-art-heist-deyoung-rembrandt-16411512.php.
9. Keraghosian, "San Francisco's Most Infamous Art Heist."
10. J. Correspondent, "Stolen Portrait Is No Rembrandt and Probably Not a Rabbi, Either," *Jewish News of Northern California*, August 25, 2000, https://jweekly.com/2000/08/25/stolen-portrait-is-no-rembrandt-and-perhaps-not-a-rabbi-either/.
11. Steve Pfarrer, "Art Heist Investigation Revived in Case of 1975 Mead Art Theft," *Daily Hampshire Gazette,* (Northampton, Mass.), February 22, 2015, A1.
12. Diane Lederman, "Amherst College Renews Hunt for Painting Stolen from Mead Art Museum in 1975," MassLive, February 15, 2014, https://www.masslive.com/news/2014/02/amherst_college_mead_art_museu.html.
13. Don Thompson, "Reputation Catches Up to Art Thief Dealt 20 Years in Prison," *Pantagraph,* (Bloomington–Normal, Ill.), July 17, 1990, 2.

Chapter 3: Opening Acts

1. "Myles J. Connor" (obituary), *Boston Globe*, July 3, 1981, 23.
2. Ted Ashby, "Rock 'n' Roll Combo Leader Has Attic Full of Weird Pets," *Boston Globe*, September 19, 1960, 9.
3. Myles Connor, interview with author, December 23, 2024, Boston.
4. Al Dotoli, telephone interview with author, October 26, 2024.
5. Ibid.
6. Al Dotoli, telephone interview with author, January 3, 2025.
7. Ibid.
8. Myles Connor and Al Dotoli, interview with author, January 22, 2025, Canton, Mass.
9. Bill Trotter, "Infamous Art Thief Revisits Criminal Past in Ellsworth," *Bangor (Me.) Daily News*, March 16, 2014. https://www.bangordailynews.com/2014/03/06/news/infamous-art-thief-revisits-criminal-past-in-ellsworth/.
10. Tom Mashberg, "Stealing Beauty," *Vanity Fair*, March 1998, 258, https://archive.vanityfair.com/article/1998/3/stealing-beauty.
11. Jack Dodson, "Myles Connor Describes Sullivan Theft," *Ellsworth American* (Hancock County, Me.), August 29, 2017.
12. C. S. Lewis, *Mere Christianity* (HarperCollins, 2001), 43–44.
13. Myles Connor, telephone interview with author, November 1, 2024.
14. Mashberg, "Stealing Beauty."
15. Curtis Prout, "William Sturgis Bigelow: Brief Life of an Idiosyncratic Brahmin: 1850–1926," *Harvard Magazine*, September 1997, https://www.harvardmagazine.com/sites/default/files/html/1997/09/vita.html.

NOTES

16. MFA Boston, "Lecture: Arts of Japan," https://www.mfa.org/event/lecture/arts-of-japan?event=128986.
17. Al Dotoli, telephone interview with author, October 26, 2024.

Chapter 4: Vengeance
1. Edgar J. Driscoll Jr., "Emerson Letter Found in Attic in Milton," *Boston Globe*, March 27, 1964, 12.
2. Forbes House Museum, https://www.forbeshousemuseum.org/.
3. Myles Connor in an undated outline for talks on stolen art from the perspective of an art thief.
4. "$1000 Reward for Stolen Tray," *Boston Globe*, March 17, 1965, 40.
5. Ibid.
6. Al Dotoli, interview with author, May 28, 2021, Canton, Mass.
7. "Spock's Museum," *Time*, November 8, 1968.
8. "Japanese House," Boston Children's Museum, https://japanesehouse.bostonchildrensmuseum.org/timeline/1913-1950/.
9. Ibid.
10. Myles Connor in an undated outline for talks on stolen art from the perspective of an art thief.
11. "FBI Joins Probe of Art Theft," *Boston Globe*, December 13, 1966, 27.
12. Myles Connor, interview with author, November 4, 2024, Boston, MA.
13. Anthony M. Amore and Tom Mashberg, *Stealing Rembrandts: The Untold Stories of Notorious Art Heists* (Palgrave Macmillan, 2011).
14. Christopher Reed, "Picking Harvard's Pocket," *Harvard Magazine*, February 1, 2000, https://www.harvardmagazine.com/2000/05/picking-harvards-pocket-html.
15. Richard O'Donnell, "Reward May Be Offered for 3 Pollock Paintings," *Boston Globe*, November 11, 1973, 3.
16. Robert Taylor, "A Growing Concern over the Theft of Art," *Boston Globe*, September 19, 1976, B1.
17. Ibid., B6.
18. "Painting Stolen," *Hull Daily Mail* (UK), March 19, 1965, 1.
19. United Press International, "Stolen Painting," *Los Angeles Times*, March 22, 1965, 3.
20. Myles Connor in an undated outline for talks on stolen art from the perspective of an art thief.
21. Katie Razzall, Larissa Kennelly, and Darin Graham, "British Museum Gems for Sale on eBay—How a Theft Was Exposed," *BBC News*, May 26, 2024, https://www.bbc.com/news/articles/cpegg27g74do.

Chapter 5: The Fugitive
1. Bob Court and George Neary, "Deadly Cobra Found in Burglary Raid," *Boston Record*, January 13, 1966.
2. "Cops Say Theft Suspect Had 'Pet' Wildcat," *Boston Record*, January 14, 1966.
3. "2 Men, Stolen Antiques Seized," *Boston Globe*, January 12, 1966, 18.
4. Ibid.
5. "Cops Say Theft Suspect Had 'Pet' Wildcat."
6. Ibid.
7. Myles Connor in an undated draft of a letter to *Boston* magazine.
8. "Flees Cops in Pants Only," *Boston Record*, February 16, 1966.
9. "Connor's Hair Nearly Halts Freedom Song," *Boston Globe*, February 16, 1966, 1.
10. Jack Kendall, "Wanted Rock-Roller Again Eludes Trap," *Boston Record*, February 17, 1966.

11   Al Dotoli, interview with author, December 23, 2024, Boston.
12   William Sonzski, "Connor's Mother Heartbroken as Son Leads Fugitive's Life," *Boston Herald*, February 17, 1966.
13   Myles Connor, interview with author, December 23, 2024, Boston.
14   Joseph W. Bradley, "Crowds Watch Back Bay Battle," *Boston Globe*, April 28, 1966, 1.
15   Myles Connor, interview with author, December 23, 2024.
16   Lawrence T. Curran, "He Was Set to Shoot as We Fired," *Boston Globe*, April 28, 1966, 3.
17   "State Trooper, Fugitive, 'Fair' After Gun Battle," *Lynn (Mass.) Daily Item*, April 28, 1966, 2.
18   "State Trooper, Fugitive, 'Fair' After Gun Battle."
19   Myles Connor in an undated draft of a letter to *Boston* magazine.
20   Myles Connor, interview with author, December 23, 2024.
21   Myles Connor in an undated draft of a letter to *Boston* magazine.
22   Letter from Myles Connor to Al Dotoli, August 16, 2022.
23   J. M. Lawrence, "John O'Donovan, State Trooper, Dies at 81," *Boston Globe*, March 18, 2012, B1.
24   Jim Morse, "Myles Connor Looks Ahead," *Boston Herald*, July 16, 1973.
25   "Asian Export Art," Peabody Essex Museum, https://www.pem.org/the-pem-collection/asian-export-art.
26   Al Dotoli, interview with author, November 4, 2024, Boston.
27   Myles Connor in an undated draft of a letter to *Boston* magazine.
28   Myles Connor, interview with author, January 21, 2025, Canton, Mass.

Chapter 6: The Boost Effect
1   Richard F. Shepard, "M. Knoedler to Move; Wyeth Chooses New Gallery," *New York Times*, January 21, 1969, 43.
2   "Wyeth Gives His Business to New Kerr Art Gallery," *News Journal* (Wilmington, Del.), January 21, 1969, 22.
3   Brian MacQuarrie, "Wyeth Touch Puts Site in Pantheon," *Boston Globe*, July 5, 2011, A1.
4   William Gerdts, *The American Painting Collection of Mrs. Norman B. Woolworth: An Exhibition for the Benefit of the Girl Scout Council of Greater New York* (Coe Kerr Gallery, 1970).
5   Bowdoin Museum College of Art, *American Paintings of the 19th and 20th Centuries: From the Collection of Mr. and Mrs. Norman B. Woolworth* (Bowdoin College; 1961), 4.
6   Georgina Schaeffer, "Be Our Guest," *Town & Country*, September 9, 2013.
7   Ibid.
8   "Woolworth Show Continues," Morning Sentinel (Waterville, Me.), March 23, 1972, 6.
9   Phyllis Austin, "50 Paintings Stolen in Monmouth Theft," *Kennebec (Me.) Journal*, April 26, 1972, 1.
10   Ibid.
11   "Woolworth's Estate Robbed of Paintings Valued at $250,000," *New York Times*, April 26, 1972, 42.
12   Austin, "50 Paintings Stolen in Monmouth Theft," 2.
13   Ibid.
14   "Woolworth Heiress Robbed at the Plaza of $750,000 in Gems," *New York Times*, October 2, 1925, 1.
15   "Noel C. Scaffa Is Indicted in Donahue Theft," *Intelligencer Journal* (Lancaster, Penn.), October 24, 1925, 1.
16   Associated Press, "Fifty Paintings Stolen from Woolworth Estate," *Syracuse Herald-Journal*, April 25, 1972, 9.
17   Ibid.
18   M. A. Andresen and T. Hodgkinson, "Environmental Criminology, Design, and Victimization: What We Know, How We Have Failed, and Where We Need to Go,"

NOTES 239

      in *Revitalizing Victimization Theory: Revisions, Applications, and New Directions*, ed. Travis C. Pratt and Jillian J. Turanovic (Routledge, 2021), 104–28.
19 Joel Bewley, "Confessions of a Master Thief," *Philadelphia Inquirer*, October 17, 2004, A25.
20 Austin, "50 Paintings Stolen in Monmouth Theft," 2.
21 Associated Press, "Third Man Freed on $5,000 Bond in Art Thefts," *Lewiston (Me.) Evening Journal*, June 12, 1973, 16.
22 United Press International, "Five-Year Pen Term Given Art Thief by Court," *Daily Courier* (Connellsville, Penn.), March 2, 1974, 8.
23 "1 Dead, 2d Critical In No. End Stabbings," *Boston Globe*, October 5, 1968, 21.
24 Myles Connor in an undated draft of a letter to *Boston* magazine.
25 Text correspondence with a family member of Richard Donati, November 16, 2024.
26 "Silver Seized in NY May Be from Boston," *Boston Globe*, October 26, 1969, 1.
27 Many details of the heist were obtained via a redacted file obtained under the Freedom of Information Act from the Federal Bureau of Investigation.
28 "Recognizable Art," *Robesonian* (Lumberton, N.C.), March 17, 1970, 4.
29 Al Dotoli, interview with author, November 27, 2024, Boston.

Chapter 7: On the Rocks
1 Al Dotoli, interview with author, November 27, 2024, Boston.
2 Ibid.
3 Obituary of Ralph Rinaldo Ranzo, January 2018, https://obits.barilefuneral.com/ralph-ranzo.
4 Al Dotoli, interview with author, November 27, 2024.
5 Ibid.
6 Ibid.
7 Bernie Murphy, telephone interview with author, January 9, 2025.
8 "Wyeth Theft Probed," *Boston Globe*, July 26, 1947, 17.
9 Pat Sherlock, "Art-Famed Olsen House Given to Maine," *Boston Globe*, July 19, 1974, 3.
10 Associated Press, "Wyeth Exhibit Draws in Japan," *Republican* (Springfield, Mass.), July 22, 1974, 5.
11 Richard Connolly, "Singer Fails to Appear at Paintings Theft Trial," *Boston Globe*, April 23, 1975, 10.

Chapter 8: A Seed Is Planted
1 Myles Connor in an undated draft of a letter to *Boston* magazine.
2 "State Police Detective Promoted," *Boston Sunday Globe*, April 9, 1967, 62.
3 Xinni Chen and Julian J. Giordano, "'Largest Art Theft': 50 Years of Searching for the Stolen Fogg Coins," *Harvard Crimson*, May 31, 2024, https://www.thecrimson.com/article/2024/5/31/fogg-museum-art-theft/.
4 Christopher Read, "Picking Harvard's Pocket," *Harvard Magazine*, May 1, 2000, https://www.harvardmagazine.com/2000/05/picking-harvards-pocket-html.
5 John F. Regan, "State Police Major, Helped Solve Many Big Crimes, 51," *Boston Globe*, May 26, 1982, 37.
6 Ibid.
7 Richard Connolly, "Seven in Alleged Vice Ring to Face US Court," *Boston Globe*, June 6, 1974, 42.
8 "Adam Worth, the Dandy Who Stole Georgiana from J.P. Morgan," New England Historical Society, https://newenglandhistoricalsociety.com/adam-worth-dandy-stole-georgiana-j-p-morganr-barons/.
9 Austin O'Malley and Kent A. Hunter, "First Facts About Classic Crimes, Mysteries, and Detective Science, from the Secret Archives of the Pinkertons," *Springfield (Ohio)*

News-Sun, July 5, 1931, 33; "Adam Worth, the Dandy Who Stole Georgiana from J.P. Morgan."
10 "Adam Worth, the Dandy Who Stole Georgiana from J.P. Morgan."
11 O'Malley and Hunter, "First Facts About Classic Crimes, Mysteries, and Detective Science."
12 "Portrait of a Woman Wearing a Gold Chain," MFA Boston, https://collections.mfa.org/objects/31040/portrait-of-a-woman-wearing-a-gold-chain?ctx=d46952d2-5f76-434b-8afc-1aadf585fc3d&idx=8.
13 "F. L. Ames's Sudden Death," *New York Times*, September 14, 1893, 8.
14 "Maria Bockenolle (Wife of Johannes Elison)," MFA Boston, https://collections.mfa.org/objects/33564/maria-bockenolle-wife-of-johannes-elison?ctx=d46952d2-5f76-434b-8afc-1aadf585fc3d&idx=6.

Chapter 9: Smash and Grab

1 Myles Connor in an undated outline for talks from the perspective of an art thief.
2 Steve Gorski, interview with author, November 4, 2024, Boston.
3 Myles Connor in an undated outline for talks on stolen art from the perspective of an art thief.
4 Bruce Macomber, dir., *Rock and Roll Outlaw: The Ballad of Myles Connor* (Howling Wolf Productions, 2018).
5 Steve Gorski, telephone interview with author, July 5, 2024.
6 Ibid.
7 Ibid.
8 Boston Police Report 208-450, April 1975.
9 Associated Press, "Rapid Art Thieves Steal Boston Rembrandt," transcript (North Adams, Mass.), April 15, 1975, 10.
10 Robert J. Anglin, "Gunmen Flee Museum with Stolen Rembrandt," *Boston Globe*, April 15, 1975, 14.
11 Ibid.
12 Robert J. Anglin, "Boston Police Expect Break in Rembrandt Portrait Heist," *Boston Globe*, April 16, 1975, 3.
13 Boston Police Report 208-450, April 1975.
14 Anglin, "Boston Police Expect Break in Rembrandt Portrait Heist."
15 Anglin, "Gunmen Flee Museum with Stolen Rembrandt," 1.
16 Ibid.
17 "The History of the Bromley-Heath Public Housing Development," Jamaica Plain Historical Society, https://www.jphs.org/locales/2005/10/15/bromley-heath-public-housing-development-history.html#gsc.tab=0.
18 Boston Police Report 208-450, April 1975.
19 Octave Durham, telephone interview with author, May 17, 2021.
20 Richard Connolly, "Singer Fails to Appear at Paintings Theft Trial," *Boston Globe*, April 23, 1975, 10.

Chapter 10: Crises

1 Robert Reinhold, "Boston Museum Names New Director," *New York Times*, March 16, 1973, 27.
2 Otile McManus, "Museum Controversy Rooted in Style, Identity, Accountability," *Boston Globe*, March 9, 1975, A9.
3 Belinda Rathbone, "Boston Raphael: Legal Art History," Center for Art Law, September 19, 2014, https://itsartlaw.org/2014/09/19/boston-raphael-legal-art-history/.

NOTES

4   Robert J. Anglin, "Gunmen Flee Museum with Stolen Rembrandt," *Boston Globe*, April 15, 1975, 1.
5   Ellen Zack, "Art Thefts in Past Year Total Nearly $35 Million," *Boston Globe*, April 15, 1975, 14.
6   Richard Connolly, "Priceless Rembrandt Recovered," *Boston Globe*, January 4, 1976, 1.
7   United Press International, "Break Due in Heist," *Lynn (Mass.) Daily Item*, April 16, 1975, 14.
8   Anglin, "Gunmen Flee Museum with Stolen Rembrandt," 14.
9   Ibid.
10 Bill Fripp, "Fine Arts Tightens Guard," *Boston Globe*, March 5, 1974, 32.
11 United Press International, "3 Gunmen Steal Rembrandt Art," *Quad-City Times* (Davenport, Iowa), April 15, 1975, 4.
12 "Latest Art Theft Is Sixth Time Fine Arts Museum Hit by Thieves," *Boston Globe*, April 16, 1975, 3.
13 Associated Press, "'Robin Hood' Returns Picasso," *Holyoke (Mass.) Transcript-Telegram*, April 2, 1969, 28.
14 United Press International, "Tip Puts Police on Trail of Rembrandt Art," *Boston Globe*, April 16, 1975, 31.
15 Anthony M. Amore and Tom Mashberg, *Stealing Rembrandts: The Untold Stories of Notorious Art Heists* (Palgrave Macmillan, 2011), 49.
16 "2 of 3 Coin Theft Suspects Released Without Charge," *Boston Globe*, November 12, 1974, 19.
17 Bernie Murphy, telephone interview with author, January 9, 2025.
18 Richard J. Connolly, "Priceless Rembrandt Recovered," *Boston Globe*, January 4, 1976, 6.
19 United Press International, "Tip Puts Police on Trail of Rembrandt Art."
20 Ibid.
21 Robert J. Anglin, "Boston Police Expect a Break in Rembrandt Portrait Heist," *Boston Globe*, April 16, 1975, 3.
22 United Press International, "Break Due in Heist."
23 Myles Connor in an undated draft of a letter to *Boston* magazine.
24 Ibid.
25 Myles Connor in an undated draft of a letter to *Boston* magazine; David Farrell, "FBI Chief in Boston to Retire in May," *Boston Globe*, April 17, 1975, 31.
26 Richard J. Connolly, "Strangler Prober Joins Defense," *Boston Globe*, October 27, 1966, 1.
27 Richard J. Connolly, "Trooper to Run Detective Firm," *Boston Globe*, August 29, 1967, 13.
28 United Press International, "Rembrandt Ransom Price is $250,000," *Pittsburgh Press*, May 12, 1975, 4.
29 Associated Press, "Everybody Wants Stolen Rembrandt," *Morning Union* (Springfield, Mass.), June 6, 1975, 7.
30 Otile McManus, "Museum Guards Reject Rueppel's Support Bid," *Boston Globe*, June 4, 1975, 67.
31 Robert Taylor, "Which Way for the Museum?" *Boston Globe*, June 15, 1975, B1.
32 William Grimes, "Jan Fontein, Scholar of Asian Art, Is Dead at 89," *New York Times*, July 3, 2017, A19.
33 Ibid.
34 "IIAS Masterclass: Jan Fontein," International Institute for Asian Studies. Archived from the original on July 3, 2017.
35 Grimes, "Jan Fontein, Scholar of Asian Art, Is Dead at 89."
36 Robert Taylor, "It Was a Topsy-Turvy Year for Art," *Boston Globe*, December 28, 1975, A11.
37 Grimes, "Jan Fontein, Scholar of Asian Art, Is Dead at 89."

Chapter 11: The Young Woman

1. "Prince Johann II von Liechtenstein (1840–1929)," Liechtenstein: The Princely Collections, https://www.liechtensteincollections.at/en/princes/prince-johann-ii-von-liechtenstein.
2. The story of Vose's visit comes from a prepared talk his son Mort delivered to the Brookline Thursday Club and the Club of Odd Volumes as reprinted in Robert C. Vose Jr., *Tales of an Art Dealer: The History of Vose Galleries Boston* (Robert C. Vose III, 2012), 110–111.
3. Diego Ribadeneira, "Rembrandt Is Sold for a Record $10.3 Million," *Boston Globe*, December 11, 1986, 1.
4. "Rembrandt van Rijn, *Young Girl in a Gold-Trimmed Cloak*," The Leiden Collection, 2018, https://www.theleidencollection.com/videos/rembrandt-van-rijn-young-girl-in-a-gold-trimmed-cloak/.
5. Gary Schwartz, email correspondence with author, December 27, 2024.
6. Gary Schwartz, *Rembrandt: His Life, His Paintings* (Viking, 1985), 168.
7. Ibid.
8. "Indubitably by Rembrandt Is Portrait of His Sister," *Springfield (Mass.) Weekly Republican*, February 6, 1930, 11.
9. Stichting Foundation Rembrandt Research Project, *A Corpus of Rembrandt Paintings II, 1631–1634* (Martinus Mijhoff Publishers, 1986), 168.
10. "Rembrandt (1606–1669)," The National Gallery, https://www.nationalgallery.org.uk/artists/rembrandt#:~:text=Leiden%20did%20not%20offer%20much,a%20workshop%20with%20Jan%20Lievens.
11. Ibid.

Chapter 12: On the Run Again

1. Pam Olinsky, "Details of FBI Arrest Made in South Hadley," *Holyoke (Mass.) Transcript-Telegram*, September 19, 1975, 15.
2. Steve Gorski, email message to author, December 10, 2024.
3. Al Dotoli, interview with author, December 23, 2024, Boston.
4. Ibid.
5. Al Dotoli, interview with author, May 28, 2021, Canton, Mass.
6. "Bastille Day Finally Comes to Boston," *Berkshire Eagle* (Pittsfield, Mass.), June 25, 1973, 22.
7. Alan H. Sheehan, "3 De Mau Mau Sentenced to Death in Jamal Killing," *Boston Globe*, August 3, 1973, 3.
8. Susannah Sudborough, "Naked Defendants, Art Thieves: Brockton Lawyer Reflects on Colorful Career," *Enterprise*, October 30, 2021, https://www.enterprisenews.com/story/news/local/2021/10/24/brockton-based-lawyer-martin-leppo-shares-his-most-interesting-cases/6111974001/.
9. Myles Connor, interview with author, December 23, 2024, Boston.
10. Ibid.
11. Myles Connor in an undated draft of a letter to *Boston* magazine.
12. Ibid.
13. Ibid.
14. Bruce Macomber, dir., *Rock and Roll Outlaw: The Ballad of Myles Connor* (Howling Wolf Productions, 2018).
15. Myles Connor in an undated draft of a letter to *Boston* magazine.

Chapter 13: High Fidelity

1. "What Do FBI's Files on Ray Patriarca Tell us About the Bonded Vault Robbery?" GoLocaProv, June 8, 2019, https://www.golocalprov.com/news/what-do-fbis-files-on-ray-patriarca-tell-us-about-the-bonded-vault-robbery.
2. Al Dotoli, interview with author, May 28, 2021, Canton, Mass.

NOTES

3   Myles Connor, interview with author, December 23, 2024, Boston.
4   Al Dotoli, interview with author, May 28, 2021.
5   Ibid.
6   Letter from Myles Connor to Al Dotoli, August 16, 2022.
7   Bruce Macomber, dir., *Rock and Roll Outlaw: The Ballad of Myles Connor* (Howling Wolf Productions, 2018).
8   Letter from Myles Connor to Al Dotoli, December 1975.
9   Macomber, *Rock and Roll Outlaw*.
10 Al Dotoli, interview with author, May 28, 2021.
11 Letter from Myles Connor to Al Dotoli, August 16, 2022.

Chapter 14: Preservation
1   Tom Sullivan and Bill Duncliffe, "Stolen Rembrandt Safely Returned," *Sunday (Boston) Herald Advertiser*, January 4, 1975, 16.
2   Richard J. Connolly, "Priceless Rembrandt Recovered," *Boston Globe*, January 4, 1975, 1.
3   Ibid.
4   Sullivan and Duncliffe, "Stolen Rembrandt Safely Returned," 1.
5   Ibid.
6   Ibid.
7   Ibid.
8   Ibid.
9   Connolly, "Priceless Rembrandt Recovered," 6.
10 Ibid.
11 Ibid.
12 Ibid.
13 Marvin Pave, "Bettering the Best—That's an Art," *Boston Globe*, January 7, 1976, 1, 32.
14 Marvin Pave, "Painting Suffered Only 2 Dents," *Boston Globe*, January 6, 1976, 6.
15 Pave, "Bettering the Best—That's an Art," 32.
16 Pave, "Painting Suffered Only 2 Dents."
17 Pave, "Painting Suffered Only 2 Dents."
18 Anthony M. Amore and Tom Mashberg, *Stealing Rembrandts: The Untold Stories of Notorious Art Heists* (Palgrave Macmillan, 2011), 105.
19 Associated Press, "Rembrandt Painting Sold for $10.3 Million," *Springfield (Ohio) News-Sun*, December 11, 1986, 22.
20 Ibid.
21 Diego Ribadeneira, "Rembrandt Is Sold for a Record $10.3 Million," *Boston Globe*, December 11, 1986, 1.
22 Jane Fitz Simon, "Art Takes on the Color of Money," *Boston Globe*, December 12, 1986, 26.
23 Ribadeneira, "Rembrandt Is Sold for a Record $10.3 Million," 11.
24 "Rembrandt van Rijn, *Young Girl in a Gold-Trimmed Cloak*," The Leiden Collection, 2018, https://www.theleidencollection.com/videos/rembrandt-van-rijn-young-girl-in-a-gold-trimmed-cloak/.
25 "Rembrandt van Rijn, *Young Girl in a Gold-Trimmed Cloak*."
26 Ibid.
27 Ibid.
28 Ibid.
29 Steve Gorski, telephone interview with author, July 25, 2024.

Chapter 15: Trials and Tribulations
1   Advertisement, *Boston Globe*, September 8, 1978, 45.
2   Myles Connor, interview with author, January 9, 2025, Woonsocket, R.I.
3   Myles Connor in an undated outline for art theft talks from the perspective of an art thief.

4   "Milton Youth to Face Hub Jury Charges," *Boston Globe*, February 14, 1967, 51.
5   "Rape Story Recanted by Inmate," *Boston Globe*, December 2, 1970, 44.
6   Alan Sheehan, "Connor Found Not Guilty in Holdup-Slaying," *Boston Globe*, December 9, 1981, 21.
7   Myles Connor in an undated outline for art theft talks from the perspective of an art thief.
8   Richard J. Connolly, "Jury in Myles Connor Murder Trial Hears Final Arguments," *Boston Globe*, March 18, 1981, 44.
9   Jerry Taylor, "Connor Acquitted But Has Skipped," *Boston Globe*, March 4, 1985, 15.
10 Letter from Myles Connor to Al Dotoli, August 16, 2022.
11 Al Dotoli, interview with author, May 28, 2021, Canton, Mass.
12 Jerry Taylor, "Connor Sentenced to Year for March Bail Jumping," *Boston Globe*, October 31, 1985, 38.
13 Richard J. Connolly, "Milton Man Denies Planning Robbery Attempt at Blackfriars," *Boston Globe*, March 28, 1979, 40.
14 United States of American v. Francis Salemme, *U.S. v. Salemme*, 91 F. Supp. 2d 141 (D. Mass. 1999).
15 J. M. Lawrence, "John O'Donovan, State Trooper, at 81," *Boston Globe*, March 18, 2012, https://www.bostonglobe.com/metro/2012/03/17/john-donovan-state-trooper/5LolGLwg2H7CE2J0EhA7ZL/story.html?event=event12.
16 Connolly, "Milton Man Denies Planning Robbery Attempt at Blackfriars."
17 "Ex-Thief Says His 'Collecting' Days are Over," *Boston Globe*, February 12, 1989, 368.
18 United States of America v. Myles Connor, *U.S. v. Connor*, 743 F. Supp. 582 (C.D. Ill. 1990).
19 Elizabeth Neuffer, "Myles Connor Sentenced to 20 Years," *Boston Globe*, July 17, 1990, 15.
20 Jay Miller, "Myles Connor Packs Beachcomber After Two-Decade Absence," *Patriot Ledger* (Quincy, Mass.), May 17, 2009, https://www.patriotledger.com/story/entertainment/music/2009/05/17/myles-connor-packs-beachcomber-after/40125436007/.
21 Letter from Myles Connor to Al Dotoli, August 16, 2022.
22 Ibid.

Epilogue
1   John R. Ellement, "Jury Rejects Art Thief's Bid to Have Antique Firearms Returned," *Boston Globe*, August 9, 2018, B5.
2   Verdict of Jury, Myles J. Connor v. Norfolk County District Attorney's Office, Norfolk Superior Court Civil Action No. 14-01322.